D0604799

CIO Best Practices

WILEY & SAS BUSINESS SERIES

The Wiley & SAS Business Series presents books that help senior-level managers with their critical management decisions.

Titles in the Wiley and SAS Business Series include:

Activity-Based Management for Financial Institutions: Driving Bottom-Line Results by Brent J. Bahnub

Business Analytics: Taking Business Intelligence beyond Reporting by Gert Laursen and Jesper Thorlund

Business Intelligence Competency Centers: A Team Approach to Maximizing Competitive Advantage by Gloria J. Miller, Dagmar Brautigam, and Stefanie V. Gerlach

Business Intelligence Success Factors: Tools for Aligning Your Business in the Global Economy by Olivia Parr Rud

Case Studies in Performance Management: A Guide from the Experts by Tony C. Adkins

CIO Best Practices: Enabling Strategic Value with Information Technology by Joe Stenzel

Credit Risk Assessment: The New Lending System for Borrowers, Lenders, and Investors by Clark Abrahams and Mingyuan Zhang

Credit Risk Scorecards: Developing and Implementing Intelligent Credit Scoring by Naeem Siddiqi

Customer Data Integration: Reaching a Single Version of the Truth by Jill Dyche and Evan Levy

Demand-Driven Forecasting: A Structured Approach to Forecasting by Charles Chase

Enterprise Risk Management: A Methodology for Achieving Strategic Objectives by Gregory Monahan

Fair Lending Compliance: Intelligence and Implications for Credit Risk Management by Clark R. Abrahams and Mingyuan Zhang

Information Revolution: Using the Information Evolution Model to Grow Your Business by Jim Davis, Gloria J. Miller, and Allan Russell

Marketing Automation: Practical Steps to More Effective Direct Marketing by Jeff LeSueur

Mastering Organizational Knowledge Flow: How to Make Knowledge Sharing Work by Frank Leistner

Performance Management: Finding the Missing Pieces (to Close the Intelligence Gap) by Gary Cokins

Performance Management: Integrating Strategy Execution, Methodologies, Risk, and Analytics by Gary Cokins

The Business Forecasting Deal: Exposing Bad Practices and Providing Practical Solutions by Michael Gilliland

The Data Asset: How Smart Companies Govern Their Data for Business Success by Tony Fisher

The New Know: Innovation Powered by Analytics by Thornton May

Visual Six Sigma: Making Data Analysis Lean by Ian Cox, Marie A. Gaudard, Philip J. Ramsey, Mia L. Stephens, and Leo Wright

For more information on any of the above titles, please visit www.wiley.com.

CIO Best Practices

Second Edition

Enabling Strategic Value with Information Technology

Joe Stenzel

WILEY

John Wiley & Sons, Inc.

Library of Congress Cataloging-in-Publication Data:

CIO best practices : enabling strategic value with information technology / [edited by] Joe Stenzel. – 2nd ed.
  p. cm. – (Wiley & SAS business series)
  Includes bibliographical references and index.
  ISBN 978-0-470-63540-7 (cloth); ISBN 978-0-470-91253-9 (ebk);
ISBN 978-0-470-91254-6 (ebk); ISBN 978-0-470-91255-3 (ebk)
  1. Chief information officers. 2. Information technology–Management.
3. Information resources management. 4. Management. I. Stenzel, Joe.
  HD30.2.C55 2011
  658.4'038–dc22

                                                    2010019067

Printed in the United States of America

10 9 8 7 6 5 4 3 2 1

Contents

Preface

Anyone working in information technology today feels the opportunities for creating and enabling lasting value, and the CIO helps define those opportunities and turn them into realities. That's what this book is about. Humanity has discovered an evolutionary tool that allows us to realize our true potential—intellectually, artistically, socially, and above all, creatively. But we must be circumspect as we explore the uses of this new tool that works as an extension of our own minds. Living as we do, on the very edge of an evolutionary horizon that once seemed far away, we must learn to respect the two native forces that have pulled human creativity in opposite directions since the beginning: (1) the drive to understand more about ourselves and our world, and (2) the desire for safety and security. Some part of us craves the entirely new; another part longs to be safe and is uncomfortable with change.

No senior executive feels the disjointed pull of these two forces more than the Chief Information Officer,[1] who seeks to create new frontiers of strategic information technology value for the enterprise, while working in an environment of service and stewardship for other people's interests. New strategic frontiers demand that the CIO take bold, decisive risks as new technologies offer competitive opportunities. Service and stewardship responsibilities demand that the CIO also take care of the day-to-day needs of people that depend on more basic information technology resources to perform what the enterprise requires of them.

Other forces distinguish the world of the CIO from executive team peers. More than any other member of the enterprise, the information technology professional works with products and services built according to designs that represent the most current understanding of the ways our world is organized. While people from other functional areas of the enterprise work within organizational structures marginally evolved from the beginning of the industrial age, IT organizations embody the principles that underlie information technology products and services—self-referencing, chaotic, morphogenic systems. The CIO must work to reconcile IT's more mature, inclusive perspective on the enterprise with the traditional views of peers that prefer the illusory safety and security of departmental silos that use command and control management policies.

Then there's the matter of the emerging role of the CIO, with its many facets in terms of the myriad expectations of the many people throughout the enterprise, which often boils down to a simple three-word question of focus. Business or technology? This book acknowledges and addresses these factors by incorporating a few basic premises in each chapter.

Premise 1: The business of the IT organization is technology, and the business of the CIO is the business of the enterprise. As such, the best practice CIO works and makes decisions in a realm of strategy, customer value creation, cost and performance management, and outsourcing partnerships while building and maintaining an IT organization that can develop and manage enterprise technology that enables strategy.

Premise 2: As a new executive role with an evolving set of responsibilities and expectations, CIOs cannot prepare themselves to learn what they need to know about the business of the enterprise without the help of non-IT experts. In addition to the chapters written by experienced, practicing CIOs acknowledged for their excellence, this book includes chapters written by performance management, accounting, and customer relationship management experts familiar with leveraging IT value.

Premise 3: The CIO is an investor of enterprise resources accountable for realizing a return on those investments. This premise acknowledges that the rest of the executive team depends on the CIO's specialized understanding and insights of information technology value opportunities. All the chapters discuss how the CIO can realize a return on IT investments—including the investment of IT's many intangible resources.

Premise 4: All enterprises are unique, and their IT organizations must align to the specific needs of the enterprise. Each chapter includes considerations for small, medium, and large enterprises across all sectors. Inherent in this premise is the understanding that all enterprises have one thing in common: Success depends on the articulation and implementation of a clear business vision and strategy. As such, the IT organization must be aligned with the enterprise vision and strategy so that it can align its products and services to realize strategic objectives. Each chapter discusses ways that the best practice CIO works to align IT products and services to fit enterprise vision and strategy.

Premise 5: All CIOs live and work in a competitive world, and customer relationship management excellence has become one of the most important competitive advantages in all sectors. The chapters in this book consistently address the importance of the IT organization's internal and external customers, and the book includes an entire chapter on customer relationship management best practices.

Premise 6: There can be no comprehensive treatment of the CIO's role as leader of the IT organization at this point in the development of this executive office. At the same time, building on Premise 4, there are common elements to CIO best practices that apply to enabling strategic value from IT in any enterprise:

- Aligning information technology with evolving business needs, and devising IT strategies that mesh with enterprise strategy
- Designing and maintaining an enterprise architecture that reflects and enables enterprise strategy
- Organizing, motivating, and managing the IT organization to focus on agile strategy execution and deliver consistently outstanding performance
- Strategic cost management practices for IT Finance that transparently reveal the operational costs of IT services to the CIO and IT customers
- Strategic performance management practices that align the work of the IT organization with enterprise strategy
- Customer relationship management practices that reflect enterprise strategy as the build value for internal and external IT customers
- Carefully selected outsourcing relationships managed according to enterprise strategy

- Calculating and managing for continuous improvement for the return on investments of tangible and intangible IT resources

CHAPTER 1 EXECUTIVE SUMMARY

Freedom with Fences: Robert Stephens Discusses CIO Leadership and IT Innovation

More often than not, the best practice CIO addresses day-to-day responsibilities with improvisational and extemporaneous solutions. Entrepreneurial innovation and creativity depend on these nontraditional, spontaneous executive capacities, but these leadership freedoms must be grounded in the general standards of professional discipline informed by each unique enterprise strategy. Product and service innovation have become increasingly dependent on the ways that information technology gives enterprise decision-makers new ways to develop an ongoing, interactive dialogue with customers through enterprise customer-facing employees. Chapter 1 addresses CIO leadership responsibilities and opportunities that promote ways the IT organization can creatively enable this dialogue between customers and enterprise decision makers while safeguarding brand integrity, assuring information security, and creating competitive advantage.

This chapter explores the CIO's challenges to promote and lead innovation for the enterprise from within the IT organization in a highly improvisational style—an unrehearsed interview format—with subsequent, relevant, fact-checked examples added to support the extemporaneous insights. In the end, Chapter 1 demonstrates the ways that best practice CIOs work from a grounded set of personal guidelines for self-discipline and inspiration.

CHAPTER 2 EXECUTIVE SUMMARY

Why Does IT Behave the Way it Does? by Bill Flemming

Chapter 2 explores IT performance management practices that align the IT organization and its resources with enterprise strategy. This chapter blends the essential elements of core business management best practices with the cutting-edge technology acumen, and discusses how the best practice CIO integrates these two skill sets. In its current form, performance management is a control mechanism that exerts its influence by aligning employees at all levels of the enterprise through a balanced set of financial and nonfinancial objectives with timely data that tracks progress and promotes better decision making to achieve those objectives. Performance management addresses group behaviors, and this chapter focuses on the ways that informed performance management practices optimize behaviors in the IT organization.

The IT organization is a business within a business for enterprises of any size or industry. Best practice CIOs recognize the ways that the enterprise IT business differs from other functional areas and departments, and they design their performance management systems accordingly. Similarly, within any IT organization, the CIO is responsible for optimizing the performance of a few basic essentials: capacity, service, IT finances, and alignment of IT business resources with enterprise strategy. This discussion examines current IT performance management challenges in the context of historical precedent by articulating the ways that the evolution from mainframe to distributed systems redefines CIO responsibilities for the ways that the IT organization behaves.

CHAPTER 3 EXECUTIVE SUMMARY

Cloud Computing and the New Economics of Business by Michael Hugos

Cloud computing represents one of the Internet's most revolutionary technologies, with transformative, disruptive influences on the ways that CIOs and their C-suite peers understand enterprise information technology. While best practices are nascent, CIOs who expect to keep their jobs can't stand back and wait for the competition to discover and master the competitive opportunities of cloud computing. Chapter 3 is a thorough, deliberate examination of all elements of cloud computing that any CIO must understand to inform and guide the enterprise executive team.

Using a balanced assessment of opportunity and risk, this chapter discusses cloud computing technology, transition considerations, performance and security concerns, and a matrix of cloud computing configurations from which enterprises can choose to optimize their strategic objectives by means of this enabling information technology. While presenting all the technology options, this discussion considers each element of cloud computing practice options in terms of how each makes good business sense in the context of specific IT settings across enterprises of different sizes and industries.

CHAPTER 4 EXECUTIVE SUMMARY

Leading with Green: Expanding the CIO's Role in Eco-Efficient Information Technology Adoption by Randy Betancourt and Alyssa Farrell

Sitting at the center of this book is a discussion of one of the most hotly debated, but potentially significant influence on global IT best practices: enterprise energy utilization and sustainability practices, otherwise known as Green IT. This chapter draws on a 12-member panel of expert contributors that provide the widest possible perspective on IT-related sustainability management, and as in the previous chapters, the presentation focuses on the business case for Green IT. There are as many different perspectives on Green IT best practices as there are regulatory environments, but the best practices are out there, and this chapter collects them into one basket.

With a focus on the business proposition, the discussion begins with examples of Green IT practices as a rapidly maturing and increasingly accepted management discipline. This chapter extends the presentation of IT performance management best practices from Chapter 2 to include essential Green IT metrics. The author and contributing experts also explore emerging Green IT innovations, opportunities and risks, the important role of public policy, and the ways that the best practice CIO and the CIO professional community must proactively engage and shape this emerging IT management discipline, with tremendous regulatory implications, for the enterprise bottom line.

CHAPTER 5 EXECUTIVE SUMMARY

Sustainability, Technology, and Economic Pragmatism: A View into the Future by Jonathan Hujsak

Building on the business case for Green IT presented in Chapter 4, Chapter 5 extends that foundation into a comprehensive discussion of enterprise IT with greater emphasis on the technology and best practice technology management. The CIO and CFO share many similarities in their responsibility profiles as service providers to virtually all enterprise stakeholders. This chapter addresses Green IT in terms of the many hard, measurable facts about the intersection of IT resources with energy and environmental concerns that CIOs must be able to readily access and understand, to develop and articulate the best Green IT practice strategies for their enterprises. Peer executives (especially CFOs), utility providers, vendors, employees, shareholder activists, and other major enterprise stakeholders already have access to these facts, and they increasingly use this information to challenge the executive team strategy.

With a focus on broad, well-developed sustainability best practices deployed by Fortune 500 enterprises around the world, this chapter explores essential definitions, terminology, technologies, employment and telecommunication trends, and security issues that CIOs can use to inform peer decision makers at any stage during the development of enterprise sustainability management practices. Integrating this detailed information, Chapter 5 presents a performance management and strategic mapping model customized for managing the sustainable enterprise.

CHAPTER 6 EXECUTIVE SUMMARY

How to Measure and Manage Customer Value and Customer Profitability by Gary Cokins

In the first edition of *CIO Best Practices*, CRM was a new competitive advantage. CRM practices have continued to evolve and be refined by the expert use of new information technologies. Three years later, CRM has become a core management practice for the C-suite. In the latest wave of social networking and ubiquitous connectivity, customers are handing CIOs information about their preferences and other sometimes-unsavory behaviors, on a silver platter. All customer behaviors add insight because not all customers are worth the time and effort it takes to please them.

The CIO's strategic partnership with the CFO has become increasingly essential for enterprise information technology to capture, organize, and leverage investments in the customer. This means that the best practice CIO needs to understand how the CFO and other senior executives translate a wide range of information about customer preferences for their financial resource allocation decisions.

Chapter 6 breaks down CRM into six sections. Parts 1 and 2 address current CRM best practices in terms of the relationship between customer preferences and shareholder wealth as a foundation for understanding customer value and profitability drivers as they relate to focused, targeted marketing delivery systems. Parts 3 and 4 move from customer analytics to deliberations about customer value determinations with a focus on customer costs and measuring lifetime customer value, such that the best practice CIO manages IT and enterprise resources as investments in the customer. Parts 5 and 6 address an increasingly outdated and incorrect senior management perception about the competing interests between shareholder value and customer value. The discussion presents metrics for assessing both customer value and loyalty, and inevitably, the ways that the CIO and CFO must work to provide comprehensive CRM information for the enterprise CMO and Sales Director.

CHAPTER 7 EXECUTIVE SUMMARY

Evolution of Networks into Networking by Karl Schubert

Chapter 7 moves full circle to pick up and more deeply explore a critical new IT development discussed in Chapter 1: The risks and competitive advantages of social networking. Like cloud computing, social networking was born of the Internet, and like so many other facets of information technology, exponential development seems to be the order of the day in terms of the body of information the CIO must digest to responsibly guide the management of this new phenomenon.

This discussion carefully explores the increasingly inextricable relationships between customers, employees, their use of personal information technologies, emerging cultural expectations and standards outside the workplace, and the ways that these factors pose opportunities and risks for the enterprise. With a focus on the business case for participation in social networking forums on both the individual employee and enterprise levels, Chapter 7 explores the business impacts of both business and social networking, the virtual world, the democratization and socialization of information, and ways that the CIO, IT organization, and enterprise can leverage the new reality of human connectivity on the Internet.

NOTE

1. This book uses the term "Chief Information Officer" (CIO) to stand for any title the enterprise might use to designate the leader of its information technology organization, such as Chief Technology Officer, and acknowledges that a person may serve more than one executive role in some enterprises.

About the Contributing Authors

Randy Betancourt (Chapter 4) has more than 25 years of experience with both program development and product management. He currently works as a client support resource for SAS IT Intelligence Group, responsible for the technical and business development of its Green IT initiative. This initiative is a project to refine the instrumentation and data collection techniques used to analyze IT asset utilization.

Randy's previous product management experiences include the expansion of capacity planning and analysis solutions for UNIX environments and network infrastructures. He holds a BA in Political Science and an MA in Public Policy with an emphasis on quantitative analysis from North Carolina State University. He can be contacted at randy.betancourt@sas.com.

Gary Cokins (Chapter 6) is an internationally recognized expert, speaker, and author in advanced cost management and performance management systems. He is a manager in performance management solutions with SAS Institute (headquartered in Cary, North Carolina), the leader in business analytics software and services, and the largest independent vendor in the business intelligence market (www.sas .com/businessanalytics/index.html). Gary received a BS in Industrial Engineering/Operations Research from Cornell University in 1971 and an MBA from Northwestern University's Kellogg School of Management in 1974. Gary began his career as a financial controller and operations manager for FMC Corporation, and he has been a management consultant with Deloitte, KPMG Peat Marwick, and Electronic Data Systems (EDS).

Gary was the lead author of the acclaimed *An ABC Manager's Primer,* sponsored by the Institute of Management Accountants (IMA). Gary's second book, *Activity-Based Cost Management: Making It Work,* was judged by the Harvard Business School Press as "read this book first." Gary's third book, *Activity-Based Cost Management: An Executive's Guide*, has ranked number one in sales volume of 151 similar books on BarnesandNoble.com. Gary has also written *Activity-Based Cost Management in Government* and *Performance Management: Finding the Missing Pieces to Close the Intelligence Gap*. Gary's latest book is *Performance Management: Integrating Strategy, Execution, Methodologies, Risk, and Analytics*. Gary can be reached at gary.cokins@sas.com.

Alyssa Farrell (Chapter 4) supports SAS Sustainability Solutions and works with SAS customers around the world to understand best practices and solutions for managing their business with environmental responsibility in mind (www.sas.com/solutions/sustainability/index .html). She participates in the Corporate Consultative Group of the World Resources Institute and the Green Tech Council of the North Carolina Technology Association, and supports the SAS Executive Sustainability Council—the leadership team that governs the SAS sustainable business practices (www.sas.com/corporate/corpgovernance/ csr-report.pdf).

Alyssa regularly speaks with trade associations, analysts, and the press about the opportunities organizations have to effectively manage a sustainable strategy and drive healthy economic growth. Prior to joining SAS, she was a senior consultant in the Deloitte Public Sector practice. In this capacity, she was a project manager for statewide and countywide systems implementations, and was responsible for user acceptance testing, change management and training, and middleware technology selection.

She is a graduate of the Eller College of Management at the University of Arizona, where she earned an MBA with a concentration in Management Information Systems. Alyssa also holds a BA from Duke University, and can be reached at alyssa.farrell@sas.com.

Bill Flemming (Chapter 2) works in a thought leadership position for the SAS Global IT Intelligence practice. As a thought leader in IT management, Bill was a pioneer in applying Activity-Based Management to IT financial management, strategic performance management to IT maturity, and reconciling system management maturity, and IT business alignment. Bill has more than 25 years of experience with both hands-on IT projects and product thought leadership. His current projects include IT Intelligent Scorecarding and IT financial management. He has published and broadcasted extensively about each subject. As a thought leader in IT business management, he embraces the opportunity to effectively manage IT. Bill currently resides in Florissant, Colorado, at 9,000 feet. In his spare time, he extensively mountain bikes and climbs "14ers."

Michael Hugos (Chapter 3), principal at Center for Systems Innovation [C4SI], mentors teams of business and technical people in practices of business agility and agile systems development, and delivers seminars and management briefings. He previously spent six years as CIO of an $8 billion distribution co-operative, where he developed the suite of supply chain and e-business systems that transformed the company's operations and revenue model. He is a recognized expert in agility and supply chain management. He won the CIO 100 Award in 2003 and 2005, the *InformationWeek* 500 Award in 2005, and in 2006 he was selected for the *Computerworld* Premier 100 Award for career achievement.

Michael earned his MBA from Northwestern University's Kellogg School of Management, and holds an undergraduate degree in Urban Planning and Design from University of Cincinnati. He writes a blog for *CIO Magazine* titled "Doing Business in Real Time," and he has authored several books including *Business Agility: Sustainable Prosperity in a Relentlessly Competitive World*, and the popular *Essentials of Supply Chain Management*. He can be reached through his Web site at: www.michaelhugos.com.

Jonathan Hujsak (Chapter 5) is head of operations research and a senior principal architect at Balance Energy, a new corporate initiative at BAE Systems North America. Mr. Hujsak has over 30 years of experience in advanced information technology organizations and initiatives at Fortune 500 companies, high-tech startups, nonprofits, universities, and research institutes. He has worked with a wide spectrum of advanced technologies, including distributed data systems, federated search engines, artificial intelligence systems, geospatial information systems, GRID computing, virtualization, cloud computing, telecommunications, e-commerce, transportation systems, space systems, logistics, and factory automation in a spectrum of domains spanning commercial, government, defense, and energy. Mr. Hujsak is currently an architect for next-generation sustainable systems, smart grids, and large-scale demand response and trading systems for the global energy industry. He holds a BS in Electrical Engineering, and attended the PhD program in Applied Physics at the University of California San Diego. Readers who wish to network for further information on topics covered in this chapter are invited to join the LinkedIn networking group titled Sustainable Community Network (www.linkedin.com), or the author can be reached at jhujsak@gmail.com.

Dr. Karl Schubert (Chapter 7) is Principal of TechNova Consulting, LLC, providing innovative ideas for technology and management development. He has served as corporate CTO and vice president for Xiotech Corporation, vice president and general manager of Daticon (a Xiotech Company), and chairman of Xiotech India, Ltd. He has a proven track record of developing leading-edge hardware, software, and combined product families and delivering them to existing and new market areas.

Prior to joining Xiotech, Karl served as a technology consultant to start-up companies associated with Austin Ventures, New Enterprise Associates, and Sierra Ventures. As CTO, COO, and Senior VP of Engineering for Zambeel Inc., he was responsible for driving technology, engineering, and operations teams to produce the first enterprise-class, 4D-scalable, NAS subsystem. As VP and CTO of Dell Inc., he architected Dell's entry into the storage business, and was responsible for guiding the storage practice through its first several billion dollars of revenue. Prior to Dell, Karl spent 14 years with IBM, when he created the company's OEM open storage subsystems unit.

Karl has been awarded a number of patents for leading-edge technological innovation in storage systems architecture, storage area networks, and other technology areas. He obtained a PhD in Engineering from the University of Arkansas, an MS in Chemical Engineering from the University of Kentucky, and a BS in Chemical Engineering from the University of Arkansas. His most recent book, *The CIO Survival Guide*, was published by John Wiley & Sons, and he is a guest speaker at professional conferences and a regular panelist in the areas of technology, innovation, and distributed international development. He can be reached at karl.schubert@technovaconsulting.com.

CIO Best Practices

CHAPTER 1

Freedom with Fences: Robert Stephens Discusses CIO Leadership and IT Innovation

F ounder and Chief Inspector of Geek Squad and Vice President for Best Buy, Robert Stephens is an articulate information technology leader and innovator who feels most comfortable and direct when sharing his insights and experiences by speaking rather than writing. This chapter transcribes a dialogue based on several recorded sessions with the editor. Section headings were subsequently assigned by the editor to indicate changes in the themes of the discussion.

THE CIO LEADERSHIP PARADOX

Joe Stenzel: As an innovative IT entrepreneur with experience in both the arts and engineering sciences, you're schooled to appreciate the vital balance between the creative

dimensions and professional disciplinary standards of CIO leadership expectations and responsibilities. Describe how this apparent paradox plays out in the current information environment.

Robert Stephens: The nature of the game has changed from the perspective of the CIO, especially in the last five years. Some of the rules for IT architecture and design are partially less formal, moving back in the direction of the mainframe, server client, and dumb terminal, but rapid prototyping is the area where innovative playfulness will soon be codified. With the development of mobile applications, smaller screens, and fewer buttons, it will be increasingly important for the CIO to avoid becoming too formal. CIOs will increasingly promote a cultural layer of playfulness within the enterprise and IT organization—a virtual sandbox if you will—as a part of the CIO's arsenal, point of view, and leadership attitude.

Balance is everything. We have freedom to innovate in play, but it has to be a freedom with fences. There's always a tendency to equate playfulness with the ignorant or the rule breakers. What about HIPAA? What about Sarbanes-Oxley? Critics will tell us that we can't playfully innovate while protecting our enterprises. They're simply wrong. CIOs get paid to help innovate and stretch. IT has become even more central to business success than ever, because the lines between an internal enterprise IT system and a customer-facing experience are diminishing all the time.

We need a balance between the formal discipline and playful innovation that characterizes the CIO, and the metaphor is really the human brain. The more we learn about the brain through functional MRI and PET scans, the more we learn that everybody is creative, everybody is methodical, everybody has varying degrees and kinds of intelligence by which we express our unique gifts—cognitive, emotional, social, ecological, artistic. Much of this is inherited, and the rest is fostered by the environment. The CIO facilitates creation of an innovative environment within the IT organization and the greater enterprise by setting the tone as a disciplined, but innovative, chief executive.

Innovation is art. Balancing is an art. As an inherently playful activity, art shows us the way to creativity and innovation. CIOs have to get things done, but business pressures place the CIO in a position of constant paradox: innovate, but keep the enterprise safe and secure. Business is how we live, and art is why we live. Back and forth, back and forth.

I'm only now coming up with the words to articulate this human intellectual dynamic. Art and playfulness are essential in life, and strategically essential in business. Art is that abstract, shapeless playground from which new ideas spring, and that's why it's so relevant to business strategy: processes very quickly become commoditized, copied, and stolen. As Picasso said, "Bad artists copy. Good artists steal." The CIO has to find a way to help enterprise employees find access to that artistic space where they develop newer, brighter, faster, cheaper forms of products and services. That's why every art historian should take an engineering class and every engineer should have that art history class—CIOs included.

This suggests that balanced leadership is characterized by highly personal frameworks for understanding disciplined creativity.

I share the conclusions drawn in Richard Florida's *Rise of the Creative Class*[1] and Daniel Pink's *A Whole New Mind*[2] about the importance of developing the right-brain, but the message I want CIOs to understand is that *everybody* has artistic capacity to some degree, especially our employees. I learned two important things in my two short years of art school. Maggie Phillips was a member of one of the first graduating classes from the Institute in the 1920s, a classmate of Georgia O'Keeffe, and my 2-D drawing instructor at the Art Institute of Chicago. She'd walk around us as we were drawing—like a football coach on the sidelines—and she would train us by saying:

> Don't look at your hands. Don't look at what you're drawing on the paper, look at what you're drawing—the real object. Your mind will draw and express the object only as well as it has come to know that object. There is no perfect line except the one you draw without editing, without that parental frontal cortex telling you the "rules." *Ignore* that voice.

This is really the job of the artist, and it's a creative, innovative intuition that I continue to remember as I work to balance the importance of creative freedoms and the inevitable leadership/disciplinary fences inherent in my work with Best Buy and Geek Squad employees and our customers. In technology, there are knowable quantities and things I can control; but in art, where new ideas arise, there are no rules—no forms codifying creativity. I can see how some people would struggle with this notion, but the key for the CIO is to understand how fences and freedoms relate to each other as a leadership function—the form and the formless. From my personal perspective as an artist, I can see how so many people struggle with the question of the relevance of art itself.[3] In art and in technology, there are no movements like the Dadaists or Surrealists anymore. All executives can be their own Institutes of Art, and this is certainly true in the world of "Executive-Interpretive Information Technology." There are no movements anymore. So what new insight am I going to meaningfully contribute to the art world/business world/CIO world?

The balance of freedom with fences includes a very personal element of self-awareness for every CIO. I now see my innovative and creative endeavors as an exercise of self-discovery. What is my style? What kind of employee do I want? What kind of system do I want to build?

The leadership relationship between art, play, innovation, and business world disciplines for the CIO is to unlock the potential of each individual in the enterprise. Some people simply aren't cut out for management, but make good technical leaders. Many CIOs are not aware of their real gifts in terms of how they can facilitate the enterprise and the IT organization through teaching. In each case, and with each person, a good IT leader recognizes these gifts and places each employee into the roles in which that person can succeed, according to his or her gifts.

This is the quest that preoccupies me now. One of my favorite quotes is from Andy Warhol, whose words released me from my guilt when I dropped out of art school to go back to work at Verlo Mattress Factory in Chicago, where I could make really good money writing software, solving business problems, and *seeing results*. Andy Warhol said, "Making money is art, and working is art, and good business is the best art." I learned that I didn't get the same kind of satisfaction in the art world as I did in business. There is nothing that is ever "done" in art, but in business I know when I've made a profit and I know when I haven't.

I think Warhol was referring to the two faces of creativity—even artists must produce materials, pay the rent, come up with money for paint. He was very overt about the notion that we have to sell ourselves. The more I study Warhol, the more I am amazed at his genius. He seems to fold massive intelligence into what we might mistake for "Pop Art," but miss incredible, practical insights. His phrase eased my guilt. I realized that I didn't abandon the true principles of creativity because I wasn't willing to "suffer" for my art. I'm not selling out; I'm following my bliss. This is part of what helps me reconcile the paradox inherent in freedom with fences, where *rules* promote creativity and innovation.

THE FENCES

Traditional executive stereotypes often emphasize disciplinary responsibilities, which seems like a good place to begin. Characterize some of the essential ways that the CIO uses information technology to discipline enterprise employees and safeguard enterprise assets.

There are always going to be paradoxes at the intersection of the CIO's disciplinary and creativity leadership responsibilities, and these paradoxes intensify as search engine technologies evolve. Unlimited information is like limitless imagination. At some point, not only is it frivolous, it becomes counterproductive.

This is a very specific pattern I see in individual employees who say, "I'm having trouble understanding how I will use any of this, and I'm feeling overwhelmed." They haven't yet learned that the same degrees of disciplinary power that can be applied to information *filtering* can be applied to creative, innovative information gathering. This is my challenge. Applying meaningful borders to information allows an employee to consume more content, where more actually means better—on the employee's own personal terms—and without a sense of being overwhelmed.

Enterprises and their CIOs are learning how to filter information to promote strategically aligned, individual employee decision-making and creativity through a process of natural selection. Examples from our everyday lives are informative here. When you have to get to a meeting, you have to keep track of time, traffic, weather conditions, the status of your car, and so many other factors. All the while, some important element can easily be forgotten as we work to trim all the margins and cut things close. Filtering is simply a set of rules and alternatives, predicted ahead of time, to be managed with information technology. The calendar, clock, and GPS in our mobile phones can talk to Google about road conditions and to our cars about fuel status. Instead of simply beeping at 10:15 to remind me to leave for my meeting, it uses available information to tell me to leave at 10:05 because I need gas, and locates the best station to get the fuel on the way to save me time. That's filtering. In my experience, most people ask if such an example is even possible, but when you think about it, the pieces are already there.

The next decade of IT will be about anticipating and connecting more and more of these pieces to organize and present filtered, meaningful information. These simple examples show how so much of our personal and work lives are based on if-then statements as the basis for unconscious rules that govern our efficiencies. The work of the CIO in this context is to identify and establish efficiency- and quality-based rules to filter and present relevant information on a real-time basis as employees and customers need it to make informed decisions. Imagine the opportunities for the CIO who sees the ways that IT can connect these relevant pieces. Another simple example: I want to receive a message when FedEx has delivered my package whether or not I sign for it; I want to be notified any time my flight schedule changes. I *want* these rules and filters as a part of my personal and work life.

Companies also provide these rules and filters to *keep* their customers. I shop at Menards instead of Home Depot because I know where

I can find everything at Menards. The store layout is an enterprise rule for customers; the rule filters and organizes the information I need to find what I want at any Menards location. More and more enterprises use these simple information filters, but the CIO should understand that over time, this filtering power is shifting from the enterprise to the consumer.

Customers increasingly maintain a set of personal, portable information-filtering rules—all their likes and dislikes. Ritz-Carlton knows what kind of newspaper I like, and of course, they have it waiting for me upon my arrival. I'm paying for that now, but when I maintain my own set of rules and I permit companies to read my rules set relevant to my interaction with them (or others), they will automatically want to apply my rules to keep my business. Instead of the rules residing with Ritz-Carlton or Northwest Airlines, they're going to reside and be managed by me in *my* account, and I'm going to release them only under another set of relevant rules, not unlike releasing medical records. The filtering system operates on a rule hierarchy, a level of complexity I'm still struggling to solve, but I'm not going to wait for my competition to beat me to it.

The CIO's role in establishing workplace filtering appropriate to employee needs is essential here. To do otherwise is to assume the irresponsible leadership persona of the maverick who gets all the credit for breaking the rules. Enterprises will increasingly celebrate CIOs who keep more and more *productive* rules in place. I tell my people several things in this regard. Number one: If you're innovating and you're not frustrated, then you're not innovating hard enough. Frustration is a sign of actual progress, not an indication of problems. Rules, like concrete highway-barriers, take a lot of energy and effort to put in place so that they really work on an enterprise level. I have respect for effective rules because I understand that they do not emerge naturally, but from a great deal of insight and a lot of hard work. These kinds of rules are unnatural; the natural universe does not generate rules without a reason; it doesn't waste energy, and neither do smart people or enterprises. People tend to take the path of least resistance; good rules conform accordingly. The energy and effort demanded by sustainable rules applies to both setup and maintenance.

What formal management rules might any CIO use to promote employee efficiencies, if not creativity?

There are a few cogent principles about rule management here for CIOs to balance their innovative impulses with disciplinary prudence. Rule One: *Understand the origin of each enterprise IT rule and codify the rule's original purpose.* Rules exist, in part, to help us avoid unintended consequences, because individuals so often focus on the linear achievement of a personal goal that may not encompass broader enterprise agendas. CIOs should formally outline rule purposes and their safeguards.

Rule Two: *Put an expiration date on every rule.* All human rules are temporary by nature, not permanent. Rules are formulated in a specific temporal environment that will change over time, and most rules will eventually need to be updated, replaced, or dismantled. These rule term limits are a check-and-balance system that forces leadership to go back to the polls and review the enterprise IT rules for relevance. Why is this rule here? Why do we still need it? Rules tend to fester unless they are periodically reviewed and refreshed. Before long, they actually promote their own unintended form of culture that insidiously takes on a life of its own and becomes institutionalized. When a rule becomes institutionalized, it ceases to serve its originally healthy regulatory purpose and becomes more like a cancer cell—genetically reprogrammed to grow and dominate healthy systems. Expiration dates are inherently healthy and empowering. They give IT and other employees the chance to keep the CIO honest.

Rule Three: *The CIO must be a reluctant rule-maker who strives for brevity and design simplicity.* This is probably the most creative of the three rules. Look at Google's start page compared to the visual noisiness of Yahoo and AOL. You might say that Google is the unorthodox one, and you'd be right; but Google maintains a different orthodoxy, where less is more. They've violently resisted any changes to that page, and we now see it as a harbinger of clean design. Following this third rule, CIOs should select new rules according to high standards such as federal privacy laws, where conditions are explicit.

When the enterprise can meet these conditions, subject to thorough review, a best practice CIO will favor breaking rules while *obeying* them. This means that employees can only break a rule by meeting strict criteria, and the CIO should *carefully encourage* this practice. There's also an extension of the second rule inherent in Rule Three, when one considers IT or enterprise policy as a rule-based system. If Twitter has taught us anything, it's taught us to keep it simple, because policy-creep is so prevalent. Constraints become the key to creativity. Twitter's 140-character limit is the source of its power. It hasn't constrained Twitter at all, and the worst thing that could happen would be for them to eliminate that constraint. We'd be left with another form of email. Google's start page emerged because Sergey Brin didn't know html. He put the search box up there in the early days and never bothered to change it because he was focused on search algorithms. I think there's a lesson here for the CIO with important implications for rule and policy management.

The collaborative CIO keeps rules refreshed and enforced by sharing the reasons that the rules were built, how the rules were built, and how to improve them. In a sense, these three rules allow the CIO to in-source enforcement and innovation to enterprise employees. "Hey, here are my restrictions and why the restrictions are in place. What solutions can you come up with based on these restrictions?" For example, the CIO cannot allow credit card information to be stored in the system, but the enterprise is trying to make it easy for the customers so that they have one less step, one fewer click. So the CIO can focus on permissible freedoms, "Here is the problem, here are my constraints. If not a single person in our smart, playful, super-connected workforce can find a solution, I'll be forced to come up with another rule."

The CIO almost plays the role of a parent when it comes to balancing employee disciplines and freedoms.

Permitting employee freedoms is a fundamental leadership style not unlike a parenting style. A parent might put up nothing but fences, but at some point a child's healthy development must include a skinned knee while learning to ride a bike, poison ivy while exploring the forest, a burned finger while playing with matches. Mistakes are our most effective teachers. I worry that enterprise leadership allows one percent of the possibilities to drive one hundred percent of the policy, and innovation suffers accordingly.

The alternative, balanced rule to the heavy-handed leadership tendency to stifle invention should be, *trust but verify*. Weigh the liability cost openly while making it easy for people to get things done. This openness actually trains the enterprise to understand why a rule is in place, why the rule makes good business sense, why the rule is important for the customer. This makes people able to challenge, follow, and enforce enterprise rules, because they *own* the rules. This promotes a culture of sharing responsibility for rule maintenance and enforcement where the CIO is no longer solely responsible, and where employees become more participatory and more compliant. CIOs who understand the freedom with fences paradox trust their employees to do the right thing under these balanced conditions for the simple reason that it costs far more energy to enforce than it does to trust.

At the same time, no CIO has the luxury of being an entrepreneurial maverick. I use different information categories to help me decide how I want to experiment and innovate. For example, one category is *knowledge about my products*, which is not confidential in terms of customer-facing support. Let's look at a support forum. All the interactions inherent with this information category are very different from credit card or financial transaction information, which needs to be guarded and protected. So I would start to play and experiment with new methods in an area like support forum information, where the company doesn't need to maintain such high security. The CIO can simply be more playful and experimental with tech-support data, using Facebook and Twitter in ways that are safe. Then, after learning from experiments in safer information categories, the CIO can pick and choose practice successes that apply to more sensitive areas.

Instead of saying, "How do we work within the sharp confines of this highly restrictive information category with many fences and gates?" the CIO might suggest to executive peers, "Let's learn how to experimentally innovate from a greener, safer information space." For example, Best Buy/Geek Squad has 14 service centers that fix over 4,000 TVs and laptops a day. We've got 20,000 service people associated with the call centers, making house calls, and working in Best Buy stores. I want to tap into everything they learn and know, and we're experimenting with a couple of theories about this safe, but incredibly valuable information category. First, I know that I have a wealth of knowledge contained in the heads of these people, but they're so busy moving from job to job and task to task that they feel they don't have enough time to move away from their invoicing screen, open up another screen, and deposit their knowledge in a new location for me to access. Even if I built such a tool, I don't think they would come.

But what if they knew that every time they typed a paragraph about what they did for the customer into the invoicing system, it would be automatically entered into a knowledge base? By proxy, they're accomplishing two things that they will value. One: They immediately realize that I've developed a system where they don't have to make an extra step. Two: I've given *them* a benefit—a system that can remember their knowledge for them and combine it with the experience of their associates. It's there for them if they ever want to look it up again.

Here's where it gets interesting, because *other* people can see it. In fact, we're going even further. Because this information is related to products, there's no need to make this information sensitive or confidential. So, let's give *customers* access to this same information so they can do self-service. Playing and experimenting even further, we're going to allow this information to be searched as a way to open it up to the broader public beyond the customer base. This allows anyone searching the information to improve the knowledge base, just like a wiki.

This is one important area where a CIO can take an information category with low sensitivity and barriers, but one that gives us important competitive opportunities and that can, in turn, give us experience to apply similar techniques to more sensitive information categories like customer purchase history. Eventually we want to learn to link these information categories. We already know what products the customer owns, so how can we turn this knowledge into a customer benefit? For example, I really like it when I use a call center that doesn't make me repeat my life story, phone number, and account number three times. In contrast other call centers seem to be psychic. The psychic ones use caller ID to trip my customer profile database, allowing the service technician to begin immediately with my concern. This is an incredibly rich, playful, experimental area for the CIO.

Chapter 7 explores the use of social networking at the workplace. But in the context of freedoms with fences, what about the employee restrictions that most companies apply regarding the use of Facebook at work or blocking access to G-mail?

All unknown things are assumed to be a threat until proven otherwise. Once Best Buy actually started interacting with customers on Facebook, it became an essential tool for us. Best Buy now has one of Facebook's most popular pages, but as the popularity of Facebook increased from its initial launch, it was not accessible to a large chunk of our Best Buy employees. Removing that restriction not only sent a message, but I'm sure it enhanced our performance. It only makes sense that any enterprise should be eating its own dog food.

Information technology has now become a powerful collaborative technology that employees experience at home in their personal lives, which leads to a very interesting question. Who's the expert now? Who's *really* the expert on the nuances of the implications of many new forms of technology? I would argue that the CIO may be at a disadvantage when compared to the customer-facing employee due to all the meetings and other executive policy-related responsibilities that create a widening, increasingly formal distance in the relationship between the CIO and the customer. We want to learn what our employees know, and we want to augment the ways that information technology can capture what they know so that we can all make better decisions.

RULES AND INNOVATIVE AUGMENTATION

Explain how a best practice CIO can use information technology to promote employee and enterprise performance and decision making.

Technology is just a set of tools developed to address our human limitations, and we've entered a period of technology as augmentation, where we're talking about an increasingly augmented reality. I'm developing a concept called *augmented expertise*, where I believe that the new leadership era is paradoxically *not* one of expertise as it is traditionally understood. Roger Martin has said, "Reality is the enemy of innovation."[4] I take that thought a step further. In the augmented expertise framework, the CIO of the future is not an expert, because as Mark Herzog says, "*Expertise* is the enemy of innovation."[5] Don't confuse this phrase with the notion that the perfect is the enemy of the good. My response to Monsieur Voltaire is, that's fine . . . if you're *not* aiming for greatness, or perfection itself. I'm in the service business; I'm aiming for perfection and world domination. I will sometimes wait before offering something until I can do it extremely well.

We're already hearing the term, "augmented reality," and I would argue that a search engine is *augmented expertise,* where Google is my long-term memory and Twitter is my short-term memory. Here's my CIO roadmap for the coming years: more *transparency,* more *openness,* more *interoperability,* more *freedom* for the employees to bring the inherent business opportunities of the most advanced cell phone technology into the workplace. It seems to take forever to standardize this kind of freedom so that the enterprise can control how employees use it. Unfortunately most business strategies are not developed fast enough to keep up with the capabilities of the latest technology. Best Buy will soon be launching a process whereby any employee can bring virtually any cell phone into the workplace, where we will install software for security and control to simultaneously balance creative freedoms for new business opportunities and customer services. Freedom with fences.

The CIO, in particular, is in many ways an enterprise politician. While most CIOs are probably leadership experts, there are many ways that we are *not* comprehensive IT subject matter experts. There's always a struggle of focus, an ongoing paradox for the CIO: whether to protect or to destroy. Borrowing a *Star Wars* analogy, listening for a disturbance in the force ultimately comes down to listening to *customers*—a trend that is unlikely to change for the next thousand years. It's been important since the beginning of the history of commerce. Customers are speaking a truth we can always count on, more so now than even five or ten years ago, because it's getting easier for them to talk to us now than ever before, and more possible for us to listen and respond in a time frame that matters to them. With so many new channels, the job of the CIO is to apply the very old rule about listening well, and to use technology to help the enterprise do old things so much better by augmenting every employee's expertise.

Talk about one of your best examples of augmented expertise from your work with Best Buy.

One day I was experimenting with an example of a new augmented reality program on my iPhone. Twitter turns on the new search engine, and I type in "Best Buy." All of a sudden I see a Tweet, "Best Buy sucks! They wouldn't take back my laptop. I hate them." Right away I click on the customer's user name and I see all these other Tweets. Four minutes ago: "Best Buy sucks!" Three minutes ago: "I can't frick'n believe this. This guy's refusing to help me."

Then it hits me. "Oh my God, he's still in the store!" So I send him a reply: "Hey, I'm so sorry. This is Robert. I'm founder of the Geek Squad. What store are you in and how can I help?" Now, I don't want him to reveal any personal information. So I give him my number, and say, "Call me."

He calls me and says, "Here's the deal. This is the second time I've brought this laptop in for repair. I got the extended warranty, and they say it's not covered. They won't let me talk to a manager."

As it happens, the manager was in a meeting and wasn't trying to evade this customer, but nobody was left to make this customer connection. I said, "Please stand by, and thank you for giving us a chance to help you. Would you let me try and take care of it?"

"Sure, I'm still here."

"Great! Don't leave the store. I've got your mobile number, and I'll call you back in two minutes."

So I called the District Manager and got the GM's mobile number. I call the GM. He comes out of a meeting, and he happens to be about 100 yards from the customer. Some other lower-paid regional employee felt uncomfortable going in to disturb the GM's meeting for the customer. This is a cultural issue, which as an IT leader, I address later.

The GM looks at the situation and says, "This guy is clearly a good customer, and he's not being unreasonable, although the customer is not being *entirely* correct." (I love that phrase, because the customer is not always *right*, but the customer should always *win*). The GM gives the guy a new laptop and decides to handle the paperwork on the *back end*. We tend to push the paperwork towards the customer instead of away. With a little bit of extra paperwork on our part, we can get Apple to reimburse the cost of the trouble that the customer's having. The next twenty Tweets from this customer were the payoff.

"Best Buy/Geek Squad are awesome!"

This kind of experience can *never* be completely automated, so we want to augment the expertise and responsiveness of enterprise employees at all levels. It's no different from my phone beeping at me 15 minutes before my next meeting. [Editor's note: Anyone watching Mr. Stephens' major public presentations will notice a microphone in one hand and his cell phone in the other hand]. Augmentation is a form of filtering, a rule system, and a form of attention control. There's this phrase coined by Linda Stone called, "continuous partial attention," which is about scanning continuously for opportunities across a network rather than about optimizing one's time by multitasking.[6] We're all continuously distracted at some level. "Did I leave the iron on?" "What am I going to get my wife for Christmas?" "I've got to get to my next meeting. Did I refuel the car?"

While acting as a filtering rule system, augmentation also liberates us to be more human, creative, and innovative—leaving the clerical, technical stuff of memory and other nonexecutive brain functions to the computers. Twitter is my short-term memory and Google is my long-term memory. Technology-liberated brains leave us with more space for dreaming about art and form and color, the wonderful meal we're going to have for dinner, when we're going to see our best friend again, and new ideas. CIOs know better than anyone else that technology can anticipate and take care of life's predictable details at home and in the workplace. We're actually going to be amazed at how *human* we become in the near future and how much more human our technology has made us. A lot of people think that technology is going to increasingly deperson- alize our lives at home and in the workplace. Nothing could be further from the truth.

THE CIO AND ENTERPRISE CULTURE

CIO leadership in the context of enterprise culture is a recur- ring theme in this conversation. Augmented expertise and information technology surely play a role in the ways that the CIO shapes enterprise and IT organization cultures.

Acknowledging that traditional CIO role expectations do not allow us to be as playful as we might like, the CIO can sometimes use industry rebels to help make the case. Co-opt the pirates within your company, or the executives who might not have the personal experience, and context for the value of playful, experimental IT exercises. For example, I just advised all senior Best Buy execu- tives that I'm going to replace their Blackberries with iPhones or equivalent models. "You work for Best Buy. How can you not be on your own premier technology? You do not want to be using a weaker phone than your average retail, part-time employee. They already have a more powerful phone than you do, and you're the executive of a billion dollar company. Come on, we should be eating our own dog food here."

The excuses are lame. "Well, some of our officers aren't technical..." This is not about being technical; we're in the business of retailing this technology. Think about the executive in charge of labor produc-tivity who uses an iPhone and installs new apps all the time. That person is going to be the first to see new ways to increase produc-tivity based on the best of our available technology—technology that's already going to be in everyone's pocket. It's not about bring-ing the executive closer to the technology, it's about directing them to see the advantages of better forms of the technology that they already own and use for their decision-making and creative activi-ties. This is how CIOs help people merge their nontechnical insights with relevant information, so that we can all learn how to be better, more facile innovators. At a minimum, the CIO is respon-sible for making sure that the other C-level executives and all company managers maintain a relevant state of personal technol-ogy in their information toolset.

The best practice CIO monitors the ways that people become too comfortable with some technologies. Best Buy is achieving a lot of recognition for new innovations, but I feel frustrated because we could have been doing these things years ago and be even more famous for our practices! The impatient side of me that wants to have immediate impact asks why Best Buy didn't adopt these practices faster. For example, most executives overuse email. Why? It's the tool they grew up with. But Best Buy executives have a *moral* business responsibility to stay ahead by remaining in touch with our employee and customer experiences. Eating our own dog food is one of the best ways to do so. You know what the Ford executive is going to be driving. For the Best Buy execu-tive and management employees, this means using the most current, best technology available to our customers.

The CIO should be aware of the first question that all employees ask in this regard. "Does that mean I have to give up what I already know?" The CIO's answer is, "No, it's about better ways of con-necting what you already know with others who have comple-mentary information. This is how you do it." I see this as the "new possible." I see this as the way that CIOs help employees self-inspire as an innovation promoting value within the company culture. Employees like to share inspirations, they communicate more readily with one another, and transform the company itself into a social information network. Innovation is really about getting people to talk to each other.

Our conversation has repeatedly referenced IT proxies as ways that the CIO can discipline peer C-suite executives, middle management, and customer-facing employees to be more creatively responsive to innovative product and service developments. How does the information technology environment promote this agenda?

Going through the more exotic forms of promoting innovation, like the Google Twenty Percent Rule, where everyone takes some portion of the workweek to promote creativity, certainly won't work everywhere. I've learned a simpler way to frame, promote, and inspire employee innovation. I see two ways to impact a corporate culture, a customer experience, or the outcome and quality of a project, product, or service: behavioral and environmental. Now there may be some classic Ivy Tower explanation to these dynamics, but this is my layman's version, based on personal experience.

Think of the behavioral impact in terms of what Steve Jobs does. He tells his people, "I want the iPhone to have only one button and a glass screen. Figure it out." Unfortunately, behavior is unreliable, most executives will never approach Steve Jobs' capabilities, and executive charisma isn't scalable. Behaviors happen on a very personal level, and seldom on a cultural level until something else helps them along. I lost 40 pounds last summer using a GPS app on my iPhone that tracked my personal mobility and encouraged me to be more physically active. My friend Dan Buettner, the *New York Times* best-selling author of the book *Blue Zone*, uses photography to tell the stories of four of the world's longest-lived cultures that have nine habits for people to get up to 10 extra good years out of life. He said, "The way you lost 40 pounds was a behavioral change, which is very rare. Most people couldn't do it because they wouldn't stick with it. Instead of getting people to consciously eat less and exercise more, I focus on environmental changes that don't even register—add more sidewalks and make sure that they're connected."

By proxy, his environmental approach achieves a change in behavior that is, in many circumstances, unconscious, more universally accessible, and therefore, more reliable. The same approach applies to promoting behaviors like bicycling or saving for retirement or a corporate innovation initiative. Rather than addressing individual employee behaviors, I believe that the CIO can more effectively set up such an initiative with an environmental approach, using the freedom with fences principles we're discussing here.

The authority of an IT proxy as an automatic enabler of enterprise creativity and innovative behavior has a huge impact on the role of the CIO. Enterprise information can be seen as the first environment, the first platform, for affecting employee behavioral changes. As such, the CIO is arguably as or more powerful than the CEO when it comes to facilitating innovative employee behaviors and having a direct impact on inspiring creativity as an enterprise cultural value.

CIOs promote innovation as a cultural value by finding new ways to connect people. Instead of asking them to use their mobile phones to perform an informational task that would help the business, just automatically link email to instant messaging. Then, sooner or later, this information-environment proxy creates a valuable new behavior. Why do we use text messaging for certain communiqués rather than email? Nobody ever attended a class about why texting is more efficient. The discovery and behavior change was unconsciously enabled by the change in the environmental proxy.

The more I study the actual processes involved in evolution and natural selection, the more I marvel at the simplicity and elegance of those processes. These processes offer the CIO some clues about how to set up similar environmental proxies through technology to promote desirable employee behaviors. We have a famous saying at Best Buy: "If a Best Buy store is not given enough signage for a certain promotion, they will make it every time." We see this over and over again in so many areas, but one of my favorite general examples about the importance of environmental proxies to guide behaviors came from watching the re-landscaping process on a college campus. After adding new contours, trees, and other amenities to improve the beauty of the campus, the administration wisely decided to simply wait and watch where people actually walked before laying out the sidewalks. Wait for the path that people actually use, and then pave that path.

RADICAL TRANSPARENCY

The C-Suite develops responsive ways for information technology to enable enterprise strategy based on emerging trends in the general economy and industry-specific environments, which include a range of elements from disruptive technologies to better customer service. How does the changing global information environment shape the formation of enterprise IT strategy?

Change is a central issue for all enterprises, and all enterprises will change over time whether they want to or not. This change comes about when the enterprise is placed in an environment that demands innovation on different terms. There's nothing like a terrorist threat or other external threat to unite internal factions. I see three forces responsible for big shifts in enterprise policy. One is proactive, based on the profit motive. "Wow! Look at the potential behind this change, and it doesn't pose any conflict with our current business. Let's line up the resources and go get this prize!" This may be a no-brainer, but it's also the most infrequent force for change. The second is reactive, based on competitive threat, where the executives say, "Oh shit, look what Amazon's doing! We've got to do this too." This force for change actually becomes very useful if you can find a way to portray it favorably by leveraging the fear.

The third and newer force is the radical transparency threat posed by bloggers and Twitter. I recently addressed the cabinet of Minnesota's governor, where they asked me about Twitter and how we listen to customers. It wasn't hard to read the intimidation on their faces, followed by the inevitable question, "Wow! What does this mean for us?" I replied, "Well, it means that you and every government executive and every other public figure and agency is at some point going to have their pants pulled down on the Internet—just like on the playground. The bad news is that it *will* happen to you; the good news is that it will happen to everyone, including your competitors and your critics." In a small social circle like high school, students live to de-pants one another on Facebook. A little bit later in life, everyone's going to know when you change your Facebook status from "Married" to "Single." These events increasingly stand out in ways that we would prefer to communicate more gradually or privately. Too bad it's all happening in real time now.

We're entering a Post-Perfect World, and Tiger Woods is the poster child for this significant stage of social evolution. First we all learn that there's no tooth fairy; then we learn that there's no Santa Claus; we learn that America's not perfect; then we learn that JFK had a mistress; and then we learned that Tiger Woods cheated on his wife. Each new step on this path of realization is another loss. At some level we all desire perfection, and at some level we were all rooting for Tiger. In the end, imperfection humanizes the world for the CIO just like it does for the rest of us. It lowers the bar. We can be more genuine and realistic about our own performance. The Germans call it *schadenfreude*, or pleasure derived from the misfortunes of others. Since no company is perfect in this Post-Perfect World, the new standard is about how hard we *try* to be more perfect, like Toyota's response to the gas pedal problem. The *transparency* of social media demonstrates how hard we try.

If your company loses *one* piece of luggage, everybody's going to hear about it. A Domino's Pizza employee picks his nose on video. Although he wasn't even doing it on a real pizza and was only joking, he caused millions of dollars in damages. But if you go online and Google "Colbert Domino's Pizza" you'll be able to watch a remarkable video. He names Domino's (one of his own sponsors), as his "Alpha Dog of the Week." Colbert saluted Domino's Pizza for admitting that their pizza was gross by using their own commercials before he sums matters up for his viewers:[7]

So to recap, Domino's old pizza's cheese:

- Did not taste good
- Had no aroma
- Was not cheese

. . . and, because they are an Alpha Dog, folks, Domino's is *not* apologizing. After all, we're the human garbage cans who bought these trash disks by the millions. Domino's is advertising that they simply weren't fit to wipe your ass with. Well folks, I have tasted the new pizza [takes another bite], and there are *so many things* I would rather wipe with it.

What really makes Domino's an Alpha Dog is not how boldly they're copping to the widespread . . . nay, *universal* condemnation of their products. Now the reasons for this shift were recently laid out by Domino's CEO, David Brandon, who admitted that though they scored high marks for service and delivery, "The weakness in our value chain with the customer was really in our core product."

So Domino's, for joining the great corporate tradition of screwing your customers and then having the balls to ask them to come back for more [Goldman Sachs, Citi, Fannie Mae, Bank of America, and AIG logos appear on screen], you, gentlemen, are my Alpha Dog of the Week.

Domino's basically allowed him to twist their press release, run them through the ringer, and come out smelling like a rose. This is what radical transparency can do by means of Twitter, YouTube, bloggers, and the other methods. Think about the ways that the press, as never before, gives us direct access to our government leaders and bypasses what Congress (government's middle management) tells us. The Fourth Estate has never been so involved in private enterprise. The Best Buy and Geek Squad ad agency is Crispin Porter & Bogusky, who are very good with challenger brands. They use an asymmetrical guerilla approach to rejuvenate brands like Burger King, when their restaurant business was losing out to McDonalds. Recognizing that the core audience was 18–24 year-old males, they developed the Whopper Freakout ad campaign where they simply took the Whopper off the store menu and filmed the boys' actual responses. This is a logical, intelligent, commonsense approach.

In this emerging era of radical transparency, Domino's can publicly demonstrate its own understanding that customers won't settle for the company advertising line any longer. We can't trust anything after Tylenol and Tiger Woods and Toyota. So what do we believe? We believe it when Domino's gives us the real video from customers about its cardboard pizza crust and tomato soup pizza sauce. This never would have been possible without the Fourth Estate. Just like Domino's, the enterprise reaps the greatest opportunities of radical transparency when it embraces those principles head on.

Remember that this doesn't mean that you have to take off your kimono on day one. Freedom with fences. Fences and filters are the ways that the enterprise defines what the brand stands for. Rules are important, but the rules need to be able to justify their own existence under all future conditions. Since this is impossible, since no policy is perfect, all policies need expiration dates so that they can be updated in a timely fashion. It's just like milk in the grocery store. The CIO needs to remove systems from the shelf before they reach their expiration date and sour the employee or the customer. Radical transparency helps us keep fresh, but only if we pay attention to and manage these new information sources.

PROACTIVE RISK PRACTICES

In a world where information technology has become a tool for increasingly aggressive attacks from the competition, how can the CIO use information technology to proactively address these threats?

In the radical transparency model, where external threats increasingly become an unpredictable force for catastrophic change, the question becomes, "How do we become more proactive like Domino's?" I don't have all the answers, but I've gathered a few clues, and the CIO is central to the solution because it all comes back to data. How can we *simulate* external threats? Can we gather the data and audit ourselves? Some people in the organization will be inspired to change through the narrative of storytelling; others require data. "I need hard facts and actionable intelligence before I change the Homeland Security Threat Level." How do we give this kind of actionable intelligence to those who need it within the business enterprise?

The constants in this interface will always be human factors such as inertia, the natural selection of environmental proxies, and inattention. This is an important issue for the CIO. For example, every time I boot up my corporate PC, I get this message that says,

> "WARNING: It is company policy that you will keep all your computerized information confidential … blah …blah … blah. Click here to accept."

I click to accept. But guess what happens after about the fifth day? I don't even read it anymore before clicking. The CIO understands why the enterprise needs to have that warning, and the CIO is about the only person responsible for the effectiveness of that important message. One solution to crisis fatigue of this kind would be to change the language of the message every day—or change the color of the background—or move the click button—or place a basic math equation to enable the boot. Never give employees the same screen twice if the routine safeguard is truly important. Mixing it up and rotating different options allow the CIO to battle crisis fatigue.

There's another time-proven but seldom-employed method for proactively responding to the threats imposed by radical transparency—the fire drill. The CEO and CIO have to run fire drills to keep their jobs in this pull-the-other-guys-pants-down Internet environment. What happens when a customer with a valid concern sends a Tweet, which then gets re-Tweeted, which then gets picked up by a consumerist, who blogs it, which then triggers a dateline by NBC? How much might that cost a company? Now the CEO and CIO can put their resistance to change in context and model the same behaviors for all enterprise employees. We've anticipated tons of scenarios—Geek Squad agents driving drunk and killing a family of four, inappropriate behavior in the home, data privacy violations such as touching customer digital property in the store and in the home—and we do this in conjunction with operations, audit control, loss prevention, and public relations. We get together regularly and maintain an evolving crisis plan, but we don't just build them to choreograph contingency plans for assigning blame; we use the plans to prevent blame.

As we're talking, Geek Squad is getting *killed* in the press about a service we offer on new PCs called "Optimization." A consumer Web site has performed its own tests and "proved beyond a shadow of a doubt" that it's a "rip-off." We've run this service for a long time, customers had perceived it as valuable, but we were actually in the process of ending it. We were going to kill it a couple of years ago, but Vista was so bad. So we had a service with a good track record, we knew Windows 7 would probably be better and negate the need for this service to some extent, and we already had the plans to kill this service. On top of all this I've actually hated the service for two years, but *shame on me* for not killing it when I wanted to, or alternatively, stepping in with the data to demonstrate its value.

What could I have done? I have a very clear answer . . . *now*. I wish that I had just gone to the store, pulled out the top-five best selling PCs, videotaped my own grandmother opening each product with a stopwatch, and document the time it took her to remove the computer, install the software, remove the crapware, and follow it with all the other things offered in our $39 Optimization service. Then I'd repeat the same recording with one of our Geek Squad agents performing the same steps. We then get to say, "We're charging you $39 dollars for something that it will take you at least two hours to complete, and you'll know you've got it right. Make your own choice."

Best Buy is an ethical company. Best Buy already dropped rebates a few years ago, and the CEO is almost ready to offer a refund. We may still end up doing this as part of our response to the blogger radical transparency factor. I keep reminding myself that I'd voiced my concern about this service in meetings for two years, and I remember seeing that the crowd has no mind of its own. Where's the one throat to choke?

This is part of the problem of managing innovation and change within the enterprise, and being aware of the human factors that resist change is critical for the CIO's own human tendencies to resist change. I should have done that videotape; I should have become my own internal blogger. Then I should have become my own internal investigative journalist to do a dateline report on Geek Squad's Optimization service. This would work to freak out the other decision makers in the enterprise, because I can tell them, "This content could have come from a real blogger. We need to either change this policy now or present its merits in a different light." All executives tend to think of audit as a financial function, but the CIO (along with the marketing group) can use informational audits to proactively keep up the pants of the enterprise.

THE CIO AND THE CUSTOMER

Like the CFO, the CIO is arguably responsible for the equivalent of an enterprise "utility," where employees and other stakeholders expect to hear a dial tone each and every time they pick up the proverbial "receiver." With the incredible number of active relationships in which CIO responsibilities may appear to conflict, how do best practice CIOs manage to strike a balance?

Relationships with executive peers, enterprise employees, IT employees, customers, competitors, and business partners all compete for the CIO's attention. As margin protection comes from value-added services, services within Best Buy have become a hybrid, where Geek Squad offers a kind of enterprise capability, like IT in most companies, but where we're also highly customer-facing. In this sense, the CIO works to be close to the "customer" within any enterprise. Without presuming to speak for the many different ways that CIOs serve their specific mission and strategic mandates in different enterprises, *all* enterprises and IT organizations have entered the service business in one form or another. More and more, the enterprise is composed of several service divisions, even those companies that traditionally see themselves as strictly manufacturing entities. If someone in your enterprise answers the phone, you're in the service business. Sending out invoices is a service.

Ultimately, every service business relies on two core capabilities: people and process. Invariably, process is driven by IT systems in

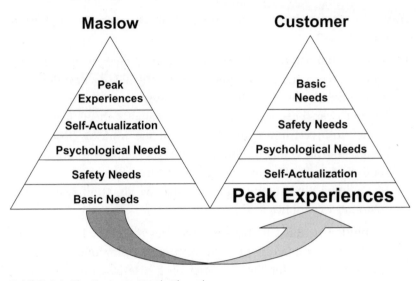

Exhibit 1.1: The Customer Needs Hierarchy

Source: *Adapted from Abraham H. Maslow, "A Theory of Human Motivation,"* Psychological Review *50(4) (1943): 370–96.*

our Knowledge Economy, and what I see as the emerging *Curiosity Economy*. In some sense, humans are only there doing tasks that the IT system has not yet become capable of performing.

In the Post-Perfect World of radial transparency, I see a reversed form of Maslow's Hierarchy, a Customer Relationship Hierarchy of Needs, as a way to resolve competitive conflict for the CIO's attention. In a conventional Maslow's Hierarchy of Needs, safety and security are the foundation (see Exhibit 1.1). The Customer Relationship Hierarchy sequences the ways employees address the customer's peak experiences by placing employee creativity and problem-solving first. One principle in this kind of practice is that whoever's closest to the customer wins. The CIO needs to work with all employees to move complexity away from the customer, not towards the customer. When it comes to the increasingly ubiquitous role that technology plays in the relationship between the enterprise and the customer, the CIO is responsible for making sure that the customer experience maximizes simplicity and minimizes complexity.

How do you achieve this with Best Buy or Geek Squad customers?

The relationship between the customer-facing employee and the customer is frequently handicapped by the outdated practices designed into increasingly short-lived legacy systems (ones that often haven't even been amortized off the balance sheet, leaving no money to invest in a better one). Someone working close to the customer who wants to improve the experience with an on-the-spot creative inspiration is told, "No. Our system can't do that. Make do with what you have." In other words, "Compromise the customer experience."

The resolution to this situation also requires the CIO's leadership to break down competing priorities so that the employee can make the best decision for the customer on a case-by-case basis. Geek Squad's motto is, *Cura et Celeritas*, which is Latin for "accuracy and speed," and synonymous with effectiveness and efficiency. I emphasize that this is a *three*-word motto: accuracy *and* speed. One word may symbolically come before the other, but the word "and" communicates that the goal of every action, process, and system should be to enable a Geek Squad agent to effectively address a customer problem on the first attempt *and* do so efficiently.

Both of these goals are noble and serve the customer well, so which one takes priority? This motto is also there to guide agent priorities whenever one business task or objective appears to compete with another task or objective. If this means giving the employee overtime to work a longer day and do things right the first time, that goal trumps more conventional determinations of efficiency standards in the Geek Squad workplace. If an agent needs to be less efficient to preserve outcomes, then so be it. The message behind this motto has held up over time, and the key to its success has been for leadership to prevent anything from being coded into decision-making and management policies when it comes to customer resource allocations that support this motto.

In terms of relationships with executive peers in this context, the CIO assumes that executive peers share customer-facing employees' creativity and problem solving priorities while remaining vigilant

for paradoxes. I use this rule to apply as a lens for discerning paradoxes as they arise. When listening to the perspectives of other
executives, I use this lens to determine whether or not any given
issue has been appropriately prioritized from the *customer* perspective. Are we complicating or simplifying the customer experience?
I go so far as to say that the customer experience is really a by-
product of the employee experience, and as such, prioritizes all
the CIO's other relationships accordingly.

If the executive team really wants the best customer experience, they
need to focus on the customer's perception of outcomes, and the
employee experience is the most accessible part of this equation
for executive management control. For example, whenever we
test a new product or service launch, I put multiple cameras on
the employees to count the number of steps or clicks or forms that
need to be completed under the constant assumption that I need
to "Twitter" their processes—I want to eliminate redundancy and
tasks that employees don't like and that don't add value to their
work for the customer. This improves the customer experience
through employee proxies, and improves the employee experience because they're less fatigued intellectually and emotionally.
No employee goes to work wanting a crappy experience. This
practice has the added benefit of helping me sort out the crappy
process from the crappy employee, so that the customer experiences neither.

I use another observation technique to sort out and perfect customer
experiences in terms of the contributions of the process and the
employee. When a single employee ignores a process, the employee
is the problem. When several employees, locations, or business
units ignore a process, the process is the problem. There's no other
way around it. This kind of employee/process phenomenon can't
be controlled, but if the CIO is smart and observes the dynamics
of these phenomena, the business can adapt and take advantage of these conscious and unconscious employee behaviors
throughout the enterprise and in the enterprise IT organization.

**This seems to be a huge leap of faith for the day-to-day work
lives of enterprise employees, both in the IT organization**

and those facing the customer. Describe some of the ways that the CIO can sell radical transparency practices to these employees.

When we look at the performance of Best Buy stores in terms of quality and reputation, we find no geographic rhyme or reason for the differences except that great, engaged leaders have great, engaged employees, and customers follow quickly behind. We're in a transition period now that can be traced to declining margins from Asian manufacturing and competition driving smart managers to adjust their management style and find new sources of revenue from areas like service. Some managers continue to struggle and pursue old habits. One of the ways to solve the problem of middle management "consistency" is through the concept of radical transparency, where customers and other employees enforce the new SOP. Enterprise transparency allows for the development of practices that bypass middle management, where executive leadership speaks directly to frontline employees. Employees can then use this to sort out conflicting messages based on old habits that they hear from their managers.

One could argue that middle management only exists until systems are developed to take their places. Radical transparency is about rapidly collapsing that middle layer and putting the CEO, CIO, and other C-Suite executives in direct contact with the customers, to more efficiently direct resources and give the customers what they want. These parties really don't want to have anyone in the middle of their relationship. [Editor's note: Gary Cokins discusses the financial elements of this dynamic in Chapter 6.] One could also argue that the traditional CIO and other senior executives have effectively (but unwisely) in-sourced the customer relationship experience to middle management. This kind of in-sourcing increases the distance between key radical transparency decision makers. While some middle management will always be necessary on a practical level, the goal is for the CIO to develop the means for middle management to enhance the executive/customer relationship, rather than get in the way.

CIOs who promote radical transparency principles understand that some employees will initially be afraid to speak up. For example, good Best Buy general managers usually post their email addresses, but some are afraid to do this. Who wants to have customers screaming at you all the time? They don't know how to handle the customer emails because they haven't set up a response process. Part of my job is to equip them with appropriate response tools as part of their working environments so that they don't feel overwhelmed. Over time, middle managers become more comfortable with transparency practices. The right IT environment promotes transparency behaviors.

When employees are afraid to post their phone number because they're going to get too many calls and become overwhelmed, the CIO and the executive team needs to remind employees that it's like cleaning out the garage. Yes, the initial clean-out is a lot of work, but it informs people about the enterprise culture and what the enterprise managers have to do to achieve *Cura et Celeritas*. After this initial investment, maintenance easily keeps it from being overrun again. Not every manager in Best Buy is perfect, but they tend to be pretty competitive, and this sets a standard. Once one or two managers take off with a new practice, the rest soon fall in line.

The general managers that have already made their email addresses available to store customers are farther along, but they're usually posting the addresses in places where customers see them on their way *out* of the store. I want to see the email address in every aisle and above the customer service desk, where the new customer service standard is a sign that says, "If your experience isn't perfect, see me or send an email to . . ."

We're evolving. Many Best Buy stores now have their own Twitter accounts, because while email remains efficient it's not as efficient as a text message. So the sign of the future will invite the customer to send an email, call a phone number (which will also be transcribed like Google Voice, and also emailed), text message, and Twitter the store managers. This invites the customer to choose how to participate in quality control, and it reminds the employee that the manager is listening.

The CIO's responsibilities for creatively, but safely, managing the enterprise identity through brand and customer expe-

rience have become a recurrent theme in this dialogue. What lies ahead, and how can CIOs prepare the enterprise and IT organization?

For a peek at the future, go to the Best Buy store locator page for a harbinger of the practice trend I'm talking about here, involving customer-facing enterprise employees. As with other enterprises, people tend to think of bestbuy.com as *the* company Web site. I think this concept is aging fast. One could argue that the fleet of iPhone application sites are now as or more important than the Apple Web site. The store locator pages of the future won't be static lists of addresses, links to Google maps, hours, and phone numbers. When a customer goes to bestbuy.com, clicks on store locator, and enters a zip code, the store locator pages are essentially customized store blogs where the general manager can now have direct control over the page and customize this heavily used customer interface. Without going through the Best Buy enterprise IS, department managers can post news, deals, Twitter feeds, photographs, and other elements of what they perceive to be customer interests, right down to the store's favorite charities.

The future of bestbuy.com is no longer the corporate home page, and customers will use the customized locator page as a portal to their local store, which feels more *personal*. We've all heard stories about local Wal-Marts in Texas selling rifles and Target Stores in Miami selling a locally sourced line of boating products—enterprise customer-facing employees instinctively know that this is the wave of the future, and best practice CIOs work to harness these employee-related insights and customer-facing opportunities.

In the end, Best Buy is creating the means to allow the customer to help us make our most important decisions through our customer-facing employees. Once these freedom-with-fences practices become the norm, the open channel to the customer will be almost impossible to manipulate. Customers will become increasingly comfortable with using these channels once they experience the degree to which they are affecting enterprise decision making. These practices will actually decrease the amount of work that employees, managers, and executives must perform.

Another important after-effect of radical transparency and enterprise identity management is the training of customers to police *each other*. Companies have started to learn that "In terms of quality assurance purposes, this call may be recorded by the *customer*." Consequently, that frontline, minimum-wage, hourly employee is learning very quickly that the customers can hold them immediately accountable. "Hey, I've got your boss' Twitter account, and my finger is poised to send a nasty message. We can do this the easy way, or we can do it the hard way." By proxy, the CIO will experience more and more pressure from the frontline managers for new systems to be able to listen and respond to customers faster. Then the CIO can turn to the CEO and more forcefully request, "Please give those frontline managers what they need to capture this customer information." While responding to the requests of these frontline managers, the CIO's responsibility becomes one of predicting different forms of possible futures. CIOs know where information system development is going before the CEOs or the GMs, so they need to skate ahead of the puck.

While employees and customers will increasingly have a finger on the enterprise Web site input and edit button, the CIO controls this functionality. For example, Wikipedia has not become a Wild West of the Internet despite its user openness. It aims for a democratic consensus, but an aristocracy comes into play when issues cannot be resolved by consensus. Rather than employ a dedicated staff of content editors and fact-checkers, sometimes the aristocracy takes over and declares martial law to lock down the page on Islam or the Profit Mohammed (peace be upon him), or a hotly debated political issue like Iran. In the event of a really big decision, the monarchy assumes control, and Jimmy Wales makes the call. All these layers can operate simultaneously when rules and filters based on enterprise policy guide employee and customer input on the Web, and the CIO introduces safeguards to protect against brand anarchy. Brand differentiation must be maintained to remain successful. The only way CIOs are ever going to understand where those fences need to go is by exercising that other brain hemisphere: by riding out on the range—(camera phone in hand) by playing on Twitter, by downloading and using mint iPhone apps, by hanging with hackers, and yes, by going to customer service conferences. Best practice CIOs don't need to become radicals, but they really need to know a few.

CIOs can use augmented expertise to direct the application of technology where superhuman employees provide a level of competitive differentiation while safeguarding the brand in the Post-Perfect World of radical transparency because the technology-augmented employees prevent dumb mistakes. All too often, the CIO and IT organization fall into the trap of simply treading water while trying to manage the budget, forgetting to look ahead to the future, and build what comes next. Ideally, the CIO has already detected what employees across the enterprise need from information systems, anticipated how systems might provide critical information, researched what is possible (and impossible), and provided an early warning toward establishing a collaborative partnership with other enterprise employees for ways to close the gap.

Yes, the CIO is tasked with reconciling budgets and doing more with less. A good CIO gets ahead of such problems in that part of the job that deals with predicting and planning for possible futures. The CIO isn't a glorified short-order cook taking orders from employees. On top of perfection and reading the future, a good CIO's job is to read minds. Welcome to the C-Suite.

THE IT ORGANIZATION

Perfectibility has been another running theme in this conversation. Describe the ways that the CIO can work to improve the awareness and performance of the IT employee, to perfect information technology services for all enterprise stakeholders.

CIOs should have the least personal inertia of anyone in the enterprise, and I see no excuses based on enterprise size, age, adherence to an operational status quo, or other factor. While a CIO may be prone to personal inertia based on a personality issue, enterprises and CEOs would be wise to look for someone with a low personal inertial moment as a basic criterion for any CIO hire.

I'm always amazed by the work of Socrates, Plato, Aristotle, and the Greek playwrights because I can't conceive of what I might do or write that would still be relevant in 3000 years. At the same time, when Plato writes in his *Republic* that a city becomes unmanageable once it grows larger than about 100,000 citizens, I feel challenged. I believe that information technology allows us to expand past some of those previous limitations because we can form vastly greater numbers of connections over greater distances than ever before, thereby redefining our human limits. The size of organizations becomes a source of opportunity rather than limitations. I understand why people still believe that big government can't be effective, but they're still thinking in terms of how government managed in the 1970s or ancient Greece. A government that knows how to use technologies of self-service could do healthcare more efficiently than we might think. Not as efficiently as we all might like to see in the time before our current Post-Perfect World, but such a government is capable of far more efficiencies than most people have come to expect, based on their dated view of size related to efficiency.

I see the same dynamics where the companies of the future no longer depend on the genius CEO because they will have very secular, agnostic, curious employees. Curiosity is the future's most important human trait. The Knowledge Economy will yield to the Curiosity Economy, where people will say, "I don't know everything, but using the power of search, both inside and outside the enterprise, I can find the *answers we need.*" The employee I now value is not the knowledge worker but the *knowledge seeker*, and this is my vision for Geek Squad going forward.

I used to think that I could train anybody to do anything, but then I learned that there are some skills that cannot be trained. These are the skills I look for when I hire. Looking at hiring from a chronological perspective, an enterprise will bring on talent at its inception. After that, leadership activities focus on recruiting better and better talent. Part of my training practice is to show my current people how to hire the best new people by asking them to look for three skills that I believe are essential for our work but impossible to train: curiosity, ethics, and drive.

Curiosity is tops for a very important reason. With the growing importance of search in the Curiosity Economy, where finding usable information is the coin of the realm, it's less important that an employee knows something than that they can locate the data that leads to an answer. I find that any subsequent training I give such employees sticks much better: They tend to be more contributive, they're more engaged, they seem to naturally do what the enterprise needs them to do. It's very easy to take this kind of employee on a long journey of expanding their points of view. It's so much easier for the CIO to get what the enterprise needs when the employees know what they're looking for and know how to look creatively while driven by their own curiosity.

As leaders, CIOs can encourage curiosity while inspiring innovation and creative thinking through playfulness, and the first thing the CIO must do is model that behavior. My nickname around here is "The Reality Distortion Field," where the message is one of permission: If I can do it, you can do it; because I'm doing it, you're also expected to do it. I first learned this working in the laboratory of a college professor. We were building a flight simulator for the U.S. Navy that turned into an after-hours video game machine. He also encouraged us to surf the new Web browsers that were coming out in 1991 and 1992. I asked, "Is it really okay for us to be using these expensive, federally-funded government computers?" He replied, "Yes! It's essential to your research. When you're playing, you're relaxing, you're opening up your mind, you're going to come up with all these new ideas. I expect you to play with this gear. Mess with it! Take it apart! Hack it!" This is how the CIO can facilitate everyone in the IT organization to use technology creatively. Take what you know and experiment.

Looking at either Best Buy or Geek Squad, describe some of the specific ways that you model and encourage IT organization performance.

Socialization is arguably a form of play, and since play is the most effective and primal form of learning, it's a huge opportunity for the CIO to build a culture of curiosity and learning within the IT organization. People learn when they work and when they play together. We now know this biologically,[8] and meetings should be fun. This doesn't mean goofy or nonproductive; it means engaging. We watch TED videos at Geek Squad, and I like to take my teams on right-brain curveball outings, like last month, when we took a tour of "The Louvre and the Masterpiece" exhibit that came to the Minneapolis Institute of Arts.

My take on effective humor is to find the serious and exaggerate it. This includes Geek Squad Agent uniforms, the cars we drive, right down to the shoes we wear—where our logo is imprinted on each sole—leaving countless reminders for customers around the world with every step an agent takes in the snow, rain, mud, or dust. Things are only funny because they're true, so the idea is to take the truth and stretch it to the point where it becomes newsworthy. But it becomes more than newsworthiness for the employees, it becomes internalized. In the beginning, employees used to complain, "Why do we have to wear a uniform? No one's ever going to see me in here fixing laptops."

That question gets answered through the agents' first-hand experiences. For example, when we introduced Geek Squad City, a national laptop repair facility, the concept started out as a gigantic, warehoused repository for efficient, quality computer repair. We weren't very far into the development process when I said, "Wait a minute . . . there's going to be 600 Geek Squad Agents here. This isn't a depot; it's a city—the largest concentration of Geeks around. Let's not lose this!" As we prepared our agents for the launch, I told them, "Hey, you're not going to find a cure for cancer in this building today, but the cure for cancer could be on the next computer you fix, and that's how close you are to history. So act like it." That's why I like the uniform. That's why we wear uniforms. It's important how we behave when no one is watching. Now Geek Squad agents like to have their driver's license and passport photos taken in uniform.

And perfect performance?

Perfect service means listening to customers, which so often means listening to complaints. But the creative approach doesn't wait for the customer to become unhappy. Rather than relying on automation as a responsive, state-of-the-art practice, a best practice CIO encourages people to build new processes that anticipate and prevent. For example, from a Best Buy perspective, rather than becoming faster at fixing a broken refrigerator, we want our employees to learn how to *anticipate* when our different models of fridges will break, and use the data to *prevent* them from breaking. The CIO and other C-Suite executives can't do this without the curious customer-facing employee who listens. Teach your employees how to swim up the food chain and work with your suppliers. "Your compressor belts fail after 9 months. Design a better belt if you want us to keep carrying your equipment." If they balk, turn to the customer. "Hey, we tried to tell Frigidaire to fix this problem, but they wouldn't listen to us. Before it leaves our store you can give us $30 to install a better belt so that it will work much longer for you." The next thing you know, we make money and the customer's happy. We're moving from automation to anticipation/prevention, which like in healthcare, is the most mature state of being.

I have all of the speeches I give around the world recorded so that my Geek Squad agents everywhere can watch them. I encourage them to be experimental the same way. Where most teams used to turn out a bullet-point email report listing the things they accomplished in the last month, I requested something different. I handed out a batch of iPod touches and told the teams in China and Turkey and Spain that I wanted a personalized monthly report format. "Instead of filming yourself sitting at your desk telling me what you did, take the camera and film yourself on the streets of Izmir in Turkey. Tell me about the city and what it's like to work there. Use the camera to show me what you do and how you succeed at your work. Let me get to know you."

The device we're employing here is to humanize the enterprise with playfulness. I send a message internally. Experimenting playfully with original ideas is a way to come up with new products and services. Just as important, the playfulness also sends important messages to the customer. We don't take ourselves too seriously, we're reasonable, we're going to give you a good experience, but we're never so arrogant as to lose either our sense of humor or our ability to listen. So no matter how big we get, our culture and our employees will still be very human in providing service to our customers.

CIOs need to serve everyone, and their relevance is central to the enterprise. This happens when the CIO rails on all levels of the enterprise to use the best, most current personal technology and teaches them the best ways to use that technology. C-Suite executives balk? Unacceptable! We need to be eating our own dog food. As I ring this bell, I credit our Best Buy CIO, who listens and gets it while trying to balance Sarbanes-Oxley and SEC laws with our commitment to radical transparency. Unfortunately, some fences are so long, high, and wide that they leave the enterprise and the CIO very few choices. Radical transparency has trained me not to harbor any illusions of control, but to aim for a goal and do my very best to fail in the right direction.

NOTES

1. Richard Florida, *Rise of the Creative Class* (New York: Basic Books, 1992).
2. Daniel Pink, *A Whole New Mind: Why Right-Brainers Will Rule the Future* (New York: Riverhead Trade, 2006).
3. Peter Schjeldahl, "The Art World Then and Now: Bronzino at the Met," *The New Yorker*, February 1, 2010, www.newyorker.com/arts/critics/artworld/2010/02/01/100201craw_artworld_schjeldahl.
4. Roger Martin, www.creativeclass.com/creative_class/2009/02/20/reality-the-enemy-of-innovation/.
5. Mark Herzog, http://twitter.com/runner_dude/status/3535831381.
6. Linda Stone, http://lindastone.net/category/attention/continuous-partial-attention/.
7. The following excerpt is a transcription of the television show that aired this segment from www.hulu.com/watch/119131/the-colbert-report-alpha-dog-of-the-week-dominos-pizza.
8. National Research Council and Institute of Medicine, *From Neurons to Neighborhoods: The Science of Early Childhood Development*, Committee of Integrating the Science of Early Childhood Development. Jack P. Shonkoff

and Deborah A. Phillips, Editors, Board on Children, Youth, and Families, Commission on Behavioral and Social Sciences and Education. Washington, D.C.: National Academy Press (2000), pp. 165–169, and Mark K. Smith, (1999) "The social/situational orientation to learning," *the encyclopedia of informal education*, www.infed.org/biblio/learning-social.htm. Last update: September 3, 2009.

CHAPTER **2**

Why Does IT Behave the Way It Does?

Bill Flemming

MAKING SENSE OF IT BUSINESS MANAGEMENT

With all the money spent on IT system management, with all the products purchased to improve IT performance, and with all the consulting dollars spent, why has the average IT organization progressed only to the point where IT management proudly boasts of proactive engagements in preventing system failures?

How *Did* IT Get to This Point?

In the 2007 edition of this book, SAS Institute quoted Gartner statistics that surveyed the degree to which different industries developed in Gartner's IT Infrastructure and Operations Maturity Model. Gartner data from 2005 showed that only nine percent of IT operations had reached the "Service" level of maturity. Nine percent! Further, 51 percent wanted to be at the Service level by 2006. What were the corresponding numbers for results released in 2008? Eight percent had made it to Service and twelve percent hoped to be there by 2012.[1] Granted, the Gartner IT Maturity Model changed to a more sophisticated version, but with a sustained industry-wide lack of progress toward achieving IT infrastructure and operations "maturity," either the paradigm is wrong, or IT leadership and their C-Suite peers haven't yet put all of the pieces in place to achieve the goal. This chapter examines the key elements of IT maturity, what the industry provides in terms of products and thought leadership, remaining gaps, and how the best practice CIO can address these issues.

The best place to start is a neglected but essential leading indicator: higher education for IT professionals. This first became obvious after speaking about IT opportunities with a newly minted Computer Science graduate student. As we spoke about system and IT business management jobs, it became clear to me that this new grad from a high-priced school had no idea what I was talking about. This lack of integrated IT system and business management curricula isn't just restricted to young graduates. Some of the answers to our neglected business management education lie in how IT professionals are educated and trained.

Colleges and universities educate and train engineers within Computer Science curriculums. Engineering expertise is required to keep the lights on and the systems functioning, but the comprehensive, strategic management of information technology is not an engineering exercise, particularly the challenging business alignment portion. Strategic IT management is a business exercise that requires a more comprehensively educated breed of manager. When hiring IT professionals out of college, most businesses hire Computer Science majors, MBAs, or Computer Engineers. Those IT engineers eventually progress into management. The curriculum for an undergraduate Computer Science major at Carnegie Mellon appears in Exhibit 2.1.

Where are the courses in Capacity Management? Service Level Management? Costing? Business Alignment? Computer Science and Computer Engineering programs train technologists but not business managers; MBA programs produce business managers but not IT technologists. If higher education is not producing IT business managers, then the answers have to come from elsewhere. To get to the answers a historical perspective is necessary.

Computer Science

- **15-121** Introduction to Data Structures (students with no prior programming experience take **15-110** or **15-117** (mini), Introduction to Programming, **and 15-121**)
- **15-123** Effective Programming in C and UNIX
- **15-128** Freshman Immigration Course
- **15-211** Fundamental Data Structures and Algorithms
- **15-212** Principles of Programming
- **15-213** Introduction to Computer Systems
- **15-251** Great Theoretical Ideas in Computer Science
- **15-451** Algorithm Design and Analysis
- one Communications course:
  - **15-221** Technical Communication for Computer Scientists
- one Algorithms & Complexity elective:
  - **15-354** Computational Discrete Mathematics
  - **15-355** Modern Computer Algebra
  - **15-453** Formal Languages and Automata
  - **21-301** Combinatorics
  - **21-484** Graph Theory
  - others as designated
- one Applications elective:
  - **15-313** Foundations of Software Engineering
  - **15-322/15-323** Computer Music
  - **15-381** Artificial Intelligence: Representation and Problem Solving
  - **15-384** Robotic Manipulation
  - **15-385** Computer Vision
  - **15-415** Database Applications
  - **15-462** Computer Graphics
  - **10-601** Machine Learning
  - **11-411** Natural Language Processing
  - others as designated
- one Logics & Languages elective:
  - **15-312** Foundations of Programming Languages
  - **15-317** Constructive Logic
  - **15-414** Bug Catching: Automated Program Verification and Testing
  - **21-300** Basic Logic
  - **80-311** Computability and Incompleteness
  - others as designated
- one Software Systems elective:
  - **15-410** Operating System Design and Implementation
  - **15-411** Compiler Design
  - **15-440** Distributed Computer Systems
  - **15-441** Computer Networks
  - others as designated
- two Computer Science electives (can be from any SCS department)

Exhibit 2.1: Carnegie Mellon Computer Science Curriculum

Source: *www.cmu.edu/academics/interdisciplinary-programs.shtml.*

43

When Mainframes Ruled

When I first entered the industry in the mid-1980s, stable, efficient mainframes were the predominant business computer. They were housed in raised-floor, environmentally controlled, glass-walled rooms typically called the Glass House. While machines were large, the business computing world was small by today's standards. The programming languages—COBOL, FORTRAN, and PL/1—were procedural and well-suited for the business applications of the era. For the most part, business applications were devoted to payroll, receivables, payables, general ledger, transaction management, batch reporting, and database management. Business applications crunched numbers quickly and accurately. The business connection was obvious. Businesses without the applications did the number management by hand—a pencil-and-paper bound method that was slow, expensive, and prone to error.

While the Glass House was centrally controlled, monolithic, and inflexible, it was stable, reliable, and almost always available. End users at the time complained about the control and inflexibility of IT, but that inflexibility and control safeguarded system management. IBM's Multiple Virtual Storage (MVS) operating system and Systems Network Architecture (SNA) network environment defined and controlled access. User transactions were entered into 3270 terminals written for Customer Interface Control System (CICS). Users claimed they were hard to use, and training costs were high. Virtual Telecommunications Access Method (VTAM) controlled peripheral access. Everyone adhered to the standards set by this MVS/SNA world. The quickest route to vendor disgrace was to offer a product incompatible with Glass House standards, and when product incompatibility brought down a production system, the vendor seldom got a second chance. Stability and reliability were paramount values for mainframe performance.

Before long, MVS could not supply all the necessary system management tools.[2] While MVS focused on control, other system management vendors such as Computer Associates and Legent marketed products for job scheduling, tape backup, report production and distribution, network management, storage management, console management, and capacity management/chargeback systems. During this era, most businesses managed for high transaction volume during business hours and tight batch windows in the evenings. System managers were concerned with hardware tuning and ensuring the availability of online environments. They were well paid and no one in the business understood them, but MVS was the operating system that ran the world. It was a perfect system management world, but not a perfect end-user world.

The hermetically sealed Glass House that no one on the outside understood was not spending time reacting to outages. MVA and SNA were built to provide an environment that set standards, and those standards ensured high availability. Network managers knew what the access traffic was going to be and where it was coming from. Unlike today, networks were not open to the outside world. Capacity Management concentrated on CPU utilization and storage needs in a controlled fashion. The Glass House was charged with providing stable environments for transactions, accounting systems, and reports. In a sense, they were completely aligned with higher business priorities. But all good things must come to an end. The personal computer and UNIX made their debuts, rapidly reordering IT system management priorities.

Desktop and Distributed Technology Explode

In the early 1990s, several technologies incubating since the 1970s had matured and gained rapid acceptance, but each of these innovative technologies depended on the other co-evolving technologies to achieve that acceptance. For example, the Internet depended on other enabling platforms, and the enabling technology that led the charge and changed all the rules was the personal computer (PC) when it debuted in the 1980s.

The PC broke rules and standards formulated for the Glass House on a number of levels.[3] IBM made business decisions about the PC that had the unintended consequence of changing the mainframe system management world forever. When IBM decided to enter the PC business they adopted a nonstandard IBM approach. To save time getting a product to market, IBM outsourced the product components, including the operating system DOS to Microsoft and the CPU to Intel. Uncharacteristically, IBM also decided to only license DOS and the CPU chips, allowing Microsoft and Intel to sell the technology to competitors in any manner they chose. Based on the business model and early marketing, IBM probably never intended or foresaw that the personal computer would become a personal *Business* computer. Early PC marketing showed a family gathered around a DOS green screen PC with a child at the keyboard as everyone beamed at the camera.[4] The PC was positioned as *flexible and easy to use* in the home, classroom, and office. The PC was slow to gain traction until Microsoft and Intel began to sell to other companies.

Without the restraining influence of the mainframe world and an attractive platform to exploit, the time frame of 1992 to 1995 unleashed the greatest era of technology innovation the computer industry had ever witnessed. Windows 3.1, Office, LANS Web browsers, the Internet "superhighway," ISPs, and client server computing all hit the market. When Microsoft introduced Windows 3.1 and Intel developed more powerful chips, PC sales gained rapid traction. That traction generated the demand for easy-to-use IT applications such as Windows. In short-order Silicon Valley, and the industry addressed that demand, albeit in a manner that created huge problems for IT system management.

In April of 1992, Microsoft released Windows 3.1. It was an instant success with three million copies sold in two months.[5] Windows 3.1 wasn't just a desktop release. It went far beyond personal productivity. Windows 3.11 for workgroups was an expansion of 3.1, which added many network capabilities for network connectivity, peer-to-peer support, and client/server applications. The Windows NT release soon dominated the LAN server market.

Shortly after Windows 3.1, Office 92 hit the market, which established the PC as a platform for professionals in most businesses. By extension, Microsoft had set new standards for Graphical User Interface use and business application interface standards. By comparison, those 3270 green screen applications began to look very tired and cumbersome.

As the PCs arrived on more and more business desktops, Bell Labs introduced another technology that took hold in the marketplace and became a key distributing component enabler,[6] a new operating environment that made it easier for developers to create software, particularly with non-procedural applications. UNIX was born, *and* it was open sourced—a new environment for small, powerful, cheaper machines that could be easily networked. No system management, baked in, none available.

A further technology with roots in the 1970s emerged as a key distributed computing enabler. Ethernet won international approval by the International Organization for Standards as the standard for LANS in 1989.[7] This acceptance made Ethernet the leader in LAN technology and spurred LAN growth in business offices connecting WINTEL machines to client/server applications and email.

The move away from mainframes toward the world of graphical desktops and client server applications hit critical mass. The ability to develop multitier applications, such as clients using Windows, database servers, and business processing across LANs on cheaper, faster UNIX servers exploded. Applications moved off the mainframe and sometimes out of the IT organization altogether. Distributed computing succeeded in breaking the Glass House monopoly of a carefully crafted environment that kept computing stable and available.

In 1993, Marc Andreessen introduced Mosaic, an Internet browser developed at the University of Illinois, and everyone with a computer had access to the World Wide Web.[8] Mr. Andreessen left to found Netscape where he found stiff competition from Microsoft and Internet Explorer. Along with browsers, search engines entered the marketplace in 1994 with WEBCRAWLER, Lycos, and a pair of 1995 births, YAHOO and Altavista. The twin technologies, browsers and search engines helped fuel the Internet explosion and later ecommerce. The growth in the Internet alone was more than enough for system managers to handle. Exhibit 2.2 shows the growth in Internet host sites from October 1991 to July 2006, where 439,286,364 sites existed.

The result for IT system management was a huge vacuum, and vendors scrambled to fill the void. Applications and the infrastructure that housed them were scattered everywhere outside the Glass House. Stability, availability, and response time became IT organization headaches, and firefighting was the new normal. Gaining visibility into the "health" of the distributed environment was not yet possible. Until

Year	Sites
10/91	617,000
10/93	2,056,000
10/94	3,864,000
1/96	9,472,000
1/97	16,146,000
1/98	29,670,000
7/06	439,286,364

Exhibit 2.2: Growth of the Web

Source: *Robert H. Zakon, "Hobbes' Internet Timeline v8.2," January 1, 2010, www .zakon.org/robert/internet/timeline/.*

1991, Legent, a leading system management vendor only offered products for the mainframe, when the company acquired Spectrum for its XCOM 6.2 product to connect disparate systems through to mainframes to share data. From there, Legent and Computer Associates, another leading systems management vendor, spent millions and millions of dollars on R&D to bring the disciplines of the Glass House out on to the wide open spaces of the new Wild West of distributed computing. "Simply put, we're accelerating CA's move into client/server," said Charles Wang, Computer Associate's CEO of the acquisition.[9]

The lack of stability in the distributed world was aggravated by another problem. Software vendors rushed products to market with both infrastructure incompatibility problems and a general lack of testing. Both situations lead to further system instability because immature products created outages that sometimes brought distributed production systems down. Without adequate tools to manage those kinds of problems, IT lapsed from the stability and predictability of the Glass House to the chaotic problems still evident in some enterprises today.

One of the first products that addressed the problem of distributed visibility to enter the system management marketplace and gain traction was brought by a UNIX hardware vendor, Hewlett Packard (HP). HP used agents to monitor the health and availability of a device. The simplest implementation was to send an agent alert to a console when the device was unavailable. As the product and monitoring industry grew, the agents read and collected a variety of metrics from system logs. Agent technology reporting alerts back to a central console become the standard for distributed operations management. The system management disciplines of backup, report management, job control, and capacity management grew more slowly because the IT organization had to first solve the acute pain of system instability—still a problem today.

Y2K and the Growth of the Enterprise Applications

As the 1990s ended, two new, self-feeding phenomena entered the fray. Programs written (either hardware or business applications) with only two digits representing the year field would potentially be rendered inoperative on January 1, 2000. Software would not be able to tell whether the year was 1900 or 2000, and some predicted catastrophic consequences if the programs and hardware weren't retrofitted or replaced with new Y2K compliant products.

Faced with enormous retrofitting costs with little upside in terms of additional functionality, many companies elected to buy new enterprise applications and new hardware. The new enterprise applications pushed IT organizations deeper into the management of business processes because the enterprise applications leveraged the new distributive technology rather than running on mainframes. Related business processes included e-commerce, enterprise resource planning, supply chain management, and customer relationship management with applications were very different from traditional accounting-oriented mainframe applications.

The physical implementation of the enterprise applications also brought a technology complexity that most IT organizations lacked the system management experience acumen to handle. Many of the "clients" were browser-based utilizing Intranet and Internet networks.[10] The applications crossed enterprise IT boundaries in the sense that business processes could be open to other businesses and consumers. Servers part of more complex architecture were placed into pools to provide specialized functions rather than simply working as a part of multi-tier application architecture. Data was far more complex, and there was more of it every day.

Applications of innovative technologies promoted new uses, more complexity, more demands for service, and wider distribution as employees worked both inside the enterprise and at home. Enterprises now primarily promote ongoing growth and innovation, finding more and more intensive uses for IT-enabled technology, along with the requisite demands for less cost and more business alignment. And system management? Best practice CIOs work to lead their IT organizations out of fire-fighting mode toward practices that increasingly enable enterprise strategies as educated, informed business partners. Enterprise IT organizations face competitive system management outsourcing pressures from managed service providers. Wherever system management responsibilities reside, the best practice CIO must remain current with new system management processes and tools entering the arena. The system management industry still lacks a coherent view of what is needed to address the demands placed on the CIO and IT organization. The following sections build just such a perspective for systems management.

The System Management Challenge

After the spine-tingling technology transformation of the 1990s and the enterprise-wide adoption of ever more complex applications, it is fair to say that the business demand for new IT enablement continues to intensify. It is also fair to say that system management as a profession still lags behind the technology transformation of the 1990s and business demands for application of the technology. It is interesting to note that the elements of technology transformation in the early 1990s took place approximately twenty years from their inception in the 1970s. While the PC would have undoubtedly been a successful product independently, other products such as UNIX, Ethernet, Internet, browsers, Client/Server, and even proprietary software applications would not have succeeded as spectacularly as they did without concurrent platform development.

From the perspective of a twenty-year cycle for system management starting from 1992, 2012 should mark the start of a system management golden era. The industry has many perspectives to consider and many products ready to mature, exploit, and integrate with other products to initiate a new era of system management. Viewed as an industry, IT system management is composed of the industry analyst community, major system management/hardware vendors, niche players, and thought leaders from IT itself.

The Industry Analysts

The industry analyst component is the vanguard of twenty-first century system management. While many firms work in this market space, SAS settled on two thought leadership representatives that have very different approaches and only join ideas at the business alignment juncture. McKinsey concentrates on managing IT as a business and promoting IT practices as strategic business enablers. Gartner emphasizes IT maturity models and approaches IT business management considerations from system management toward business alignment. McKinsey is steering non-IT business managers toward IT business alignment and Gartner is steering IT engineers through the engineering maturity processes to achieve IT business alignment.

During the Glass House era, business applications were primarily devoted to accounting and online financial transactions. The business value was more obvious, and the technology was far narrower in application compared to the enterprise applications in play today. With the broader, enterprise-wide applications, the need for strategic intent is now even more acute. McKinsey therefore emphasizes the articulation of strategic themes. In the article, "Innovations in IT Management," McKinsey states that IT generates value on two complementary levels: (1) core assets of hardware, software, and processes, and (2) value in use.[11] "Value in use" refers to business applications that are optimized to yield maximum investment value.

Optimizing investment value here means that the enterprise establishes a value on the IT organization and its resources through a series of metrics that determine the economic value of the IT investment to the business. While metrics are not hard and fast, important measures determine the cost-to-revenue ratio, strategic value, and competitive edge. McKinsey also advocates measuring *operational value* by putting key performance indicators (KPIs) on the operational level of the business, such as "on-time delivery."

In a second article, "Managing IT in a Downturn: Beyond Cost Cutting," McKinsey emphasizes delivering increased value to the business as opposed to merely cutting cost.[12] As the IT organization and its resources increase in value and integrate more deeply into business processes, it becomes harder to cut costs and easier to increase value. After IT has engaged in efforts to streamline application portfolios, reduce infrastructure costs, and outsourcing, what remains is to create greater business impact through better management of sales and pricing, sourcing and production, support processes, and performance management (PM).

McKinsey continues their strategic focus via metrics in a third article, "Assessing Innovation Metrics."[13] While most enterprises value innovation, most don't measure it. Those enterprises that actually measure innovation generally depend on eight metrics to make their assessment. Innovation metrics provide strategic direction for innovation activities, guide allocation resources, and improve innovation performance. Interestingly, McKinsey noted that few enterprises tracked the relationship between innovation and shareholder value. Companies track revenue growth, customer satisfaction, and percentage of sales, but less than one-third track the relationship between innovation spending and shareholder value. Only the best companies pursue and measure innovations as a portfolio, and track the entire innovation process as inputs.

The Gartner Maturity Models approach to IT system management thought leadership begins from the polar opposite of McKinsey. Gartner maturity models aim directly at where system management has consistently felt the most pain from the early 1990s through to today: the inability to keep IT infrastructure up and running. Because of infrastructure redundancy and other safeguards, entire production systems seldom go dark. Rather than fight system-wide outages, the IT organization fights a continuous stream of small outages. Fighting small or large outages is expensive, time consuming, and a drain on services. Gartner reports that fifty-one percent of IT budgets are spent on system management and support of product applications.[14]

The Gartner IT Infrastructure and Operations (I&O) Maturity Model is a matrix with people, processes, technology, and business management on the left axis, with the maturity steps called Survival, Awareness, Committed, Proactive, Service Aligned, and Business Partnership across the top of the matrix. *Survival*, of course, is absence of any formal strategy or functions, an extremely chaotic, immature environment. *Awareness* indicates a level of insight that system management improvements are both possible and necessary. The IT organization is aware of needs, has some basic tools in place, but faces a big job for system management maturity. *Committed* requires an investment in both tools and processes. Real progress is made with the *Proactive* stage, where the IT organization implements processes, standards, domain management, and project management. The *Service Aligned* IT organization begins to implement customer and business services and management, which is essential to attaining a business partnership. IT organizations at the *Business Partnership* stage of maturity focus on business processes, business optimization, and business contribution metrics. Business Partnership practices overlap with the McKinsey perspective practices. The Business Partnership stage cannot be attained without an infrastructure foundation that is as well managed, stable, and available as the mainframes were in the Glass House.

How mature has the IT industry become? Exhibit 2.3 shows the results. I&O maturity levels will differ across industries, enterprise size, and business strategies, but the exhibit is an estimate of I&O maturity at each level with a prediction of progress by year-end 2012.[15] Gartner states that sustainable maturity develops over years, but CIOs and their IT organizations face rapid return on investment (ROI) expectations of four to six months. The answers to another Gartner survey that polled CIOs in 2006 for the reasons behind their lack of progress are still as revealing and relevant:

- Lack of senior management support
- Lack of practical implementation guidelines
- Lack of time to develop a thoughtful approach
- Lack of hierarchical reporting structure
- Lack of effective organizational communication[16]

Timeline	Survival	Awareness	Committed	Proactive	Service Aligned	Business Partnership
12/2007	<2	45	30	15	8	<1
12/2012	<2	30	35	21	12	<2

Exhibit 2.3: IT I&O Maturity

System Management Vendors

System management vendors have always been on the fault line between industry advances that are a step or two ahead of enterprise adoption and the fight to keep infrastructure up and running. The system management tool market is large and lucrative because the need for these products and services is obvious, the pain is acute, and the large ROI is easy to justify. The vendors aim their products and services at the heart of the most critical distributed computing model problems: lack of infrastructure stability and operational firefighting. With homogeneous environments that were widely distributed and extraordinarily complex, monitoring and managing within that model was a massive challenge. As the industry matured beyond firefighting and chaos, vendors expanded their respective legacy products and acquired technology to round out their offerings.[17] Their subsequent offerings followed the Gartner maturity models building from infrastructure management toward business alignment and management, as opposed to the McKinsey perspective that linked IT practices with enterprise strategic intent.

If the history of business computing since 1992 tells us anything, the lesson would be that the problem to be solved is bigger than any single vendor or any single sector in the industry. The large system management vendors bring strong solutions in certain areas while other portions of the solutions seem to be isolated (Portfolio Management), an afterthought (Capacity Management), or nonexistent (Financial Management). The next plateau for the system management vendors coincides with the next rung on the Gartner scale, Service Management, and is marketed to a segment of IT that is complex and labor intensive.

Vendors have their own particular slant on service management. Whether marketed as Service-Oriented Architecture (SOA) or Business Service Management (BSM), the heart of the offering is a service catalog of IT offerings. Simply put, offerings are assembled to create a business application. The underpinning of the application is a contract that specifies the parameters of the offering, usually in terms of availability/response time/throughput (A/R/T). Such contracts may have chargeback provisions to be paid to IT and penalties paid to the end user if IT fails to meet service levels. Vendors are expanding products to provide varying amounts of automated provisioning with a set of common goals: minimize service costs, minimize developing and building service/business processes, reuse services, and of course, keep IT customers happy.

Niche Vendors

Niche vendors tend to be smaller startup companies plugging holes in the system management market that the megasystem management vendors address poorly, if at all. Service management is the core offering of most niche vendors, along with the customer's ability to transparently calculate the cost of service. Most of these offerings also have a dashboard of the service and financial results, and many of the niche vendors align with Information Technology Infrastructure Library (ITIL) consultancies.

A review of the products offered in this space reveals overlap with the larger vendor service management products. Service catalogs and service-level management are standard. Niche vendors differentiate their services most markedly in terms of the costing/chargeback engines. Cost of service and transparency are usually key components of financial management, but not for SAS. Nor is reporting results in a dashboard PM. If costing is limited to service while ignoring capacity management and other important IT costs, the niche is a bit too narrow. The tool is rendered to the tactical, rather than strategic, level.

IT Management

This discussion now turns to the very individuals responsible for IT system management and who perform the work day in and day out. Giving advice is much easier than implementing advice. SAS gathers IT management perspectives from conferences, publications, and one-on-one interactions. Everyone in IT management seems to agree on one idea: The Business is First. Always. Most IT managers want "actionable" metrics. Others avidly look for ROI Management. The front runners are taking a strong, disciplined approach to cost cutting and financial management.

In 2007, Intel presented "The Road to Enterprise SOA" at America's SAP Users Group (ASUG), which discusses how the enterprise followed a maturity formula to attain SOA.[18] The project was driven by a SAP upgrade and a need for master data management. This situation is emblematic of current system management: grappling with the complexity of the enterprise applications and gaining a solid system management foundation. Intel's desired state was service portfolio planning, which would lead to cost savings in service re-use. The steps on the path were infrastructure consolidation, virtualization, instrumentation, service taxonomy, and value dials—a great start, but a very engineering-centric approach that would dovetail in the future with business services planning driven by service portfolios, and enable Intel to roll out applications faster and cheaper. The process began in 2001, and by 2007 was paying substantial dividends.

At the P100 conference in Orlando, Florida in January 2009, two major themes were cost-cutting and financial management. A panel of CIOs participated in a discussion devoted solely to cost-cutting. Their attitudes reflected a bit of McKinsey and a bit of Gartner. Panelists cited big savings of up to 33 percent in managed services and hoped to gain the same with virtualization. They stressed strengthening their infrastructure. Cutting costs was only part of their management emphasis. Demonstrating business benefits and using metrics were equally important, and participants expressed a desire to do a better job. Participants generally wanted to look and plan further into the future, some as far as four years. Industry analyst perspectives on the benefits of both maturity and business alignment were well represented.

Madge Meyers of State Street Bank presented a vision that clearly stood out. She also re-articulated the idea that an optimized infrastructure reduces costs. (In the spirit of disclosure, State Street Bank is a SAS customer.) In the domain of financial discipline, State Street is a clear front-runner. Under the rubric of governance, State Street established a model of end-to-end business cases and ROI management. This model produces self-funding enhancements, cost transparency, and charge back by usage.

In the broader context of SAS client and sales engagements, calls, and conversations, the typical IT organization is still ratcheting their way up to a level of proactive management, where they manage daily threshold infrastructure exceptions that could affect availability or service and implement an effective long-term capacity management forecasting system. The inability to forecast capacity across the enterprise is crippling to many IT organizations. This kind of effort is most always managed by engineers, and the proactive/capacity projects are rarely visible outside of the originating group, much less tied to business strategy.

Four IT Business Management Domains

Distributed computing sent shock waves through IT and system management from which IT has yet to fully recover. Industry analysts, system management vendors, niche vendors, and IT management all have perspectives on partial solutions, but none of the stakeholders espouses a complete model or the means to integrate all the perspectives. The essential management pieces are obviously missing and must come from new management approaches. This section explores the four IT business domains of capacity optimization, service level management, financial management, and business alignment as they apply to the current IT industry environment. SAS established these four domains based on ITIL version 3, our own thought leadership, and industry analyst feedback to form a hybrid model with invigorated focus and emphasis. The enhancement of these four domains will help lead to the transformation of IT system and business management into a stable, available, and business-aligned model. This section discusses the four domains in terms of the current state and emerging opportunities to expand the management of each IT business domain, to fulfill its promise and enable the other domains to fulfill their strategic promise.

Capacity Optimization

Current State: When discussing capacity management, people often misunderstand the term *capacity*. As an essential IT management domain, capacity in this context means maintaining enough infrastructure to meet business computing requirements where *infrastructure* means network bandwidth, connections, server capacity, data storage space, even power and cooling. Capacity management does not refer to human resources, office space, desks, or parking places. From the SAS perspective, capacity optimization is a desired state for capacity management in terms of demand management and availability management. IT organizations have long been hampered in this area by their inability to create an enterprise view of servers, networks, and end-to-end enterprise business applications performance and metrics. A direct result of the rapid acceptance of distributed computing in the early 1990s, a heterogeneous, extremely complex infrastructure is now spread out across the globe, and managed and monitored by heterogeneous systems tools. Large companies generate vast amounts of performance and utilization metrics data, which they are unable to consolidate into a single enterprise view. Without enterprise views, it is nearly impossible to forecast capacity and business needs or to synchronize capacity with service views. The end result is that capacity management is usually done poorly—machine-by-machine or location-by-location—or not done at all.

A broader problem emerges when capacity management is performed server-by-server, location-by-location, or through educated guesswork. Inadequate capacity management acts to prevent business alignment by improperly sizing applications, burdening service management, and destroying financial projections. Capacity managers either buy too much infrastructure or undersize capacity, only to make a panic buy later. Most often, capacity managers either overbuy pooled infrastructure or buy oversized infrastructure to host a single application. Capacity managers work under the premise that oversized infrastructure will deliver the necessary performance and stability while preventing service disruptions during production times. Buying infrastructure sized for cost efficiency can lead to disruptions if managers can't assimilate the views needed to manage for performance.

Opportunities: Beyond the inherent promise to provide adequate infrastructure to run the business, capacity management presents business management opportunities in terms of both cost management and alignment to the other three business domains. Armed with end-to-end views of servers, capacity managers can provide a quick and large ROI by eliminating excess server capacity through server consolidation. Server consolidation requires both a current utilization baseline and a time series forecast of utilization extending out a year.

Consolidation is a solid maturity approach utilized by forward-thinking businesses. In addition, many IT organizations look to virtualization as a cost reduction initiative, and are correct in looking to virtualization for cost gains. Best practice capacity managers properly size virtualization allocations to maximize the cost management opportunity (i.e., not too big nor too small) by studying the allocation utilization rates and forecasting their growth. Not involving capacity managers in virtualization projects is a missed opportunity. After determining the optimal capacity, managing to that level wrings out the costs of idle capacity and also eliminates panic infrastructure buys. Buying in panic mode never results in a smooth, cost-efficient implementation, and enterprises often come dangerously close to impacting service levels. A recurring theme in this section is the interconnectedness of the processes across these four management domains. Capacity management should not be performed in the isolation of an engineering silo. To achieve greater levels of IT maturity, capacity managers must cross-pollinate and be cross-pollinated by performance measurement information flowing into and out of the four other IT business management domains.

For example, capacity managers need financial information beyond budget allocations for capacity buys. Determining the cost of capacity not only promotes more effective capacity management but also provides foundation costs for service management and service management contracts. The cost of capacity includes the cost of utilized capacity, reserve capacity, and unused capacity. Attacking unused capacity without distressing service levels is a combined capacity, service, and financial management exercise. Capacity managers must also determine capacity in nontraditional ways. Predicting the exhaust rates of standardized services and the growth of business services create other ripe opportunities.

Service Management

Current State: From thirty-five thousand feet above the landscape where fine details are obscured, the various approaches to service management appear more alike than different. The differences sometimes appear to be more of a marketing exercise. From that altitude, service managers appear to build catalogs of IT services (Premium Web Service, Bronze Network Access, etc.) and assemble those components into business service contracts that specify service parameters in terms of availability, response time, throughput, and service hours. System management and niche vendors sell this approach, which appears to also follow the engineering focus of Gartner IT Infrastructure and Operational Maturity Model. Only a small minority of IT organizations has achieved this level of maturity. Best practice service managers remain vigilant for several issues while implementing this large and very necessary IT business management domain.

Service managers ignorant of the true cost of service are driving in a thunderstorm without windshield wipers. It's hard to see, and the risk of collision is unacceptably high. For example, service managers run into cost mismanagement issues when they enter into service contracts with business users who cost more than specified by the contract. Some niche vendors already address a portion of this issue, but service managers generally fail to make the connection between IT operational budgets and the planning process for new and ongoing services, as well as the connection between capacity management and service level management.

Opportunities: The capacity management section discussed the value of forecasting for optimizing infrastructure over time. Forecasting provides equal value for service management. Service reporting and financial measures are inherently reactive. Forecasting service level performance, future capacity needs, and cost of service growth augment service management practices. In addition to forecasting, a management structure that contains value measures is another essential opportunity for more mature service management. Reporting cost and service results are inadequate without knowledge of the degree to which the IT organization succeeded in terms of key enterprise strategic objectives and the metrics that track them. Meeting business goals and objectives are the ultimate measure of IT value. Forecasting performance is engineering; applying intelligence to enabling and meeting business strategy is a new level of business maturity for IT management.

Financial Management

Current State: We don't need to discuss IT financial management from thirty-five thousand feet. So neglected is the subject that I doubt it would even be visible from that altitude. Most CIOs and their IT organizations need to get down on their hands and knees at weed level to see the primary problems. Most IT organizations manage their budgets in spreadsheets. Spreadsheets are easy for individuals to use, inexpensive, and most everyone already has one. But as widely distributed spreadsheets quickly lose their effectiveness, they become very expensive. Difficult to consolidate into department views and then into an enterprise view, widely distributed spreadsheets result in inaccuracies, and a large percentage of expense planning is lost. The wide use of spreadsheets for IT budgeting can be traced to adoption of corporate budget systems that are not tailored for IT organizations and resource management. In addition, IT also budgets in another management area where the spreadsheet inaccuracy is even higher: planning and managing the portfolio of new and existing business service projects. Large corporations have hundreds and hundreds of such projects trapped in spreadsheets that they ruefully call "the swamp." With the utmost difficulty and many complete failures, financial managers attempt to reconcile the hundreds of spreadsheets into an accurate, consolidated view, and then reconcile the consolidated portfolio view to the operational budgets.

Trapped within this swamp are the answers to essential IT management questions with enterprise-wide strategic implications: On whom are we spending, and what are we spending it on? Was the spending justified? Optimized? How are we prioritizing IT support, service, and spend? How do we plan future IT resources and services? How do we minimize unused IT resources? How does this information inform overall decision making for IT, business units, and the bottom line?

Opportunity: The opportunity is to create an IT financial management system for a service-oriented IT organization. IT financial managers may continue to use a spreadsheet for individual operational and portfolio project planning, but they put all the data in one foundation to preserve its integrity. Financial managers then combine financial data with capacity and service data, which provide financial intelligence to the other IT business management domains in a usable format for optimizing their own strategic management decisions.

Capacity managers need to know the cost of capacity, including unused capacity, and cost of the support processes necessary to manage the infrastructure. Service managers need to know the cost of service, unused service, and who consumed the service, including relevant support processes for both the standard service catalog components and each business service.

Business Alignment

Current State: True business alignment, or in Gartner terms, business partnership, is still an illusion as borne out by Gartner statistics. They report that less than one percent of IT organizations achieve their Business Alignment stage of maturity—a very small number in any survey sample that includes best practices. Two factors account for the lack of business alignment in the IT industry. First, vendors do not supply IT organizations with the support they need for developing portfolio management and system management tools that span metrics collected by various enterprise and IT monitoring and management systems. IT vendors focus on building maturity from the infrastructure management up—a purely engineering focus. What tools exist for financial and business management are neither integrated nor applied by IT managers seeking to solve their business challenges. Second, despite IT analysts pointing the industry toward aligning visions and techniques, the most important alignment achievement must include participation by the business intelligence community for new IT strategies with supporting applications.

Opportunities: Because true examples of business alignment are rare and few people in the industry have actually seen a single example, the opportunity for business alignment is far greater than most CIOs realize. This IT business management domain opportunity means that as a key strategic enabler for most enterprises, CIOs would manage the IT organization like a business with a business. CIOs and their IT organizations will a create value axis for every IT product and service from the performance metrics in each of the four IT business management domains. Business objectives that IT products and services must enable will be traced back to overall business strategy through these metrics. Enabling these strategic business objectives will carry a negotiated price tag to build and support after implementation. That negotiated price tag must fit within the ROI calculation of each business objective. CIOs will determine support costs through business user volume and service estimates, which IT will translate into service and capacity levels. Once built and implemented, the applications and their related IT services will be measured, forecasted, and optimized from business objectives, service results, costs, and business strategy.

The IT transparency illustrated here requires a different set of tools and processes that have yet to be broadly discussed in the IT market. While the rest of the enterprise is either already using or receptive to strategic performance management (SPM), many IT organizations have yet to reach this stage of business maturity. The utilization metrics increases in value when associated with strategy, initiatives, goals, and objectives that are mapped to other IT management domains.

PUTTING THE PIECES TOGETHER

While IT has made strides toward monitoring and managing infrastructure on the machine level, management is often done with multiple tools in multiple locations. In order to enable the four IT management domains with the required infrastructure metrics, best practice CIOs work to consolidate the metrics trapped in isolated tools and design new IT infrastructure metrics data management tools to access, integrate, aggregate, analyze, and manage large quantities of IT resource performance data from hardware, operating system software, networks, Web servers, databases, and applications.[19]

Step One: IT Infrastructure Metrics Data Management

IT resource performance metrics are generated by the logging mechanisms inherent to IT resources or are created by the Enterprise Systems Management tools used in managing IT infrastructures. Everything needed to analyze IT resource performance data from multiple sources for capacity planning and forecasting, consumption metrics for financial management, service-level performance measures, seasonality analysis, and enterprise IT performance summaries should be included in the initiative.

As demonstrated in Exhibit 2.4, SAS collects resource data, normalizes across platforms, and publishes the data for use by multiple users across the IT management domains. Of course, data management must scale to enterprise demands. When faced with multiple-system management tools, locations, or perhaps no tools at all, inherent to the SAS IT Resource Management server is the ability to natively extract information from many industry standard operating systems and systems management tools. Native support is the predefined ability to translate source data into a SAS representation for storage in the performance database. Data is retrieved from its native data source and brought into the IT resource data warehouse, where IT metrics are represented exactly as they are extracted. In the detailed level of the performance database, it is likely that IT data metrics are available for analysis and reporting on a per-polling cycle or per-event basis, as would be necessary for daily proactive management of a stable system. As detailed level data is retained, it is reduced—statistically summarized into aggregation levels that require incrementally less storage, enabling longer term storage as would be required for capacity management time series analysis. Any part of this data warehouse definition can be modified, added to, or deleted from at any time.

The staging transformation invoked by SAS IT Resource Management adapters extracts the raw IT resource performance data, performs any calculations and conversions that are required by that adapter, and loads (stages) the resulting data into tables in the IT data mart. Staging jobs can be run interactively or scheduled to run in batch mode, depending on the enterprise requirements. An aggregation transformation specifies how data is to be transformed and stored so that it can provide analysis and report-ready IT resource performance data.

For example, an aggregation transformation provides specifications for filtering data, calculating statistics, performing rolling accumulations, and ranking and grouping (classifying) the data according to user specifications. For any given adapter, SAS IT Resource Management generates transformations that create information maps referencing the data needed to create and view reports.

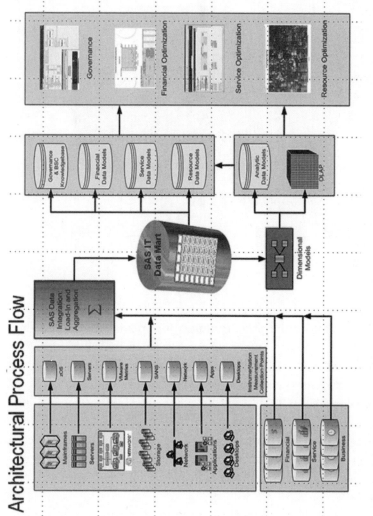

Exhibit 2.4: Enterprise Systems Management Tools for Managing IT Infrastructures

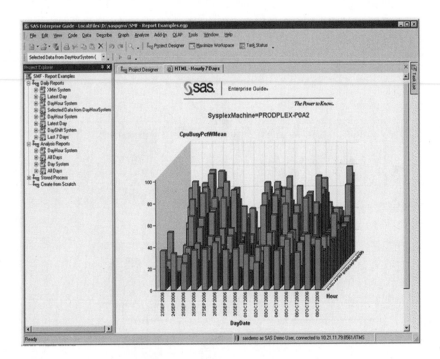

Exhibit 2.5: Data Reporting Tool Accessibility

Simple summary aggregation tables and the information maps for those tables are the primary inputs for creating IT resource performance and capacity planning reports such as CPU utilization, threshold analysis, and peak period analysis. SAS offers a collection of easy-to-use query and reporting interfaces for different types of users and recipients (e.g., capacity planners, IT infrastructure analysts, IT operations managers, senior IT management for business alignment, financial managers, and service-level management). Whatever the IT management domain, data must be accessible to a wide variety of reporting tools and visualization techniques as represented in Exhibit 2.5.

In summary, IT data management must aggregate data into enterprise and domain management views, regardless of the source of the data. Data must be accessible to other tools as necessary as well as reporting and visualization tools. IT data management is the foundation that the capacity, service, financial, and business alignment management domains are built upon.

Step Two: Capacity Management for Risk, Expense, and Quality

Lack of senior management support, practical implementation guidelines, time to develop a thoughtful approach, hierarchical reporting structure, and effective organizational communication—of these five major barriers to IT maturity, the lack of time to develop a thoughtful approach and the lack of effective organizational communication are more symptoms than root causes. If CIOs and their IT organizations found the time to develop a coherent articulation of enterprise-relevant IT business thought expressed in terms of business measures and ways IT resources enabled those business measures, IT/business communications would mature quickly.

As a business within a business, mature CIOs expect enterprise business users to provide the IT organization with business plans based on specific technology request and commensurate measures that demonstrate the ways that the technology resources provide and enable their strategic objectives. Best practice CIOs expect those business plans to address the four IT business management domains to facilitate the development of appropriate metrics and ongoing communications about performance results and related IT service forecasts. In short, thoughtfully developed business plans that promote strategic communications must include business measurable goals and objectives for the alignment domain, volume estimates for the capacity domain, service requirements for the service management domain, and the price the technology user is willing to pay for capital investments and ongoing services expenses for the financial management domain. Adequate capacity enables technology business plans and service levels. Well-managed capacity promotes financial management. Capacity management has other benefits as well. Here is what Martha Hays and Margaret Churchill have to say:

> Critical IT systems are managed by monitoring day-to-day activities to ensure they are performing within stated utilization and performance thresholds. Responding to system alarms causes the operations team to react to the problem and implement an immediate change. These changes may cause unforeseen consequences on other parts of the environment, resulting in a ripple or cascade effect across the enterprise.

A capacity management process will instill a discipline of preparing for the future and planning for appropriate changes well before the system alarms go off. This allows the IT organization to predict when thresholds will be reached and prescribe the right changes. By doing so, better decisions can be made about server consolidation, hardware procurement, and service level management.[20]

The discipline of capacity management reduces risk and expense in a far-reaching manner. SAS places capacity as the first IT management domain to emphasize that mature capacity management (1) addresses instability problems endemic since the advent of distributed computing; and (2) pulls IT much closer to the service management, financial management, and business alignment domains. Hayes and Churchill expand the implications for the CIO and IT organization, where the figures they reference appear in Exhibit 2.6:

Forecasts provide advance notice that an outage or other type of problem is likely to occur. Once the predictions have been made, what is the best way to prevent the problem from actually occurring? Modeling delivers this capability through what-if scenarios that identify the impact of planned or unplanned changes to the system in areas such as workload levels, workload patterns, server configurations, network infrastructure, and storage arrays.

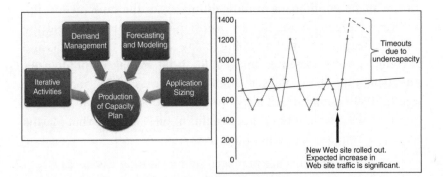

Exhibit 2.6: Hayes and Churchill on Capacity Management

Source: Martha Hays and Margaret Churchill, "Paper 6151 Forecasting + Modeling: A Partnership to Predict and Prevent Capacity Bottlenecks," Computer Measurement Group Presentation, 2006, Volume 1, (Computer Measurement Group), www.daschmelzer.com/cmg2006/PDFs/033.pdf.

IT firefighting is expensive, time-consuming, and distracts the organization from spending time on innovative solutions that add value back to the business. However, IT fire prevention is seldom practiced. The combination of forecasting and modeling, as part of a capacity management process, provides the insight needed into future IT events, and effectively prevents the IT fires.

Indeed. One begins to wonder how much of the IT organization's budget has been spent firefighting in the last seventeen years. And more:

The combination of these two methods also extends capacity management from a silo or server-centric view, to a broader end-to-end view. This allows predictions to be made about utilization, response time, workload growth, workload changes and infrastructure modifications.

For example, today's systems may be running within acceptable thresholds, and a linear trend shows that there is enough capacity on the servers to sustain a 5 percent fixed workload growth over the next three months. However, this trend does not account for a spike in demand that is expected for the upcoming holiday season. By using a time-series forecast, we can predict that the servers will bottleneck at the beginning of the peak shopping season. A model is built from the forecasted data and is used to evaluate several configuration changes that could support the increased workload. This analysis allows us to plan for the changes needed to the system to support the seasonal demand. With ample time before the peak season starts, we have the time to properly procure and plan for the changes, avoiding emergency procedures and expensive procurement. We have maintained user service and utilization levels—and have prevented an IT fire.

How does IT move from firefighting to a thoughtfully determined, well managed capacity that provides for service levels and financial management?

Capacity management evolves once an organization has implemented a PM system that focuses on monitoring current systems and reacting to alarms that result from exceeding utilization thresholds or service levels.

Since there must be an actual historical basis for the predictions, the data captured from performance monitors is required for the capacity planning process. Even if systems monitoring and event management are taking place, the resulting data must be stored for analysis and reporting purposes.

A great deal of capacity management information can be uncovered from basic analysis of the system and event data. These include the following:

- Which systems are experiencing outages or exceeding utilization thresholds?
- Is there a pattern based on time, day, month, etc.?
- Are the events consistent with changes in workload?
- Is there correlation between multiple events?
- When an issue occurs, what is the impact on the other systems?

For further analysis, data can be captured from the system monitors and stored in a centralized performance data repository. Since information from heterogeneous systems may have been collected at different time intervals and in different time zones, an extraction, transformation, and load (ETL) is used to "homogenize" the data. Once done, reports can be created that provide detailed historical analysis. These reports are useful to show a correlation of past events and past system responses to those events.

Once the data is captured, forecasting and modeling can be done. ITIL, however, does not differentiate between the two, as depicted in Figure 1. In practice, the two methods are different even though they use some of the same terminology.

Capacity builds on IT performance metrics. After performing a basic analysis of the infrastructure and establishing baselines, the role of forecasting becomes increasingly important. The CIO and IT organization perform forecasting on the baseline to predict normal business growth and from business plans that pass along volume predictions to capacity and financial managers.

A common report generated from historical data is a linear trend. This is the quickest and simplest report and is supported by spreadsheet software. Trend lines are based on an average of three or more historical data points extended to some future point. Trend lines are appropriate when future system behavior is expected to be at the same rate as the historical data with no seasonality.

In cases of seasonality or expected workload changes, trends will provide erroneous results. This is depicted in Figure 2. The forecast would indicate that there is sufficient capacity to support the system. However, when a new Web site comes online, the Web server is unable to handle the traffic. As a result, the trend provided an incorrect result since it was not able to predict the impact of this workload change.

Business decisions based on this trend will result in a false confidence that the system will continue to operate properly. As a result, basic linear trending is not recommended for making predictions of complex systems. For systems that experience pattern changes due to seasonality or planned business promotions, robust forecasting like time series with seasonality, trend, and event correlation is recommended.

Another problem with the linear trend is that it can't be used for systems that are close to experiencing a bottleneck. These systems will start queuing and/or consuming additional system overhead. This will cause the utilizations to skew, which will not be identified through a linear trend. Notice how a prediction of seasonal behavior from the chart above would have resulted in underestimating the capacity needed.

Time Series Forecasting analyzes time series variables and forecasts future values by extrapolating trends and patterns in the past values of the series or by extrapolating the effect of other variables on the series. With the use of sophisticated statistical software, a forecasting model can be developed and customized to best predict your time series. In the IT environment, these time series are easily obtained from your performance measurement data which has been stored and summarized in a capacity database (CDB). By choosing the proper time intervals (day, week or month) and variables as input, your historical data can lead you to a justifiable forecast of capacity requirements. Forecasting is accomplished through the following:

- Storing and summarizing the data
- Analyzing the data to determine seasonality and other patterns
- Selecting an appropriate forecasting method
- Generating a forecast, which includes expected business projections and events.

In addition to data management, analysis and forecasting tools are essential to capacity managers. Forecasting the complex enterprise applications is a set of intricate tasks, not the least of which is picking the proper statistical to fit the forecast problem. One approach is to hire statistical talent. Another is to use statistical software that analyzes the data and the problem and selects the best statistical approaches for you. After integrating statistical management approaches, capacity managers expand their roles by sending capacity data to financial managers and receive costing information in return. The next step is service management, because service managers would be ill prepared without capacity service level forecasts.

Step Three: Standard Services as a Foundation to Business Services

Stepping into service management requires the leveraging of the previously built IT data management foundation. Since service contracts are the underpinning of the services that the IT organization provides to enterprise business users via their business plans, cost of service is crucial to contract negotiation. Determining how much each business is able to pay for the IT business service is one building block in determining the value IT provides to business users.

Building an array of standard services based on the technology silos that all the Computer Science majors manage is a natural starting point. Network engineers manage networks as a service. The IT organization independently manages Web servers as a standard service. Standard services are those IT components that enable the business plans submitted by the business users. Standard services can be turned into "branded" services by attaching differing levels of value to each service, such as premium, gold, and bronze service levels, with price and performance gradations for each level. In terms of IT management, each standard service requires an internal contract that specifies the level of service, the cost we wish to manage to, and a capacity plan. Monitoring the results is essential.

With a stable set of standard services, service managers match business plan requirements in terms of availability, response times, and throughput to the catalog of services and determine the price when the business plan passes through capacity to ensure that the volume estimates in the plan can be supported. Agreement on services and costs constitute the elements of a service contract. Planning each contract is an exercise in capacity, service, and financial management.

Financial Management: A New Era

Financial management specific to the IT organization has received less thought and support than either capacity or service management. Very few IT organizations have found effective solutions for financial management challenges. Most IT organizations find that even the budgeting applications are ill suited for IT management. Tools for planning the capital and expense of business user new project portfolios are nonexistent. The result: IT manages budgets and projects in a swamp of spreadsheets. There are several reasons for the dependency on spreadsheets, but primary among them is the General Ledger (GL). The GL has other important purposes in the custodial role of finance that center on external reporting and internal controls. It has its own highly controlled environment with many rules governed by external reporting and tax requirements. Since the GL is optimized for external and tax reporting purposes, it is a poor tool for internal analysis and reporting, especially for the service-focused business of IT management.

Assuming that the best practice CIO manages the IT organization as an internal company separate from those business units consuming IT services, the resulting perspective clearly emphasizes the four IT management domains as the basis of the IT Value Axis: If IT services are being purchased, what does the customer expect from IT? What would IT as a supplier provide? The customer would expect:

- Consistent service delivery as specified in contract
- Consistent quality
- Competitive pricing

As an external supplier, IT would provide:

- Adequate capacity to assure consistent service delivery as required by contract
- Robust processes to provide consistent service
- Invoices with prices and supporting documentation of services provided

In such a business relationship, the price that the customer is willing to pay is based on perceived business value and a benchmark of prices and services offered by other IT suppliers. Customers are willing to pay for what their business services consume but not for waste or excess capacity. Excesses are not allowed to inflate the price. If the *price* is too high, the customer finds other alternatives. It is critical to note that the cost to provide the service does not establish the price for a profit-oriented IT provider. Independently, market conditions set prices, as it does for the rest of the business. The profit motive drives the supplier's desire and willingness to provide the service. Profit equals revenue minus cost. For a high enough price, an IT service provider purchases whatever capacity it needs to make a profit. When prices are too low, IT service providers redeploy resources to a more profitable market and potentially stop offering the service. If *profitability* is low, IT service providers are highly motivated to improve the efficiency of their operations. If profitability is too low, the service provider leaves the business.

IT financial management must address the costing of services, processes, and business services while bridging that data into a project portfolio planning environment that anticipates project capital costs (essentially new capacity and development costs), projects the ongoing expense of the capitalized costs, and delivers a projected financial impact on existing capacity for capacity managers. Key ingredients of the model depicted in Exhibit 2.7 are:

- Standard financial and statistical forecast models used for planning
- Fixed and variable qualifications available in both cost and plan model
- Planned capital expenditures and commitments used to manage depreciation
- Interactive scenarios used for simulations
- IT planning process that can be integrated with enterprise planning as a separate loop
- Department ownership of the loop
- Comparisons of operational and financial results available for monitoring and management

As depicted in Exhibit 2.7, the planning process allows planners to retain the front end use of Excel but without the consolidation

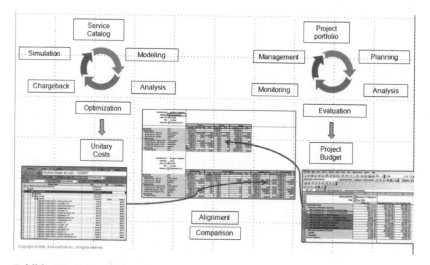

Exhibit 2.7: IT Financial Management Process

headaches associated with free-floating spreadsheets. Planning data is housed within the SAS foundation but displayed in Excel. Project managers plan individual projects by assembling the anticipated standard service components. Within the spreadsheet are the costs for the services, the existing capacity, the unit costs, entry for the new volumes, and the impact on capacity. Conditional highlighting displays when capacity is impacted. Projects are consolidated for project directors and capacity managers as shown in Exhibit 2.8.

Central to the financial management system is the conversion of operational budgeting into the costing of services, processes, and capacity. The tool used for this conversion is Activity-Based Management (ABM). An IT ABM analysis starts by identifying the resources deployed in the IT organizations. Typically, these are recorded in the GL for each IT department—usually the only relationship between ABM and the GL. The SAS ABM model begins with GL costs by department and by account as its first view, retaining the original GL view to provide a firm common starting point and for correlation with external financial reporting. However, it then also provides a parallel view of resources that better reflects operational requirements and realities.

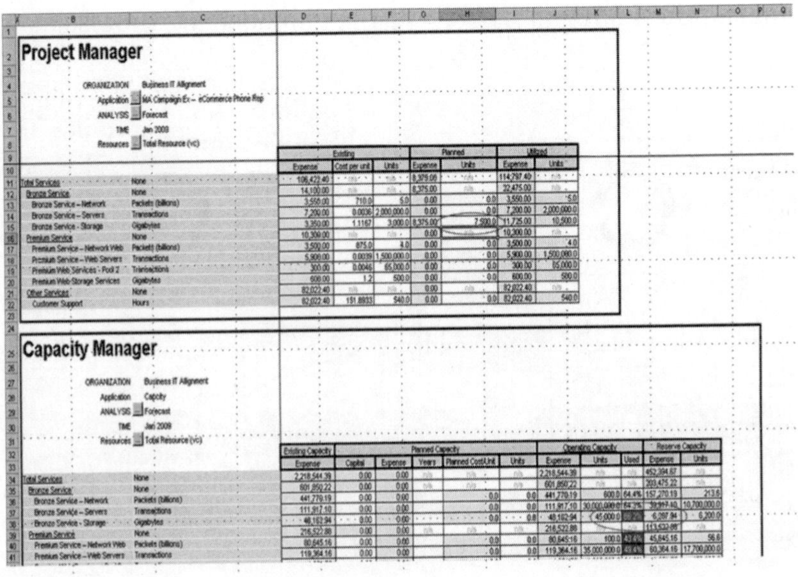

Exhibit 2.8: Project Consolidation for Directors and Capacity Managers

Regrettably, the level of GL data detail is both greater and lesser than the optimum set required for ABM. Where there is too much detail, such as accounts required for tax reporting, these details can be aggregated. Where there is too little detail, such as for asset depreciation, a well-designed ABM model uses its capabilities to split these costs to a more appropriate and useful level to support decision making. The reorganization is accomplished in the transition between the GL view and the new operations view.

This operationally focused view reorganizes resources and their costs to align them with operational resources—it captures resources in terms of teams of people, types of equipment, and other more operationally natural categories. This operational view is designed for use and easy understanding by operating personnel. At the same time, all costs are easily traced and reconciled to traditional financial views, which aggregate into a robust and comprehensive resource view that is also verifiable. This provides IT managers with a view of what the resources that they deploy actually cost in terms that they easily understand and use for decision making purposes. This view is also the foundation for subsequent views of activities and services. The overall model cost flow and management views are shown in Exhibit 2.9.

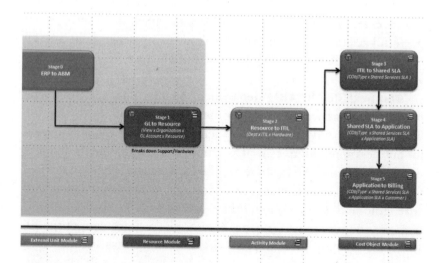

Exhibit 2.9: IT Cost Flow Model

IT components are tracked separately because they constitute a significant cost and play an essential part of IT business services. For these components, the cost recorded in the GL is usually aggregated to a level not useful to operations management. For this reason, component information is obtained from asset registers or other sources to identify the current costs of components at a sufficiently granular level to support service level agreements and capacity forecasting models.

After establishing an operational view of resources, the next step is to assign these costs to the work that these people do. This model uses existing ITIL process definitions as activity definitions. Using the ITIL process definitions provides a sound, common basis for measuring predictable, repeatable IT processes. ITIL processes are a necessary component in the IT maturity process. Without them, it would be difficult to attain a proactive, service-oriented, value-driven IT organization. Resources are traced department by department to the ITIL processes representing the work performed by people from each department. At this level of detail within the departments, this work is considered in terms of activities. Later, using reporting tools, costs are easily reported at the organization-wide ITIL process level. After these costs have been assigned, the costs of ITIL processes become available. Since the ITIL costs are tied to the operations resource and financial resource views, people can observe more powerful relationship costs with breakdowns by department and by types of resources either by the operational view or the financial view of cost.

The next step in ABM deployment enables tracing costs to the products and services provided by the IT organization. Following the business plans, service level agreements contain the value definition for business applications as well as service level requirements. In addition to documented SLAs, there may be more general standard services offered as a cost savings or legacy services not yet formally documented with customers. Even without formal documentation, IT should ascertain cost and service performance for internal management purposes. ABM methodology requires a cause and effect tracing of costs. Consumption metrics often provide the best basis for this assignment.

Standard services may also be traced to specific services, where they are used as components of a broader business service offering.

At this point, cost analysis of services becomes available for service cost trend and service unit cost trend. With the relationships to ITIL processes, components, and people resources already established, these services can be analyzed by ITIL process and/or the resources consumed. Conversely, resources can be analyzed in terms of the services that ultimately consume them.

In the final step of ABM deployment, services are assigned to customers based on usage consumption metrics. Cost metrics are now available by customer. As these are added to the relationships already calculated in the model, a rich analysis base becomes available to help users and providers understand the operations and relationships to operating results. Since the symphonies that IT plays are business applications covered by SLAs, the results can be used for both value reporting to customers and also for internal IT optimization. In summary:

- Activity-Based Modeling is used do define, manage, and change the cost model and scenarios.
- The cost model contains operational and project data to derive costs, notably time per position to produce project costs.
- Costs assignment rules are defined on operational drivers.
- The cost model is populated, integrating financial data from financial systems and operational data from operational systems.
- Web reporting and business reporting are also used.

A sample of an online analytical processing (OLAP) cube extracted from ABM and posted to a dashboard appears in Exhibit 2.10. The subject is the costs associated with a branded standard service—Premium Web Servers. The cost transparency shows three main cost categories: the business services (projects) consuming the service, overhead reserve costs, and excess capacity costs. The next level of cost categories breaks down the individual hardware components of the service and the ITIL processes consumed by the branded, standard service. The data is essential for financial management.

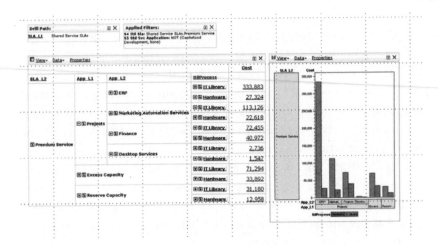

Exhibit 2.10: ABM-Extracted OLAP Cube Posted to Dashboard

Step Four: Strategic Performance Management

PM isn't necessarily the last step in achieving IT management maturity and business alignment. PM can and should be applied throughout the maturity process. Let's review the key issues. CIOs identified the lack of organizational communication and the lack of time for thoughtful planning as barriers to IT maturity. Educational institutions generally prepare either IT engineers or business managers but not IT business managers. The distributed computing technology adopted in the early 1990s that neglected to include system management as a part of the business model put IT in a twenty-year cycle of attempts to overcome that neglect. Enterprise applications are complex, expensive, deeply embedded into business processes, and therefore demand a new business/IT relationship that is still evolving. And lastly, no one, not the system management vendors, industry analysts, niche vendors, or IT management, has a complete answer to the best practices at this stage of IT maturity. We do know that CIOs and their IT organizations have not comprehensively focused on the IT business management domains or applied business analytics to those IT management domains. In other words, CIOs are still learning to use business tools with IT tools for a complete picture.

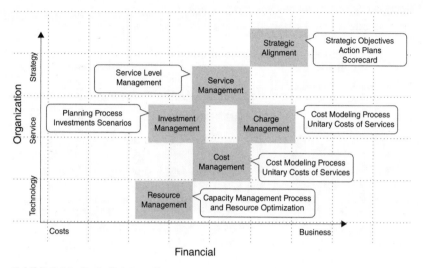

Exhibit 2.11: Strategic Integration

PM has three discrete measure areas to communicate throughout the IT organization and to enterprise business partners: (1) business strategy, goals, and objectives; (2) IT internal engineering and management strategy, goals, and objectives; and (3) the cross-section of the business and IT strategy, goals, and objectives (see Exhibit 2.11). Suffice to say that PM requires a foundation as do the other IT management domains. PM is not a matter of placing metrics in a spreadsheet. PM provides the deliberate linkage between the management centers of business enablement ROI, business objectives, IT service contracts, capacity management, forecasting, and IT service cost transparency. Gary Cokins writes that many application failures are tied to the lack of a strategic view and the lack of a forward view. Let's tie the pieces together with examples.

PM metrics drill down from broadly stated metrics to lower levels of detail following the path of organizational intent through to group performance. Metrics should contain, at a minimum, a target to manage toward the actual achievement and a performance calculation that expresses how close the actual achievement came to the target. In Exhibit 2.12, PM is managing the performance achievement for three essential IT domains that link IT to the business: business objective measurements, IT service level performance, and the cost of the service.

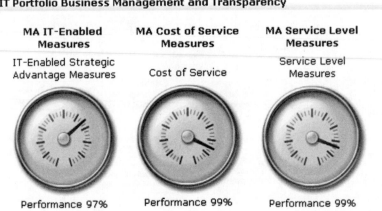

Exhibit 2.12: Executive Dashboard PM View

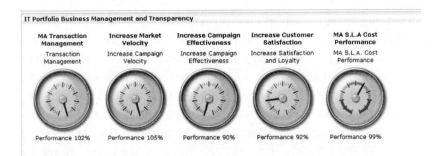

Exhibit 2.13: Marketing Automation Drill-Down

For an executive view, this dashboard is probably sufficient. For other levels of the business it is not. Tracking the business performance requires three levels displayed in four examples of detail. The second level measures business objectives that justified the investment in Marketing Automation. While there is more business detail in subsequent drill-downs, the dashboard icons link directly to the original business case objectives for the Marketing Automation investment decision (see Exhibit 2.13).

The drill-down on the cost performance provides more insight by delivering an OLAP cube summary of the cost of providing the service of a business process in the Marketing Automation. Financial transparency detailing the costs of providing the service is attained by presenting standard service consumption by infrastructure component and the IT system management processes that were expended in supporting the infrastructure components in the service (see Exhibit 2.14).

Measuring business objectives, service contracts, and the cost of service is a major step forward for IT maturity. It is, however, only part of the maturity picture. IT internal engineering and management must be brought into the PM picture. Let's start with the business of capacity management. Capacity has several management objectives that look for cost savings and service improvement. Capacity managers must manage to keep excess capacity as low as possible through consolidation and virtualization and forecast as accurately as possible (see Exhibit 2.15).

View▾ Data▾ Properties				⊡ X
			Year	⊞ 2008Q4
SLA_L4	SLA_L1	StdSvc_L1	StdSvc_L2	
MA Campaign Exe – eCommerce Phone Rep	Infrastructure Based	⊟⊞ Standard Service	Bronze Service – Network	$39,737.73
			Bronze Service – Servers	$69,847.32
			Premium Service – Network Web	$5,398.40
		Subtotal		$114,973.45
	None	⊞⊞ None		$253,688.56
		Subtotal		$253,688.56
	Process Based	⊟⊞ Standard Service	Bronze Service – Network	$14,782.73
			Bronze Service – Servers	$37,596.60
			Premium Service – Network Web	$33,370.58
		Subtotal		$85,749.91
	Subtotal			$454,411.92

Exhibit 2.14: Standard Service Consumption

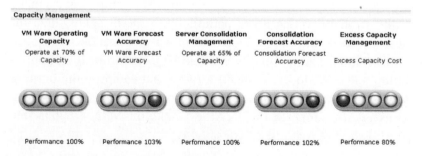

Capacity Management				
VM Ware Operating Capacity	**VM Ware Forecast Accuracy**	**Server Consolidation Management**	**Consolidation Forecast Accuracy**	**Excess Capacity Management**
Operate at 70% of Capacity	VM Ware Forecast Accuracy	Operate at 65% of Capacity	Consolidation Forecast Accuracy	Excess Capacity Cost
Performance 100%	Performance 103%	Performance 100%	Performance 102%	Performance 80%

Exhibit 2.15: Capacity Management Objectives

Appl Type	Resource Class	Resource Group	Resource Lev 3	
		⊞⊡ **Router**		91,804
		⊟⊡ **Servers**	⊞⊡ **Server A**	59,694
			⊞⊡ **Server C**	31,264
	⊟⊡ Hardware	⊞⊡ **Disk**		3,687
		⊞⊡ **Network – Web**		2,628
		⊞ ⊡ **Web Servers**		45
			⊞⊡ **Hardware Administration**	18,181
			⊞⊡ **Network Support and Mgmt**	15,977
⊡ Excess Capacity			⊞⊡ **Mainframe Support and Mgmt**	14,954
		⊟⊡ Hardware Group	⊞⊡ **Distributed Capacity Planners**	1,476
	⊟⊡ Support		⊞⊡ **Network Capacity Planners**	1,351
			⊞⊡ **Storage Capacity Planners**	1,224
			⊞⊡ **Mainframe Capacity Planners**	1,191
		⊞⊡ **Support Group**		29,311
		⊞⊡ **Administration and Finance**		24,158
		⊞⊡ **Software Group**		13,288

Exhibit 2.16: Excess Capacity Visualization with the Financial OLAP Cube

Excess capacity is a cost that IT must absorb, and the IT organization must manage excess as close to zero as possible. In Exhibit 2.16, the financial OLAP cube depicts the excess capacity costs by device and the IT system management services engaged in managing the excess capacity. Excess capacity isn't simply idle components, but components that are utilized to some degree but underutilized beyond the overhead capacity built in for headroom.

Service management must manage the twin centers of standard service and business services to a level of cost and service performance determined as a part of the IT organization's business management and planning. Standard services are managed to internal IT service contracts and are measured as a part of good IT business management. If the standard service is not performing to specifications, then the business services won't perform to contract specifications either (see Exhibit 2.17). Excess capacity can also be managed in the business-facing side of IT: in the standard services that comprise the business services. IT "sells" the standard services. Excess capacity here is similar to excess inventory. In this OLAP example, this service has far too much excess capacity (see Exhibit 2.18).

Shared Services Performance

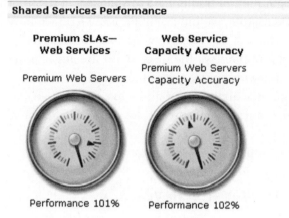

Premium SLAs— Web Services	Web Service Capacity Accuracy
Premium Web Servers	Premium Web Servers Capacity Accuracy
Performance 101%	Performance 102%

Exhibit 2.17: Shared Services Performance Dashboard

View▾ Data▾ Properties				▣ ✕
				Cost
Service Type	**Appl Type**	**Application**	**Resource Class**	
▣ **Premium Service**	⊟▣ **Projects**	▣▣ **ERP**	⊞▣ <u>Support</u>	<u>334,600</u>
			⊞▣ <u>Hardware</u>	<u>25,798</u>
		⊞▣ **Marketing Automation Services**	⊞▣ <u>Support</u>	<u>114,207</u>
			⊞▣ <u>Hardware</u>	<u>20,714</u>
		⊞▣ **Finance**	⊞▣ <u>Support</u>	<u>72,224</u>
			⊞▣ <u>Hardware</u>	<u>41,471</u>
		⊞▣ **Desktop Services**	⊞▣ <u>Support</u>	<u>2,734</u>
			⊞▣ <u>Hardware</u>	<u>1,570</u>
	⊞▣ **Excess Capacity**		⊞▣ <u>Support</u>	<u>70,329</u>
			⊞▣ <u>Hardware</u>	<u>33,937</u>
	⊞▣ **Reserve Capacity**		⊞▣ <u>Support</u>	<u>30,579</u>
			⊞▣ <u>Hardware</u>	<u>12,937</u>

Exhibit 2.18: Excess Capacity

Has the application of traditional PM supplied all the information and tools necessary to make intelligent decisions? Do we have all the tools to judge which of our management domains impacts success or failure the greatest? Have we the tools to test the impact of proposed changes to our initiatives and forecast the results? In other words, can we apply advanced analytics to PM and move PM planning and interpretation from educated guesswork to confidence interval based analytics?

We can. SAS calls it *Intelligent Scorecarding*.

CHANGING THE WAY IT BEHAVES

The CIO and IT organization spend significant time, effort, and money designing and implementing strong, proactive programs to build effective capacity, service, financial, and alignment practices. You convinced your business users to provide business objectives along with their requests for IT investments. From those business objectives IT has created service, cost, and capacity contracts and spawned a broader set of internal management objectives. Now IT and its business partners are measuring alignment metrics up and down the value axis. In spite of all the planning, the measurement results indicate you are a little short of expectations. The programs didn't produce the results everyone had bet their bonuses on.

What do you do now? IT has been steered in a new direction, and while results are adequate, improvements must be made. Do you stay the course, adjust the course, or is a new, improved course needed?

If it were possible . . . to know which assumptions and initiatives were correct and which were wrong . . . to know which measures had the greatest impact on success, which assumptions failed, and to what degree . . . to know how much better we might understand the ways that IT was doing the right things, measuring the right things, and selecting measures reflect the correct strategy in the proper portions . . . to know when changes needed to be made (as they inevitably do) . . . could we then predict the impact of those changes before the changes are made?

This chapter is not just about SPM. It is about SPM and Intelligent Scorecarding for IT, which gives IT an additional tool, honed specifically for IT, to help steer IT management and initiatives in the direction that provides the most value for the business. Poorly conceived and ill-applied SPM undermines the achievement of optimized results, or even worse, becomes the wrong tool addressing the wrong problem. Deliberate and judiciously applied SPM is absolutely necessary for effective and efficient strategy execution.

IT strategy that addresses system management issues while knitting an effective business relationship with IT customers has proven to be an elusive goal since the end of mainframe dominance in the early 1990s. To understand the ways that SPM and Intelligent Scorecarding applications address this strategic IT management goal, we have to rummage through several subject areas and cross-pollinate germane material throughout four main themes:

1. IT and SPM
2. Management domains in the PM context
3. Analytical performance management
4. IT analytical PM

Addressing the Challenges of IT and Strategic Performance Management

SPM for IT is more than just generating and reporting a mishmash of stovepipe metrics. Reporting historical performance while ignoring correlation or forecasting is not a better way forward. SPM is not magic. It is part art, part science. SPM has its own lessons learned from how businesses applied it to handle business problems. SPM and analytical performance management (APM) do not have much of a history in IT management applications, so we have to extrapolate and garner insight from its use in other areas of the business. The art of SPM eventually leads us to the realization that the IT organization's business users are trying to solve very similar business issues as IT managers. The users just have a little more problem-solving experience in this area.

In its simplest form, SPM without Intelligent Scorecarding provides the linkages to ROI, objectives, and IT enablement, which contains a simple view of the business/IT value axis. The value axis is broad enough and layered enough to not only contain the business/IT value axis but also reflect an internal IT management model that covers the four essential IT management domains of business alignment, capacity management, service management, and financial management discussed earlier in this chapter. The value axis is important because most application failures lack strategic perspective—such application failures look to correct current issues and fail to address future conditions. While the IT organization's business partners must justify the acquisition and purpose of strategic business applications, IT is not excused from understanding and contributing toward that strategic perspective, which is the crux of business/IT value axis alignment.

Accordingly, the CIO's contribution to the value axis starts when IT first begins to process new business application goals and objectives. The best practice CIO uses the following steps to translate the application into empirical values that can be implemented and measured:

- Business application goals and objectives
- Determining the price to be paid for IT enablement and ongoing service
- System projections of volume, data storage, and other criteria
- Service level requirements
- Impact on capacity: infrastructure, capital, and expense
- Measurement system

Sounds easy enough, unless your IT organization hasn't matured into a service provider or learned to manage IT like a business. In that case, the steps on the value axis won't be attainable in the short term. IT organizations all too often manage by engineering expertise that translates into technology stovepipes. Managing by engineering and technology stacks is an effective and efficient approach given that we educate and train engineers by discipline rather than educating and employing generalists. What is not provided, especially as engineers are promoted to management, is an enterprise management view of IT organization responsibilities—a management view of IT not taught in most management programs. Earlier sections articulated the perspectives researched by two key members of the analyst community, McKinsey and Associates from a business perspective, and Gartner taking an engineering approach. While these two perspectives start from different ends of the maturity process, both promote the conclusion that IT should be run like a business. The following discussion fills in the space between these two perspectives.

SPM provides more than just linkages between ROI, objectives, and IT enablement. The benefit is far, far greater, and the job demands more than mere linkages. Engineering disciplines in IT are typically awash in internal key performance indicators (KPIs) generated by monitoring and management tools that don't necessarily address the obstacle that stymies most IT organizations from maturating into business-oriented enterprise service providers: firefighting infrastructure failures. Neglected, or missing altogether, are the business-oriented KPIs from service management, financial management, and business/application strategy.

Although many CIOs and their IT organizations have very little applied experience with SPM, the business side of the house generally has similar communication and management holes. SPM synchronizes business and IT improvements to create value. Since misapplication or under-application of SPM can lead to undesired outcomes, Gary Cokins lists three questions that enterprise and IT leadership should use SPM for focusing value creation and synchrony:

1. What products or service lines should we offer or not?
2. What markets and types of customers should we serve or not?
3. How are we going to win and keep winning?

When business is good, choices are easier; when business is bad, choices are harder. Many executives have found themselves on new ground that makes decision making more challenging than in the past. Enterprises have discovered that many of the products they have in the marketplace are basically commodities that offer little difference in terms of quality or functionality. Consumers choosing between cell phone A or cell phone B or flat screen 1 or flat screen 2 have little to lose (or gain) between brand choices or where to make the purchase. One transaction seems as good as the other.

Compounding the commoditization of products and services, enterprise and IT executives find themselves managing organizations that are complex and constantly changing. Their strategies often fail due to the lack of communication. Interest consequently spiked in SPM because businesses faced eight major chronic problems that needed resolution:

1. Failure to execute strategy
2. Unfulfilled return on ROI promises from transactional systems
3. Escalation in accountability (consequences) for results
4. Need for quick trade-off decision analysis
5. Mistrust of the managerial accounting systems
6. Poor customer value management
7. Dysfunctional supply chain management
8. Broken budgeting process

How were these issues addressed through SPM? The most typical activity was the reporting of standard information at standard frequencies. A simple, widely used example is reporting sales by geographic region each quarter.[21] Executives see how many flat screens 1 and 2 were sold, when and where, on a quarterly and regional basis. Adding just a bit more sophistication, managers and executives can drill down into the data and see trends, patterns, or anomalies that need attention. They see that flat screen 1's numbers were trending up in the Chicago area in August, but most likely they wouldn't make a connection with the Cubs stretch run for the pennant, know why flat screen 1 was chosen over flat screen 2, or know which flat screen was the most profitable model of the two. Additional sophistication adds executive alerts for responsible managers when parameters approach established preset performance levels. The Cubs were eliminated (again), sales nose-dived, and the alert was sent.

Since the IT organization's maturity has been surveyed, measured, and critiqued, it is fair to ask about the maturity of SPM application in businesses. More Davenport statistics:[22]

- Integrated SPM across the entire organization: 37%
- SPM throughout the enterprise, but not integrated: 32%

■ SPM in some areas: 24%

■ Nothing: 7%

It seems that almost all enterprises use PM and reporting to some extent. Most reporting, however, is not built on the foundation of a balanced scorecard or strategy maps. In other words, enterprise strategy is generally not embedded in the reporting system. Without the underlying relationships of major enterprise strategy initiatives, deliberate to the extent that investments measurably impact enterprise objectives, the result is often a loose knit system of KPIs, for ill or good, displayed on an executive dashboard that does not demand the attention of the decision maker.

A comparison of the eight major chronic problems that drove enterprise executives toward SPM and the problems faced by CIOs and their IT organizations today reveals striking similarities. A deep and persistent topic for the CIO over the last fifteen years has been the failure of IT to execute strategy on two principal levels: system management and customer value management. A key part of IT's customer value management breakdown is centered on the "unfulfilled return on ROI promises from transactional systems." Even as unfulfilled ROI shows up as a major driving force on the business side of the ledger, enterprise executives point the finger at IT costs rather than service delivery and optimizing IT system value by those very same systems. The keys to costing too much? (1) Mistrust of the managerial accounting systems; (2) a broken budgeting process; and (3) dysfunctional supply chain management in the form of disconnected engineering silos.

Few CIOs question that their IT organizations face daunting cost and PM challenges. System management problems that affect business performance and drain cash continue to plague enterprise IT. As any firefighter will tell you, it is cheaper and far more convenient to prevent fires than to put them out and repair the damage. When any organization finds itself reflexively reacting to one unforeseen event after another, the employees find it very difficult to muster the energy and resources to move strategic imperatives forward. The toll exacted in the case of such an IT organization is a group of people, no matter how talented or well-led, who are unable to overcome the system management challenges wrought by the rapid technology changes of the 1990s and Y2K-spawned enterprise applications that have burrowed so deeply into enterprise business processes (and yes, those same applications that failed to produce a ROI).

As the CIO and the IT organization seek to solve system management and business alignment issues, APM is the approach that can provide the tools to form, test, and forecast strategy that aligns enterprise strategy with IT enablers. Earlier sections identified four key IT management domains, which are also the building blocks of IT management maturity and the basis for SPM Intelligent Scorecarding.

Best practice CIOs recognize the importance of business management opportunities and how those opportunities should be strategically managed and measured, both to enable business end users to gain ROI for their IT investments, but also to enable strategic internal IT resource management. Intelligent SPM doesn't necessarily use capacity management as a starting point, but capacity management is the starting point for IT management maturity. Intelligent Scorecarding addresses the challenge faced by best practice CIOs to balance the right capacity at the right cost, to provide strategically enabling IT services, and to measure the impact on enterprise business objectives. Best practice CIOs and their IT organizations develop capacity management from an engineering silo into partnership with other IT enterprise business management domains and cement system management maturity with strategic enterprise business priorities. For example, after determining the optimal capacity level, actively managing the capacity to that level wrings out the excess capacity costs of idle capacity and also eliminates panic infrastructure buys. Determining the cost of capacity not only effectively manages capacity but also provides foundation costs for service management and service management contracts. The cost of capacity includes the cost of utilized capacity, reserve capacity, and unused capacity. Capacity managers must also determine capacity beyond the traditional manner. Predicting the exhaust rates of standardized services and the growth of business services remains a ripe opportunity for the best practice CIO.

Coupled with cost, service management is the most visible and measurable portion of the IT organization. All IT resource users have to be able to articulate what the IT organization should provide, how much is it going to cost, and why it is needed. Thus far in the marketplace, service reporting and financial measures have been reactive in nature, as has been most IT-related enterprise PM reporting. Forecasting service-level performance, future capacity needs, and cost of service growth moves service management from looking in the rearview mirror to using a GPS. Best practice CIOs may not avoid all the problems, but they can manage them. Forecasting provides value for service management. Best practice CIOs use one other opportunity for service management: the IT-related strategy management structure must contain enterprise business value measures. Reporting cost and service results are inadequate without knowing progress toward enterprise business strategy objectives. Meeting business goals and objectives are the ultimate measure of the ways that IT enables enterprise strategic value. Applying intelligence to enabling and meeting business strategy is a new breed of IT management.

When capacity management has additional tools that include the cost of capacity (including unused capacity), the cost of the support processes, and the strategy metrics to manage toward enterprise strategic objectives, capacity emerges from the cocoon of an engineering silo as an IT strategic enabler. When service management considerations include the cost of service, unused service, who consumes the service, relevant support processes for both the standard service catalog components and each business service, along with strategy metrics, the financial domain becomes the pinnacle of the new IT management model of business alignment.

Because many CIOs and IT organizations have little experience in applying either SPM or Intelligent Scorecarding to business alignment, best practice examples are rare. Most examples of business alignment center on portfolio management, which has been disconnected from true financial management and SPM as just another silo. The opportunity presented by business alignment is far greater than typically imagined. As one of the key strategic enablers of most enterprises, IT would be managed like a business while performing as a part of the greater enterprise. IT products in the form of applications that enable business processes enjoy the same benefits as other enterprise-wide management tools. Enterprise leadership creates a value axis from the performance metrics from each of the IT management domains. Each IT organization responsibility must have business objectives that trace back to overall enterprise business strategy, enabled by the CIO. This enablement must have a pre-established price tag before implementation of any new IT products, projects, or services. That price tag must fit within the ROI calculation of the enterprise business objectives, where the support costs are determined by the volume and service estimates articulated by the IT resource users, which the CIO and the IT organization translates into service and capacity levels. Once built and implemented, IT applications and related services can be measured, forecasted, and optimized from business objectives, service results, costs, and business strategy.

Intelligent Scorecarding and Analytical Performance Management

Thomas Davenport articulated four key points that he considered the Holy Grail of APM:

1. In an ideal world, consider or control for all possible variables that might have a substantial effect on financial performance (customer relationships, employee attitudes and behaviors, level of innovations, value of brand equity, and the others) for one overall equation that described the relative contributions.

2. No longer would organizations report metrics simply because they are familiar or because a standard balanced scorecard format suggests them.

3. Business strategies (those in a strategy map) would be testable.

4. Firms would also be able to predict the impact of increases or decreases in non-financial performance.[23]

Davenport suggests that enterprises statistically test relationships in business strategies through PM reporting: where that reporting would be more creative, relevant, and valuable than the sales stats for flat screen TVs and other conventional performance reporting. Businesses would know what worked *and* what failed, and modify their strategies accordingly. Davenport suggests applying statistical analyses to variables in PM, with demonstrates dramatic results. Carrying his work further, SAS shows *how* to perform the analysis.

Let's examine some Davenport examples. Each example tested two variables, one financial and one nonfinancial:

- Hilton: Five percent improvement in customer retention results in a 1.1 percent increase in annual revenues at a typical property.

- Harrah's: For each 1 percent growth in its share of customer gaming budgets, its share price increases by $1.10.

- Best Buy: Discovers that for every tenth of a point on a five-point scale increase in employee engagement at a particular store, operating income rises $100,000.

- Victoria's Secret: Finds that raising its average conversion rate by 1 percent brings more than $35 million in sales and $15 million in operating profit.

In a couple of more sophisticated examples where two variable analyses were performed with controls to focus the results:

- Toronto Dominion Bank: Controlled for customer service-financial performance of its branches, the bank finds that customer service equals 19 percent of the variation in branch profitability and further finds that service improvement only affects profitability in the middle of service rankings; incentives are aimed at the middle.

- Store24: Creates a balanced scorecard and a strategy map for a program titled "ban boredom" on the assumption that entertained customers buy more; the program does not work; it lowers profitability even when controlled for demographics and income levels, but the program works where employee skill levels are high.

As discussed in Chapter 1, enterprises regard the relationship between customer satisfaction and loyalty, employee satisfaction, and product capability as key indicators in driving financial success. Most businesses measure them to some degree. Other nonfinancial variables are less common. For example, a tech services company found that the average time it takes to close a case is a strong predictor of gross margins. An oil refiner found uptime closely correlated to profits.

Intelligent Scorecarding takes the best of APM and embeds itself in the strategy map of a scorecard. Most businesses have avoided the rigor of a balanced scorecard or the complexity of the strategy map that evolves from a balanced scorecard. Balanced scorecards impose a structure that might be too confining for IT. The first edition of *CIO Best Practices* discussed an IT balanced scorecard. Seeking a way to guide the implementation of IT maturity, SAS subsequently labored on that scorecard, complete with a strategy map, for another year or more. While strategy maps have value, SAS has found that the approach does have its flaws. A strategy map is a map, nothing more. If one is planning a car trip and uses an atlas to map the route, travelers can rest assured that the map is accurate but cannot be assured that the chosen route is the best route. These maps are not designed to identify traffic patterns, bottlenecks, construction zones, or factor in weather forecasts. Neither are strategy maps. No history to look back on. No forecasting to rely on. No indication which part of the plan is more important than any other.

Intelligent Scorecarding removes the tediousness of designing a scorecard, balanced or otherwise. CIOs and their C-Suite peers can design visually, drawing relationships as the path forward is more clearly articulated. As executives design strategic IT measurements, the tool applies statistical techniques to measure results and predict the impact of changes. By building the statistical measures and forecasts of the relationships into the strategy map, Intelligent Scorecarding overcomes a major shortcoming of strategy mapping, which gives equal weight to all relationships, whether financial or nonfinancial. In addition, Intelligent Scorecarding removes uncertainty associated with making changes in strategy by forecasting the impact of proposed changes with confidence intervals.

Designing Intelligent Scorecards can be done either by working from the top down or by building from the bottom up. Working from the top down is the easier and surer method. In honing this tool for IT, SAS works from the top, beginning with the four IT management domains of capacity, service, financial, and business alignment. Each domain is a "perspective" in the strategy map. As in any strategy map, thought must be given to the relationships between the management domains. The trick is to settle on the order of influence between domains.

NOTES

1. Donna Scott, Jay E. Pultz, Ed Holub, Thomas J. Bittman, and Paul McGuckin, "Introducing the Gartner IT Infrastructure and Operations Maturity Model," Gartner ID Number: G00147962, October 2007, confluence.arizona.edu/.../introducing_the_gartner_it_iInfrastructure+and_Operations_1479621.pdf.

2. Paul McCann and David Migliore, "What is MVS?" November 3, 2005, http://searchdatacenter.techtarget.com/sDefinition/0,,sid80_gci212618,00.html.

3. Tom Hormby, "What a Legacy: The Origin of the IBM PC," August 11, 2006, http://lowendmac.com/orchard/06/ibm-pc-5150-origin.html.

4. IBM, "IBM Personal Computer," Brochure 1982.

5. Google search for "Microsoft Windows 3.1 Sales History," www.google.com/search?hl=en&tbo=p&tbs=tl%3A1&q=microsoft+windows+3.1+sales+history&aq=f&aql=&aqi=&oq=.

6. Michael Hauben and Rhonda Hauben, "On the Early History and Impact of Unix Tools to Build the Tools for a New Millennium," *Netizens: On the History and Impact of Usenet and the Internet* (Wiley-IEEE Computer Society Press, 1997), www.columbia.edu/~rh120/ch001j.c11.

7. Brevard User's Group, "History of the Ethernet," LAN Networking Networks Packet Xerox, http://bugclub.org/beginners/history/EthernetHistory.html.

8. Marcus Kazmierczak, "History of the Internet," September, 24, 1997, http://mkaz.com/ebeab/history/.

9. "Legent Corporation—Company History," www.fundinguniverse.com/company-histories/Legent-Corporation-Company-History.html.

10. Steven Chan, blogs.oracle.com/images/Architecture%20Diagram%20R12.png.

11. Michael Bloch and Andres Hoyos-Gomez, "How CIOs Should Think about Business Value," *McKinsey Quarterly*, March 2009, www.mckinseyquarterly.com/How_CIOs_should_think_about_business_value_2307.

12. James M. Kaplan, Roger P. Roberts and Johnson Sikes, "Managing IT in a Downturn: Beyond Cost Cutting," *McKinsey Quarterly*, September 2008, www.mckinseyquarterly.com/Managing_IT_in_a_downturn_Beyond_cost_cutting_2196.

13. Vanessa Chan, Chris Musso and Venkatesh Shankar, "Assessing Innovation Metrics: McKinsey Global Survey Results," *McKinsey Quarterly*, November 2008, www.mckinseyquarterly.com/McKinsey_Global_Survey_Results_Assessing_innovation_metrics_2243?pagenum=5.

14. Michael Smith and Kurt Potter, "IT Spending and Staffing Report, 2009," Gartner ID Number: G00164940, January 27, 2009, www.gartner.com/DisplayDocument?doc_cd=164940.

15. See note 1.

16. Gartner, Incorporated, April 4, 2006/ID G00138514.

17. Jean-Pierre Garbani and Peter O'Neill, "The Megavendors in IT Management Software," Forrester Research Incorporated, May 21, 2008, www.forrester.com/rb/Research/megavendors_in_it_management_software/q/id/43904/t/2.

18. Gregg Wyant, Russ Heinsen, "Intel and the Road to Enterprise SOA," 2007 ASUG Annual Conference, Session 1601, presented by Intel Corporation.

19. Joseph Hatcher, "Overview of SAS ITRM Resource Management 3.1.1," *Introduction to SAS® IT Resource Management 3.1.1*, (Cary, NC: SAS Institute Inc., 2007), support.sas.com/documentation/onlinedoc/itsv/intro311.pdf.

20. Martha Hays and Margaret Churchill, "Paper 6151 Forecasting + Modeling: A Partnership to Predict and Prevent Capacity Bottlenecks," Computer Measurement Group Presentation, 2006, Volume 1, (Computer Measurement Group), http://direct.bl.uk/bld/PlaceOrder.do?UIN=2037913568ETOC=RN&from=searchengine. All subsequent Hays/Churchill quotations and exhibits come from this presentation.

21. Thomas H. Davenport, "The Rise of Analytical Performance Management," SAS Institute White Paper, www.sas.com/resources/whitepaper/wp_5596.pdf.

22. *Ibid.*

23. *Ibid.*

CHAPTER 3

Cloud Computing and the New Economics of Business

Michael Hugos

nternet-based technology is driving economic change at a level not seen since the spread of industrial technology in the late nineteenth and early twentieth centuries. What became known as "Web 2.0" and the business and consumer applications it brought about have continued to evolve, and what has emerged is now known as cloud computing, software-as-a-service, and social media. There is as yet only a short history of using these technologies and they continue to evolve. So we have much to learn, but it is quite clear that they are leading to disruptive changes in the way we communicate with each other and in the IT infrastructures that companies use to support their business operations.

The spread of cloud computing is an excellent example of the phenomenon known as "creative destruction," which was popularized by the economist Joseph Schumpeter.[1] Schumpeter pointed out that in capitalist economies, there are waves of change where the introduction of a new technology or new process for doing things upsets and replaces the previously dominant technology and the people and companies who used that technology. Cloud computing is having this effect on vendors who sell traditional versions of computing technology, and on the people who make their living operating this technology.

Companies that have large investments in traditional in-house computing technology will not abandon those investments immediately, nor should they. The transition of companies to cloud-based technology will be quicker for some and slower for others, depending on their individual circumstances. But the change will happen. History shows over and over again that resistance to the spread of new technologies is almost always futile (and often fatal). People and companies that resist are finally forced out of business and replaced by others that do adopt new technology. Clearly the best strategy for people and companies is to actively explore the opportunities for cloud computing, begin appropriate projects to gain experience in its use, and understand its strengths and weaknesses.

A COMBINATION OF TECHNOLOGIES CREATE CLOUD COMPUTING

Since the turn of this century, several different but related kinds of information technology have been evolving rapidly, and they are now being combined to make it possible to deliver computing resources on demand to companies almost anywhere in the world. The combination of technologies, such as the Internet, Web browsers, server virtualization, parallel computing, and open source software, produces a whole new set of possibilities for delivering computing resources. The term "cloud computing" is now used to describe the result of combining these technologies. IT vendors are offering combinations of these technologies to companies that want to outsource some or all of their traditional IT operations such as running data centers and operating traditional application packages, like enterprise resource planning (ERP), customer relationship management (CRM), and other business support applications.

SOME WORKING DEFINITIONS OF CLOUD COMPUTING

The exact definition of cloud computing is still evolving. Cloud computing is both a model for delivery of business computing services and a method for managing and operating computing hardware and software infrastructure. Different IT vendors put their own spin on their definitions, but they share more commonality in their definitions than differences. Here are several working definitions:

- "Consumer and business products, services, and solutions delivered and consumed in real time over the Internet" (IDC)[2]

- "A style of computing where scalable and elastic IT capabilities are provided as a service to multiple customers using Internet technologies" (Gartner)[3]

- ". . . a broad array of Web-based services aimed at allowing users to obtain a wide range of functional capabilities on a 'pay-as-you-go' basis that previously required tremendous hardware/software investments and professional skills to acquire." (Jeff Kaplan)[4]

- ". . . a way of utilizing resources wherever they may be when you need to use them. In that sense you just need to insure that your networking, security, and hardware infrastructure are robust enough to deliver the resources when needed, but just as important, your applications need to be able to execute well in that environment. To me, it is having what you want, when you want, through your virtual desktop no matter where you are." (Frank Enfanto)[5]

From these definitions and lots of other definitions (do a Web search on "cloud computing definition"), there are three characteristics that everyone seems to accept when it comes to describing cloud computing. Everyone agrees that cloud computing has the characteristics of:

1. **Practically unlimited computing resources.** Resources such as computing power, data storage space, and additional user sign-on IDs for applications are available on demand as needed, and this enables a high degree of agility and scalability in meeting evolving business needs.

2. **No long-term commitments.** Computing resources are immediately available and they may be used as long as needed and then retired because they are acquired on a month-to-month or even a minute-to-minute basis.

3. **Pay-as-you-go cost structure.** Because there are no long-term commitments, the cost of cloud computing resources is a variable cost, not a fixed cost; cost fluctuates depending on the amount of usage.

CLOUD COMPUTING HAS THREE COMPONENT LAYERS

The pace of change in cloud computing technologies is rapid. Certain components are changing so fast that the names and technical details of how they operate alter significantly every six to twelve months. Nonetheless, it is possible to group cloud computing technologies into three basic categories or layers. These layers support each other, and the relationships between the layers and the way each layer operates are relatively stable. We will use these three layers to create a basic model of cloud computing and provide a stable framework to discuss cloud computing technology (see Exhibit 3.1). The three layers of technology used in cloud computing are:

1. Hardware virtualization
2. Data storage and database management
3. Applications and application development environments

Hardware virtualization is a term that refers to the abstraction of computer resources so that many different computers or application servers seem to be available to run different application system, even though there may be a much smaller number of physical computers actually present. The term "virtual machine" (VM) refers to a software implementation of a computer or application server that executes programs like a real physical machine. Hardware virtualization enables companies to optimize the use of physical server resources and improve server administration. Virtualization is a common practice on mainframes and is becoming widely available for other computer architectures, such as computer servers built from low-cost computer chips

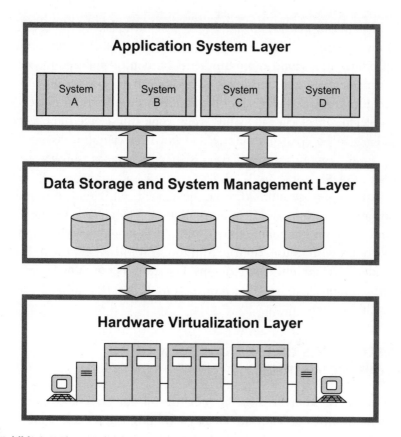

Exhibit 3.1: Three Technology Layers of Cloud Computing

and commodity hardware. In the cloud computing world, this layer is also referred to as infrastructure-as-a-service (IaaS).

Data storage and system management based on hardware virtualization is far more efficient and flexible than was possible before. Instead of buying a new physical server to host each different database, different databases can be supported by different virtual machines. The processing power of these virtual machines and the storage capacity of these databases can then be dynamically changed based on actual business requirements as they occur. In addition, these different virtual servers can be set up to run different operating systems, such as Linux or Windows, as needed. In the cloud computing world, this layer is also referred to as platform-as-a-service (PaaS).

Applications and application development environments can leverage hardware virtualization and data storage and database management capabilities in a cloud computing environment. Application systems to support different business operations can be hosted on virtual machines that are scaled up or scaled down hour-by-hour as needed to meet business user demands. New copies of a given application system can be created instantly and put into operation as needed. In cloud computing this layer is referred to as software-as-a-service (SaaS).

Application systems can be developed on cloud computing platforms that support different programming languages, testing platforms, and system management tools, depending on what system developers wish to use. Google, Amazon, and Microsoft provide some popular development environments. Popular programming languages that are supported are languages such as Java, PHP, Ruby on Rails, and C#.

IMPLICATIONS OF THE TRANSITION TO CLOUD COMPUTING

The momentum created by the pressures of our present economy is driving us inexorably toward cloud computing. Larger companies are creating their own internal clouds and smaller companies are moving to clouds from external service providers. The twin concerns of performance and security are valid, but they are not excuses or reasons to prevent the switch to cloud computing. Vendors are rapidly delivering tools to respond to and manage these concerns.

The move to cloud computing is the most profound change in IT since the emergence of the Internet. Big changes are occurring in the mission of in-house enterprise IT organizations and the way they are run. The bulk of staff in these organizations are presently devoted to performing traditional IT functions such as operating and maintaining data centers, data networks, and PCs, as well as the monitoring and enhancing of application systems that are hosted in those data centers or running on desktop PCs. Adoption of cloud computing will shift most of these traditional activities out of enterprise IT groups and into the cloud service provider organizations.

The information technology profession as we have known it for the last 40 years is dying; its obituary is already written. Companies are transferring the risk of high-ticket technology investments—like wholly owned data centers and internal application hosting—to highly focused and specialized service providers. Who's looking after the network? A service provider. Who's monitoring application performance? A service provider.

With the move to cloud computing, in-house IT professionals in most enterprises face big changes in their careers and risk to their job security and earning power. The spread of cloud computing is creating disruption on a level commensurate with the degree of change it ushers in. Just as some IT professionals in the 1980s resisted introduction of personal computers in their companies, and some IT professionals questioned the value of the Internet in the early 1990s, some IT professionals now resist the introduction of cloud computing in their companies. New technologies like these reduce demand for certain traditional skills, and they change the way the IT profession is organized.

Cloud Performance and Security Concerns

As it was one hundred years ago with the debate about whether to rely on outside vendors to provide electric power, the two main concerns in today's debate about cloud computing revolve around issues of performance and security. Because of the demand for new IT operating models created by economic imperatives of our global real-time economy, there are many technology vendors creating products to address these performance and security concerns.

New startups and established IT vendor companies are developing products that provide performance monitoring tools for cloud computing environments. Cloud computing service providers are purchasing these performance monitoring products in order to support the growth of their cloud computing businesses and to assure their customers that they can monitor performance and deliver consistent and high levels of service. For many application systems there are already adequate performance management tools available. In other cases there are still significant technical issues to be addressed, but if the history of technical development in the last several decades is a guide, we can safely assume there will be rapid progress made on these issues in the next few years.

IT vendor companies are rolling out suites of new products that enable companies to provide better security for cloud computing environments. They offer products for cloud intrusion prevention and for global threat correlation. Using these products, companies can create computing and collaboration environments that integrate in-house IT infrastructure with cloud-based application systems, and they can exercise a high degree of control over who enters those environments and what information those people have access to.

As these products rapidly improve, they become analogous to good brakes on a racecar; the better the brakes, the faster you can drive the car. Good performance monitoring and security protection enable companies to go faster and faster in setting up new cloud computing applications because they don't have to worry about performance and security concerns that would otherwise slow them down.

Cloud Computing Drives Creation of New Businesses

Under the relentless pressures of economic necessity and unpredictable market conditions, companies simply have to find ways to shift the cost and risk associated with basic IT equipment and operations to outside vendors. These vendors can then amass huge demand for their services, make the investments, and build the data centers needed to create new economies of scale that deliver computing services at lower and lower price points. Cloud computing data centers are evolving into factories that supply computing power, data storage, and application systems to drive the rest of the global economy.

Plans to simply cut IT budgets and try to keep operating expenses down until business rebounds will not work. If companies restrict IT operations and IT is seen and used only as a cost center instead of part of what creates and delivers the company's value proposition, then a company will not be able to roll out new products in a timely manner or keep up with changing desires of its customers or respond quickly enough to new threats and opportunities.

It will not be a winning move for business or IT executives to take a position analogous to the in-house electric power people from one hundred years ago. Instead, a far better move is to find ways to be part of enabling the transition to the cloud and moving your enterprise toward a more variable cost operating model. There are many opportunities for people who can show companies how to move to cloud computing and, at the same time, how to address the performance and security issues that go along with this move. When companies make this move they will have much more money to spend on doing the things their customers pay them for and creating the evolving stream of products that keep them connected and relevant to their customers and earn them profits.

This shifting of functionality to outside service providers must happen in order for in-house IT organizations to redirect their time and money toward working with the business units to use IT as part of what creates and delivers a company's value proposition to its customers. IT in the form of social media is fast becoming the way that companies spread the word about their products; traditional print advertising is losing its effectiveness. IT in the form of customer support and relationship management systems is how companies connect with their customers and build long-term relationships. And many companies produce products such as financial services, consumer electronics, smartphone and Internet applications, and entertainment and consumer services of all sorts that literally are built and delivered as IT themselves.

A useful analogy to think about is this: Universal access to low-priced electric power made possible by the spread of electric utilities drove a wave of innovation, not only in how businesses operated but also in the products they developed. From the 1910s onward, the introduction of thousands of new products using technologies such as electric motors and vacuum tubes became possible because everybody had dependable electric power. How many companies were created to build and sell products built with components like electric motors and vacuum tubes and transistors? What business innovations and new products can you now imagine based on universal access to low-priced cloud computing power? How many new companies will be created to develop and deliver those products?

A BUSINESS STRATEGY BASED ON AGILITY

This section and the rest of this chapter expand on agile IT system development methods and agile IT architecture principles, discussed in Chapter 3 of the first edition of *CIO Best Practices*. Cloud computing can be considered primarily as a cost-saving technology, and can be used here and there on cost cutting projects and quick fixes to provide point solutions for certain operational problems. Or cloud computing can be understood in the context of an overall business strategy based on agility and responsiveness. Cloud computing certainly provides cost savings in some situations but cost savings is not the most important benefit. The real value of cloud computing is the way in which it can be used to support a strategy of business agility.

A strategy of business agility puts responsiveness before efficiency. It emphasizes the ability to make continuous incremental changes and adjustments in operating procedures to respond as the world unfolds, so as to best fit new conditions. It also emphasizes continuous exploration of new business opportunities followed up by rapid growth into new markets when exploration shows a business opportunity to be profitable.

An Example of Business Agility

Here is a case in point; suppose a company, GrowMore Corporation, spots an opportunity to leverage its existing expertise and supplier relationships to launch a new product line for a market adjacent to its traditional markets. In order to do this, the company wants to set up a new business unit with branch offices in key geographical locations. It wants to have sales offices in these areas, and it wants to support the sales staff in these offices with a CRM system that enables sales-people to prospect for customers, create presentations and proposals, and follow up with prospective customers in a timely and organized manner. GrowMore Corp. also wants to collect sales and prospecting information from all the regional offices and store it in a single database at headquarters to provide for overall reporting and tracking of sales and business development activities.

The new product line will need some customization for individual customers so that it best fits the customer's unique needs, but GrowMore Corp. does not want to staff all these offices with engineers to do this customization. Instead of sending engineers out with sales-people to make calls on prospect companies, the company wants to set up videoconferences. This way their salesperson on site with the customer or prospect can arrange for videoconference interaction between an engineer and a customer, and the engineer can interview the customer and collect the information needed to configure the product.

In the old days, management of the new startup business unit would have submitted a support request to the company IT organization. The IT organization would then have sent out a business analyst to evaluate the request and study the needs of the new business unit. Then the request would have been prioritized against requests from other business units, and since existing business units typically get priority in the allocation of available IT resources, the startup unit would likely have to wait until the next budget cycle before it could get funding for the IT services it needs.

Then, when the funding and IT resources became available, there would be a process of designing and developing the needed software or evaluating possible packaged software solutions. Then there would be the purchasing and installation of the needed hardware and the communications networks, and finally, the rollout of the new system and accompanying user training. During that time, months or even years would have passed. In many cases, the window of opportunity for the new business would have closed, and the solution delivered would be too late or would not effectively address business needs that had evolved and changed during the time it took to build and roll out the system.

Instead of all this, management of the new startup business unit can go directly to relevant cloud services providers and start using one of their SaaS offerings within a matter of a few hours or a few days at most. Unlike the old days, there will not be any big upfront cost involved (no capital expense allocation needed) and the cost of oper-ating the systems will vary, depending on the amount of usage. That way, there is no sunk capital cost if the business idea doesn't work out, and there is not much in the way of system operating costs. If the new business does work out, then operating costs can be paid for out of sales revenue.

Using cloud technology and SaaS applications, the opportunity exists for this new business unit to put together a system by combining SaaS applications for their CRM needs and their video conferencing needs. They can add other industry-specific SaaS applications to their systems infrastructure as needs evolve. Or the new business unit can develop some unique custom applications as justified by the value proposition, and those applications can still run in the cloud, so there is no need to buy computer hardware and staff up the new business with IT people to operate that hardware.

Implications of Cloud-Enabled Business Agility

Cloud-Enabled Business Agility lowers the cost of sales for a new business unit in a way that then makes it possible and profitable for the unit to pursue smaller deals that were previously not profitable. The company can build a base of business from many smaller deals, which may be easier to get instead of having to go after only the larger projects and fight all the competition that goes along with getting those larger deals. These are some of the benefits of using an agile business strategy and the technology that enables such a strategy. The case study later on in this chapter further illustrates these ideas of agility.

Cloud computing has great cost cutting potential in certain situations, and at the same time, it's important to keep the larger business strategy in mind. The agility benefits far outweigh the purely cost-saving benefits. If an enterprise strategy calls for improving its ability to bring new products to market and its capability to expand geographically and open new offices, then cloud computing is a powerful technology for attaining these objectives.

Using cloud technology to enable new business formation and new product development creates what could be called multi-national small and medium businesses (SMBs) because with cloud technology, SMBs can now be truly global, where 10 years ago they could not afford the IT infrastructure to support global operations in an integrated fashion (see Chapter 5 for specific examples of this trend). For instance, small and medium sized businesses can open new sales offices in countries around the world, and conduct local sales campaigns in a way unthinkable before cloud computing. Opening new country sales offices simply means paying for more people to use a cloud-based CRM package and a cloud-based teleconferencing system. Specialists at company headquarters can back up salespeople with in-depth technical support without having to fly people around the world to meet with clients.

USING THE CLOUD FOR BUSINESS ADVANTAGE

Companies need IT infrastructures that enable them to operate more efficiently and accommodate continuous, incremental changes in business operations. To that end, many companies are already using server virtualization, and some are also using service-oriented architecture (SOA) to better leverage their existing IT investments and get additional flexibility and responsiveness from their existing systems infrastructure.

Companies are now at the point where they need to move on from an internal focus directed at maximizing use of IT resources to an external focus on supporting collaboration and new product development through use of cloud computing. Companies are moving from internally focused SOA projects to externally focused Web-oriented architecture (WOA) projects, where they begin using SaaS applications and combining them with internal applications that support collaboration with other companies to drive their growth.

This will happen because cloud and SaaS vendors are becoming more and more like utilities, offering reliable computing power and basic applications like email, ERP, CRM, and a growing array of industry-specific applications. Over the coming years, these vendors will develop economies of scale and expertise that enables them to offer their services at a much lower cost than what most companies would spend to deliver those services internally.

Because of these developments now and over the coming years, companies will outsource more and more of their basic IT operations to manage their costs for basic IT services. This will, in turn, enable companies to shift more of their time and attention to doing things with IT resources that add value to their products and provide meaningful differentiation in the eyes of their customers. IT will be used to deliver competitive advantage.

Cloud computing thrives in entrepreneurial environments where leapfrogging the competition is a daily motivator. Innovators need tools that fit their fast pace, their work-anywhere mentality, and their collaborative instincts. Cloud computing sets the stage for corporate innovation. Freed from lengthy implementation projects, moribund legacy applications, and armies of consultants, IT personnel can turn cloud computing into a competitive advantage.

Cloud computing offers significant advantages in its low startup costs, quick delivery of computing resources, and its pay-as-you-go cost structure. In addition, it offers ease of management, scalability of systems as needs grow, and device and location independence so people can access these systems from many different devices, such as a PC or a smartphone like a Blackberry or iPhone. And finally, cloud computing enables rapid innovation in companies to respond to evolving markets.

Many SaaS vendors and cloud service providers come to enterprise IT from the consumer IT side, and that means they are already focused on providing that customer-friendly interface that makes their software and services easy to learn and use. They bring the simplicity developed through their consumer experience, apply it to the corporate world, and continuously integrate with mobile devices such as Blackberries, iPhones, netbooks, electronic book readers, and iPads. These mobile devices are quickly becoming the new interface between people and the online world.

BUSINESS APPLICATIONS WITH THE GREATEST POTENTIAL

Apply a pain-versus-gain measurement to determine which applications could work well in the cloud. If your company is a startup operation then, almost by definition, most applications will be good candidates for cloud computing because of the advantages described earlier in the GrowMore Corporation case study.

If you are starting with an established company and existing infrastructure of in-house systems, then applications with the following characteristics are good candidates to start exploring cloud computing:

- Standalone applications with a low business risk if something happens and the system goes down or if system data were compromised or stolen

- Applications that are expected to have highly volatile and hard-to-predict workloads

- Situations where there is a need to collaborate and share information with an extended value chain of business partners

- Applications where there is a need to perform periodic data analysis on high volumes of data

- A platform to try things out quickly and at low cost, such as to field test a new application system or to create test and development environments for building new systems

- Situations where there is a need to conserve on capital expenses

An example of a standalone, low-risk application is a system like a simple Wiki blog site to support information sharing and knowledge management within a company. Another example is a system that allows people in field offices to collect and share data and update business planning models or a system for use by the human resources group to pilot a new recruiting process.

An example of applications with high volatility and usage patterns that are hard to predict is when a company launches a new product or a new product promotion and puts up a Web site to support that effort. If a site will only be up for six months or so and be prone to high spikes in traffic volume, then why spend the money and resources to sustain the site indefinitely, and why tie up systems infrastructure to support the peaks in usage volumes when that infrastructure will be underutilized during the non-peak times?

For instance, a fast-food restaurant chain might decide to promote special low-priced value meals by establishing a Web site where customers can check for specials and see the location of nearby restaurants offering these specials. The site would be heavily accessed when certain specials are offered, but it is hard to predict the actual usage volume. In such a case the company could employ a cloud services provider to set up the Web site. The service provider could quickly set up the Web site and provision that site with computing power and data storage capacity as needed. This way the restaurant company would only pay for the actual usage it incurred, and its usage costs would drop during periods of low customer activity.

Clouds also make sense where business is conducted based on shared data and where rapid feedback is needed. An example of this need to collaborate and share data with an extended value chain of partners could be a healthcare company that wants to share data on patient care and outcomes with a network of pharmaceutical companies and medical service providers. The healthcare company can make the data anonymous by blanking out the names of patients and then load the data into a cloud-based system where all relevant parties can access the data and apply cloud-based analytics to sift through the data for important patterns and trends.

Applications where there is a need to perform periodic data analysis on high volumes of data are also good candidates for cloud computing. For instance, an energy company doing geographical analysis to search for new oil fields could set up the compute-intensive portions of this operation using a cloud-based system. When large databases of information come in from its field exploration units, the company could ship this data up to the cloud where it would be processed and the results returned for in-house analysis. The company could strip out location-related data, so even if the data were stolen, it would not reveal sensitive information about where a promising new oil field might be located. In this example, the company would only pay for the computing resources used for the job when the job was run without tying up money in idle infrastructure when there were no jobs to run.

Many companies are already using cloud solutions (IaaS and PaaS) to quickly provide their in-house application development groups with testing and development environments. Instead of going through all the expense and time of purchasing the hardware and software needed to develop new systems, the development groups of these companies can get what they need immediately and pay for it only as long as their need lasts. As one senior enterprise architect at a major corporation put it, "You can buy a gift card on Amazon and use it to set up your own data center." Cloud service providers such as Amazon, Google, Hewlett-Packard, IBM, Microsoft, Rackspace, and others offer immediate provisioning like this.

CLOUD RISK CONSIDERATIONS

There are a number of issues to consider when deciding which applications to put in the cloud and which cloud service providers to use. Those issues and their related risks tend to group up into the areas of system and data security, performance management and service level agreements, and vendor lock-in.

The issue of system and data security is perhaps the most frequently discussed IT risk. There are risks that data placed in the cloud can be compromised or stolen by third parties. Yet it is also important to see these risks in their proper context: the state of security that presently exists within many companies. Many companies have data security issues that are equal to or even greater than those faced by cloud service providers. In-house data center operations are cost centers, they are always under pressure to cut their costs, and that means all their security issues cannot be addressed.

Data center operations and security are part of the way that cloud service providers and SaaS vendors earn their profits, so these companies are far more inclined to invest in security. Data and system security are issues that these provider companies have been working on for some time, and because their systems live in the cloud outside corporate firewalls, they get attacked thousands of times every day. This experience gives cloud service providers more security experience and better security procedures than that enjoyed by the average corporation.

CIOs and CTOs should also remember that the greatest security threat to systems and data, whether behind an enterprise firewall or in the cloud, is something known as "social engineering." Social engineering refers to the various practices used to interact with system users, data center operators, and help desk staff to illegally gain access to passwords and user IDs. There are many ways that people can be tricked into giving away passwords and IDs to unauthorized parties who then use this information to gain access to the systems and data they want. Enterprise IT organizations are just as vulnerable to social engineering as cloud service providers. Protection against social engineering is more a matter of managing human nature and maintaining effective policies for administering system access information.

Performance management of cloud-based systems is an area that can make in-house IT staff uneasy. They are used to having more direct control over the actual computer, communications hardware, and operating systems that drive the systems their companies have used up until adopting the cloud. They worry that once systems are moved to a cloud environment, there will be no way to monitor and control the user response times and other performance characteristics of those systems. They feel that their companies will just have to accept whatever performance levels the cloud services vendor may offer and make the best of it.

Since high levels of performance and satisfied customers are central to the profitability of cloud service providers, companies are investing in technology that allows customers to monitor and manage many of the operating parameters of cloud-based systems as discussed in Chapter 1. Cloud service providers are working with technology companies (Akamai, Cisco Systems, F5, IBM, and Nimsoft to name just a few) to design and install technology that monitors and displays real-time information, showing how well a given cloud application is performing. This technology enables in-house IT staff to respond and make adjustments as system slowdowns and other problems appear.

Performance management technology will continue to improve as more and more use is made of cloud systems. Technical problems have technical answers, and technical advances can happen quickly when there is sufficient demand. Performance management is a justifiable concern of cloud customers, but it is not an obstacle that should prevent companies from making effective use of cloud systems.

SLAs that guarantee certain levels of system performance are constantly evolving. At present, cloud service providers and SaaS vendors do not offer strict guarantees on their service levels. When service outages do occur, the vendors offer to reimburse customers for the cost of their services during the period of the outage, but they do not pay penalties that would reimburse customers for loss of business revenue or costs they incur because of a service outage.

Again, it is important to see the issue of SLAs in the proper context: comparing the performance records of cloud service providers and SaaS vendors with the performance records of in-house data centers. In many cases there is no formal measurement of the service levels provided by in-house IT organizations. In-house systems go down or their response time slows down, and people in a company just accept that as a fact of life.

The quality of in-house systems performance is directly related to the sophistication and training of in-house IT organizations. While large enterprises can afford large and well-trained IT staffs and sophisticated data centers, many (maybe even most?) enterprises get by with underfunded data centers, poor automation, and understaffed IT operations. IT staffs at these companies do the best they can with what they have, but they also make no guarantees about the quality of their service or the reliability of uptime for their systems. For these companies, a cloud provider may be an improvement in quality of service.

Lock-in is another risk in cloud computing that companies need to assess. Cloud computing often uses a different systems architecture than that used by traditional in-house systems. So once a system is put in the cloud it is not a simple matter to bring it back in-house or to move it to another cloud. Before selecting a cloud provider or a SaaS vendor, it is important to evaluate the stability and longevity of that company, understand their pricing model, and project the likely ongoing costs associated with using their applications to run your business.

Once again, it is important to see the issue of cloud provider lock-in by using an appropriate context: Lock-in already exists with traditional in-house systems and software. Once a company makes a commitment to use an ERP system and installs the software, there is a large degree of lock-in that comes along with that decision. It is expensive and time consuming to install an ERP system, and once done it is very unlikely that a company will go to the expense of uninstalling that system and switching to a different ERP system. The same goes for making a commitment to build company computing and communications infrastructure. Once the technology from a given vendor or small group of vendors has been installed, it would require a great effort to switch to the technology of different vendors.

Over time it may actually be easier to switch from one cloud provider to another than it is to switch from one software vendor to another for your in-house systems. This is because clouds, by definition, are able to create virtual computers that you use to run your applications. As long as the operating system used by the virtual computers of one cloud provider is the same as the operating system used by another cloud provider, then it is possible to move the program code from one provider to another and expect that application system to work. Many cloud providers use a version of the Linux operating system. Other cloud providers use the Microsoft Windows operating system.

Moving data from one cloud provider to another is the other issue to consider when thinking about moving your application system to a different cloud provider. Cloud providers such as Google and others are endorsing open standards (such as HTML 5.0) that make it easier to move data from the databases of one provider to the databases of a different provider. These same data transfer standards are also making it easier to move large amounts of data back and forth between in-house systems and cloud systems.

CLOUD COST CONSIDERATIONS

The cost of using cloud systems is often compared to the cost of buying and operating the system hardware and software in-house, and the answers provided depend on the depth of the analysis that is done. On one level, a person can simply compare the rate for renting the use of a virtual server from a cloud provider and compare that with the cost of buying a real server. After a certain number of months it would appear cheaper for a company to own and operate that server in-house. Therefore, if the application system it will power is expected to be used longer than that number of months, it might be more prudent to build and operate the system in-house rather than in a cloud.

A senior enterprise architect, Rick Pittard, who works at a global 100 corporation, has been investigating this issue and working with some cloud-based applications to learn more. Assessing his corporation's cloud service provider, he observes that, "Hardware costs for short term projects, up to two years, are less expensive than purchasing and operating our own. Systems that will operate for longer than two years may be more cost effective to operate in-house."[6] Then he went on to add another insight, "but at three years you are getting close to replacement of the equipment, and if you go through the replacement cycle to upgrade your hardware, then there is no cost advantage to running it in-house; you might as well use a cloud provider instead."[7]

People often forget to add all the indirect costs that go along with purchasing, installing, and operating their own computer equipment. The indirect costs add up to much more than the purchase price of the hardware. In their cost analysis, people need to include all of the related costs such as:

- **People and electricity.** What is the cost of the people in procurement who negotiate purchase prices and support contracts; what are the costs of the people in IT who operate the equipment; and what are the costs of the electricity and air conditioning and rent and operation of the data center where this equipment is located?

- **System administration and asset tracking.** What is the cost of the people who maintain the system databases and do the system upgrades; what is the cost of the people who manage the software licenses and hardware leases; and who then dispose of these assets at the end of their useful lifespan?

- **Opportunity cost.** What are the costs of not doing other things with the money spent on the above two areas? Are there other places where you could use that money for better return? About 70 percent of most company IT budgets goes to maintenance of existing systems and infrastructure. Maybe by using cloud services, a company can reduce this percentage and spend their money on things that produce a higher return.

None of these costs address what may be the biggest cost of all: the cost of senior management time. If senior management in IT and operations spend most of their time on operations staffing, data center build out, and equipment leasing and installation, is that a good use of highly paid management time? Maybe it would be better if they spent more time figuring out how to use technology to sell more of the company's products and services, reduce operating expenses, and use IT for competitive business advantage.

CASE STUDY: SELLING "DESIGNER CHOCOLATES"

This company makes well-known chocolate candies and sells them through a variety of retail channels. It sells a lot of candy, but profit margins on candy are always being squeezed. Then some smart marketing people in the company spotted a business opportunity to sell "designer chocolates," cookies, and drinks through cozy storefront locations in upscale neighborhoods. The company won't sell as much this way as through traditional channels, but it will get a much better profit margin. It is an opportunity for the company to supplement its traditional business with a new business that can generate big profits for some period of time, but no one knows for how long.

What would you do if you were the CIO or the COO and you were asked how you were going to support this new designer chocolate business? Here's what you could do; here's how you could create an agile IT architecture and leverage it to move quickly and support this new business venture. Imagine that Exhibit 3.2 is what your existing infrastructure looks like; it was created over the years to support your traditional manufacturing business.

The key to meeting the company's needs for launching the new business is to leverage existing systems as much as possible, to hold down costs and speed up delivery times for new systems. You could use server virtualization to better utilize existing servers and avoid having to buy any new hardware. You could also use an open-source, bare-bones store point-of-sale system to support basic store operations.

You could set up a simple network using IaaS at each store to connect cash registers and PCs to the Internet. Using that connection

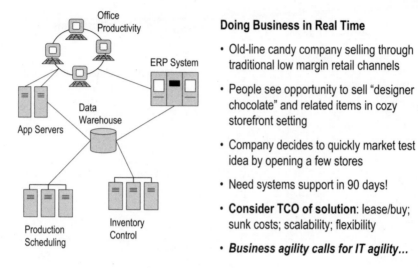

Doing Business in Real Time

- Old-line candy company selling through traditional low margin retail channels

- People see opportunity to sell "designer chocolate" and related items in cozy storefront setting

- Company decides to quickly market test idea by opening a few stores

- Need systems support in 90 days!

- **Consider TCO of solution**: lease/buy; sunk costs; scalability; flexibility

- *Business agility calls for IT agility...*

Exhibit 3.2: Case Study: Selling Designer Chocolates

and employing agile IT system development methods, you could use SOA to hook in functionality from the existing inventory control system to manage store inventories and use the existing ERP system to handle accounting and financial reporting. A new supply chain database (a data warehouse) could be created using PaaS to store and report on all the business transactions related to store operations. This would provide the data needed to learn and continually adjust and improve operating processes of the new business. Exhibit 3.3 illustrates this approach.

You deliver the first version of the Store Support System needed to open a few stores to test the concept, and guess what? The concept is taking off! Business is good, and now the folks in marketing and sales want to open up more stores and add some new features and products to the business model. Once again, you are asked to deliver the systems capabilities needed to make the expansion possible. But still, nobody knows how far this expansion will go or how long this business will last.

How would you use agile IT architecture to keep supporting the growth of this business? Given the uncertainty of the business, it's probably not wise to buy more servers to support more stores, because

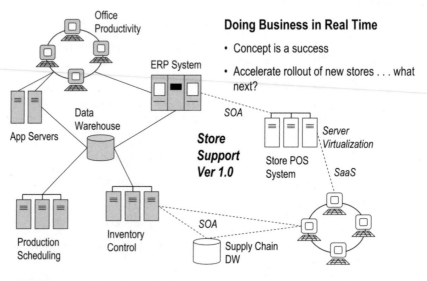

Exhibit 3.3: Designing the Network

you would have to take on the cost and the risk of building out your data center, adding more system backup capability, and hiring more staff. Instead, you could use a cloud services provider to deliver all the computing power for the stores on a pay-as-you-go basis. This leaves you free to cut back on computing services if the business were to take an unexpected turn and not grow as expected.

You could also combine the needs of the new business with needs of the existing business and look at retiring older IT architecture in favor of using more cloud computing and SaaS to meet changing company needs. This would turn fixed operating costs into variable costs and reduce any need for capital to purchase IT infrastructure. Operating costs would rise somewhat as business grew, but operating costs would also drop if the business did not grow as expected, so cash flow is better protected. The company would not have to incur the risk of a big investment in IT infrastructure at this stage when the business is going through significant changes and long-term needs are hard to see. Exhibit 3.4 illustrates this approach.

These diagrams illustrate how a lot of companies are going to evolve their systems architecture in the coming years. Using these techniques and technologies enables companies to move quickly, yet

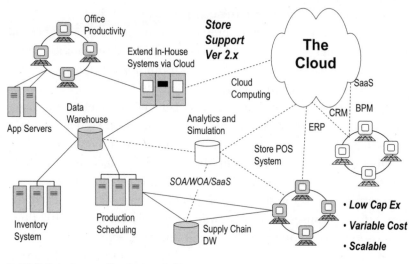

Exhibit 3.4: Augmenting System Agility

also minimize their investment risk in case a new business doesn't pan out. These approaches are stable and scalable. They enable an organization to move quickly. Ready or not, this is what the future of responsive enterprise IT infrastructure looks like.

DESIRABLE CHARACTERISTICS OF NEW IT ARCHITECTURE

In the present economy, companies are looking for ways to cut IT expenses, yet the real opportunity is to find ways to manage total company expenses in such a way that they track with the demands of business operations. Saving 10 or 20 percent on a company's IT budget is relatively small savings compared to using IT to save 10 percent on the operating expenses of the whole company or using IT to grow company revenue by 10 or 20 percent.

Companies have the opportunity to power their business operations with systems infrastructure that meets three operating standards:

1. Low capital expense
2. Variable cost of operations
3. Scalable computing platform

Low capital expenses are the order of the day in business because revenue and profits are under pressure, credit markets are tight, and loans are harder to get, so there is less money for capital investments. Also, because we're in a period of rapid technological change, making big investments in technology is risky because it might result in your company investing in technology that becomes obsolete a lot faster than expected. Best practice CIOs are learning to get systems in place without a lot of upfront capital expense. Smart executives are learning to shift their investments from the building of facilities like data centers to delivering new business operating capabilities instead.

Committing to the standard of a variable cost operating model is very smart because it's a great way to protect company cash flow. Pay-as-you-go operating models mean operating expenses will rise if business volumes rise, but just as important, operating expenses will drop or stay small if business volumes contract or don't grow as big or as fast as expected (you only pay more if you're making more and you pay less if you're making less). In this economy, where it is so hard to predict what will happen next and where companies need to keep trying new things to find out where new opportunities lie, variable cost business models are best for managing financial risk.

Committing to scalable systems infrastructure enables companies to enjoy the benefits of the first two standards. A scalable systems infrastructure enables a company to "think big, start small, and deliver quickly." Company executives can create strategies with big potential and try them out quickly on a small scale to see if they justify further investment. Companies can start with targeted 80 percent solutions to address the most important requirements first, then build further features and add more capacity as business needs dictate.

PUBLIC CLOUDS, PRIVATE CLOUDS, AND HYBRID CLOUDS

Although the exact definition of cloud computing is still being debated and different parties are offering slightly different visions, the cloud computing model has a handful of characteristics that are always present: massive scalability; provisioning of computing resources on demand; a pay-as-you-go cost structure; multiple systems and multiple users supported on the same computing infrastructure; systems and data available from anywhere with Internet connectivity; built-in disaster recovery; and software oriented toward customer ease of use.

Three models of cloud computing can be defined within this broad vision of cloud computing:

1. *Public clouds* are owned and operated by third parties and located in data centers that are outside of companies that use them. Multiple companies share the resources of these cloud computing data centers; they are each assigned their own virtual resources based on a common set of physical resources. Public clouds are provided by companies such as Amazon, Hewlett-Packard, IBM, Google, Rackspace, and Salesforce.com.

2. *Private clouds* are owned and operated by a company or a cloud computing provider, but they are built for the sole use of a single company. Private clouds utilize the same technology as public clouds, and they are often built to enable an individual company to maximize the use of its computing resources and be more responsive to company needs than was possible under the traditional IT operating model.

3. *Hybrid clouds* are combinations of multiple clouds that are both public and private. These clouds are created by individual customers to meet their specific needs. For instance, a company may decide to create a hybrid cloud to combine a CRM system provided on a public cloud operated by SalesForce.com with an ERP system running on their private cloud, and they may further extend this hybrid cloud by combining it with the Google cloud to provide their employees with the collaboration and productivity tools provided by Google Apps. Hybrid clouds like these sometimes use the services of a cloud aggregator.

Up to this point, this discussion has focused on the use of public clouds and the business reasons for using them. For many startup companies it makes sense to start immediately with the use of a public cloud, instead of investing precious capital in building their own data centers. By doing this, they avoid the distractions of running commodity computer hardware and software, and are able to concentrate on developing their unique value-added product or service that will be the profit generator for the company.

But for existing companies that have already made significant investments in systems infrastructure that they run in-house, the choice of how to proceed with the use of cloud technology is not so clear. They can consider the choices of creating private clouds or using hybrid clouds.

Private Clouds

Many industry analysts believe that private clouds will be attractive to in-house IT groups for the foreseeable future because of concerns about governance, data security, and performance management.[8] Private clouds also offer large companies an inviting way to consolidate data centers, cut technical support and operations staff, and increase server utilization. Typical server utilization inside corporate data centers ranges from as low as 2 percent up to around 10 percent, and implementing a cloud can raise those levels to 60 to 70 percent,[9] saving the need to buy a lot of additional servers.

There is a case to be made that private clouds don't need to be quite as automated and self-served as public clouds to deliver value to companies in the form of increased server utilization and faster user provisioning. Instead of using online Web request forms to provision computing services for a new application system, employees of a company could just send an email to their IT provisioning group with the request. The in-house IT organization could get it done and email the requestor back in a few hours with the confirmation and information they need to start using the newly provisioned system.

There is also a case to be made that larger companies enjoy certain economies of scale in the IT operations, and they can provide IaaS and PaaS less expensively than those services could be obtained from outside cloud service providers. In this circumstance, private clouds make good business sense for certain categories of services.

Private clouds may not need to run entirely on uniform hardware the way public clouds do. For instance, IBM has experience building private clouds that use products such as Tivoli on its mainframes, Windows and Linux on its servers, and Websphere transaction management and SOA and MQ Series for message sharing between these different platforms. By doing this they are able to create fit-for-purpose clouds and increase the utilization of each platform.

Building a private cloud in the typical heterogeneous enterprise environment offers advantages such as:

- It enables IT organizations to leverage existing infrastructure and get cost-effective use of their previous IT investments.
- Placing cloud computing inside the corporate data center eliminates many of the issues that accompany the use of public clouds such as data security, performance management and SLAs, and concerns about regulatory compliance.
- Private clouds also have the potential to obtain a lower cost of use, since they don't have a profit margin added onto their services, as is the case with public clouds.

In building their private clouds, companies can take an approach that allows them to invest in their private cloud as the first step on a journey to become comfortable with a cloud operating model. Companies may feel that external cloud environments have too many unknowns and too much risk until they become accustomed to this new operation model. Private clouds are a good way to test maturity and reliability of the technology. Companies can develop trust in the technology and the pubic cloud providers they work with on a limited scale. They can learn to deal with different regulatory, data control, and security issues. Over time, the in-house private cloud versus public cloud mix goes from 90-10 to something like a 50-50 mix or even a 20-80 mix. Large companies will probably not get to an all or nothing situation regarding their use of public and/or private clouds anytime soon.

Hybrid Clouds

A company may have a private cloud to share IT resources across multiple applications and increase utilization of the servers in their data center. Suppose that a company starts to experience a surge in user demand for one of their applications. By using a hybrid cloud they can quickly and cost effectively expand the capacity of the servers in their private cloud. They can draw upon the power of a public cloud to handle the increased user demand and maintain good system service levels for the people using it.

To create a hybrid cloud, companies need to put the infrastructure in place that will allow them to integrate public clouds with their private clouds while still maintaining security and performance management capabilities. IT vendor companies (Cisco, Itricity, Juniper Networks, and Nimsoft to name a few) are making the technology that allows companies to do this. This is the underlying infrastructure companies need for hybrid clouds. Integration of cloud applications and in-house systems requires an effective method for maintaining security, monitoring performance, and passing data back and forth between the cloud and the in-house systems. Perimeter security in hybrid clouds can be provided by a number of methods, such as data encryption and virtual private networks. Many in-house IT groups are already familiar with the use of this technology.

Most cloud vendors provide robust tools to help manage system performance in the cloud. This is their business, so they invest heavily in performance monitoring and reporting capabilities that often are superior to what companies have in-house. Once in place, this infrastructure becomes the base for new business models. It allows rapid expansion and contraction of computing power as business needs change, and it also provides the security, performance management, and regulatory compliance needed to operate hybrid clouds.

Cloud applications are, by their nature, relatively easy to integrate with other systems because they are built with well-defined application interfaces, known as application programming interfaces (APIs). Compared with the task of integrating different in-house applications, integrating cloud applications with in-house applications is often easier because the APIs of cloud applications make it easier to import and export data and pass that data back and forth between the cloud and in-house systems.

ISSUES TO CONSIDER WHEN THINKING ABOUT PRIVATE CLOUDS

Private clouds have all the issues associated with public clouds, and they require significant upfront capital investment to set up. They have the same problems with monitoring and managing performance. They have the same problems with the risk of vendor lock-in (particularly with respect to the virtualization technology used)[10] and the question of whether that vendor will keep up with the pace of technology change in the marketplace.

It is a huge challenge for internal IT organizations attempting to build private clouds because they often have not dealt with the business-process reengineering aspects of private clouds. The information technology infrastructure library (ITIL) is a popular set of best practices that are widely used to run the in-house data centers of individual companies. ITIL practices are going to clash with cloud practices because ITIL is very manually intensive, and clouds, by definition, must be highly automated in order to achieve the levels of user self-service and the rapid infrastructure provisioning required for meeting user service requests.

At present there are few, if any, in-house IT organizations that can match the operating discipline, automation, and resultant efficiencies of the big cloud data centers being run by vendors such as Amazon, Google, IBM, Microsoft, and Rackspace. Cloud vendors invest in their infrastructure and in automated systems administration capabilities, to achieve great economies of scale and operating efficiency. In-house IT groups are always being squeezed to save money and to cut their operations budgets, so they are challenged to create the economies of scale that public cloud vendors can achieve.

As Irving Wladawsky-Berger put it, most company data centers are a hodge-podge of different technology reflecting the company's history with different vendors and its mergers and acquisitions. He pointed out that they look like what most factories looked like before the advent of lean manufacturing practices. The engineering disciplines promoted by lean manufacturing and implemented by the Japanese and Germans have set a standard that every other manufacturing company needs to match if they want to achieve world-class productivity and cost efficiency levels. Companies need to adopt similar practices regarding their equipment and the layout and operations of their data centers.

Public cloud vendors are bringing this same discipline to bear on their cloud data centers. The public cloud vendors have implemented a new world-class level of practices and use of equipment that in-house IT groups must also adopt if they wish to achieve the same level of productivity and efficiency. Based on his experience over the last couple of years, senior enterprise architect Rick Pittard put it this way:

> Size of data centers is important but may not be as central to gaining economies of scale as having a standardized hardware and operating system environment. Size and standardization are both necessary to get real economies of scale. If you have size, it can reduce cost if you also have standardization, but without standardization, size alone will not reduce your costs. Without standards, the diversity of hardware makes it very hard to move into a cloud environment.[11]

Cloud computing by its nature requires a lot of innovation; it demands steady innovation to make it work and to make it easy to use by a mass consumer market. Public cloud vendors in the business-to-consumer world have innovated rapidly and done so over the last several years, in spite of our difficult economic situation. Where in the corporate world has so much changed in so short a time? The innovation cycles of public cloud vendors are usually much shorter than most corporate IT lifecycles; most companies work on five- to six-year lifecycles or longer. It will be a challenge for them to keep up with the pace of change initiated by public cloud vendors.

The rapid innovation cycles of public cloud providers like Google and Amazon are driven by real-time customer feedback loops. As discussed in Chapter 1, customer feedback drives their innovation in a much more effective manner than the feedback that drives traditional IT vendors and in-house IT groups. That is because the central business of cloud service providers is to make money by responding quickly to customer desires. In-house IT groups do not have that stimulus, and they are not seen as profit centers in their companies, so they do not have access to the same levels of investment to improve their service offerings.

If not used carefully, private clouds can defeat the central purpose and the value proposition that cloud computing provides to companies. With private clouds, companies still have the distraction of buying servers, building data centers, and operating enterprise systems. In-house IT staff is still focused on running existing technology and systems instead of figuring out what new technology and systems the company needs.

THE CLOUD IS A PLATFORM FOR MANAGING BUSINESS PROCESSES

In this real-time global economy with short product lifecycles, companies need to be good at bringing new products to market, and they need to be good at tailoring existing products to keep up with shifting customer preferences. In their ongoing search for new products and new markets, companies engage in growth by expansion of existing business units and by mergers and acquisitions of other companies. Business processes need to be flexible to accommodate these activities.

The value proposition delivered by most companies (unless they are themselves cloud service providers) lies in the way they manage their business processes, not their technology. It lies in the way they tailor their processes to meet constantly changing market conditions. Technology is a means to this end, but technology is not an end in itself.

Although the cloud is certainly a platform for managing the delivery of computing services, that perspective is more from the traditional technology-oriented view. Another way to look at the cloud is from the business perspective of companies that use the cloud to support their operations. From their perspective, the greatest benefit they can gain comes not from cost savings in technology, but from the revenue they earn by being more responsive to changing customer desires; the revenues they generate with faster roll out of new products and successful expansion into new markets.

In addition, it is important to remember that companies are much less self-contained and much less vertically integrated than they were 20 years ago. Companies have been steadily outsourcing non-core activities so that they can concentrate their time and money on doing the value-added things that produce the product or service their customers want. As a consequence, most companies are dependent on a network of suppliers that provide support services. And for companies

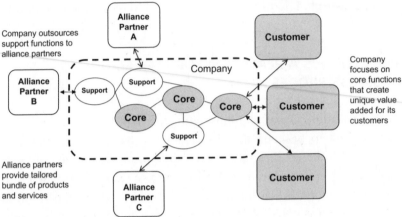

Exhibit 3.5: Interconnected Enterprises

to manage their business processes effectively, they need to find ways to effectively collaborate with their supplier partners. Exhibit 3.5 illustrates the interconnectedness that now is the norm for most companies.

The cloud is not about new technology so much as it is about new business models. The business model in Exhibit 3.5 shows how companies are evolving away from self-contained organizations that perform all their core and support activities internally. Companies are becoming enmeshed in networks of suppliers and customers, and to paraphrase a famous saying, no company is an island. No company can succeed all by itself. Companies depend more than ever on effective collaboration with its supplier partners. Business services need to be delivered in a reliable and predictable fashion, and it is the flow of information back and forth between companies via the cloud that makes this possible.

The cloud is an ideal environment for companies to build and deliver an inventory of business services targeted to individual market segments and specific customers. Business process management (BPM) is the foundation for offering business services over the cloud. Using BPM, companies working together can assemble an appropriate bundle of business services needed to best serve certain kinds of customers. BPM systems can then monitor performance of these inter-company services and provide all parties with the real-time reporting and transparency they need, so as to continually adjust the business processes that deliver these services as conditions change.

BPM systems tap into and monitor the data that flows between the transaction processing systems used by companies. For instance, consider a business process like that which receives orders, routes the orders for fulfillment, ships the ordered products, and then bills the customer. There are several transaction processing systems involved: a Web-based product catalog and order entry system; an order routing system; an order fulfillment system; a billing system; and an accounts receivable system. You can think of the workings of each of these individual systems, but to really understand what is happening and optimize the whole process of taking orders and serving the customer, you need to see and understand how all these systems work together. A BPM system can show you a unified big picture view of the data flowing between these systems, and it can spot bottlenecks where data flow slows down or where problems develop that affect the efficiency of the whole process.

A recent report from Gartner states, "By 2013 dynamic BPM will be an imperative for companies seeking process efficiencies in increasingly chaotic environments."[12] It also says that more and more customer-facing processes will be configured based on specific knowledge about the customer, and suppliers will use BPM to tailor their processes on a just-in-time basis to meet the evolving needs of customers. In other words, BPM systems deployed in a cloud environment become the way that companies working together in value chains deliver a constantly changing mix of responsive products and services to customers. Cloud-based BPM becomes the basis for effective cross-company collaboration to deliver personalized and specialized processes that support individual customers.

BPM and SOA are two sides of the same coin: BPM is the business view; SOA is the technology view. BPM allows companies to model their business processes and combine and streamline them. SOA allows companies to reuse software assets and cost-effectively create systems to support redesigned business process flows. Companies can use SOA or WOA to integrate across different clouds and integrate cloud applications with internal company systems.

BPM allows companies to break their business processes into collections of interconnected tasks. This is an important step in enabling them to extend their operations beyond their own company boundaries, to embrace services provided over the cloud. In this way, they can outsource certain processes and tasks so that they can concentrate on their core value added processes and continue to improve them and invent new ones.

In a world where products and services quickly become commodities and where profit margins are constantly being squeezed by this commoditization, it is the ability to continuously tailor these products and services that will earn companies an additional profit margin on top of the diminishing margins offered by those otherwise commodity products. The driving force of the responsive economy of this century is coming from the unleashing of innovation via cloud services that are quickly becoming available all over the world. Scientists can collaborate on health and environmental problems; businesses can cooperate to deliver tailored products and services worldwide; and in these business networks, companies can focus on doing what they do best and rely on other companies to perform the complementary tasks that are a part of delivering the finished product to the end-use customer.

It is through this agile process of continuous response to changing customer desires that most companies will differentiate themselves and find most of their profit opportunities. You could call the profits generated in this way as the "agility dividend." Real-time global markets are continuously adjusting the price of commodity products towards their cost of production, just as real-time stock markets continually adjust the price of stocks. So it is in the agility dividend that most companies will find their best opportunities to generate profitable revenue that is above the prices set by global markets.

AUTOMATE ROUTINE PROCESSES, FOCUS PEOPLE ON HANDLING EXCEPTIONS

Companies are like fish swimming in oceans of data. There is simply not enough time for people to handle or review standard information that records just the predictable, expected operations occurring in a company. Routine, standard data and procedures for handling it must be driven by automated transaction systems that support the company's standard operating procedures. Computers handle routine situations much better than humans because they never get bored by the routine, and they scale up quickly as transaction volumes increase.

People in a responsive organization need to devote their time to handling nonstandard data. Nonstandard data is any kind of data that is different from what is expected: data that for any reason does not conform to the rules built into automated transaction systems or the performance parameters built into performance monitoring systems. When a company's systems encounter this kind of data, people quickly get involved. The greatest opportunities for any organization lie in the way they detect and respond to unexpected problems, threats, or opportunities.

Use computers to do what they do best. Let them handle the day-in, day-out moving of routine data related to basic transactions such as purchase orders, invoices, account balances, order status, address changes, and so on. Wherever there are people doing routine data entry or repetitive work of any sort, this is an opportunity to automate. Computers do this sort of work much better, faster, and cheaper.

Use people to do what they do best. What they do best is think, communicate, and solve problems. We don't need to build excessive amounts of complexity and cost into new computer systems if we free up people from routine work and give them the data and training they need to solve complex problems and handle the exceptions to routine operations. We don't need artificial intelligence in our systems when we can apply the real intelligence of people who are trained, motivated, and empowered.

Most business operations are routine, and repetitive work that can be handled with relatively simple sets of processing rules can be applied to business processes with BPM systems. The BPM systems can be used to move and monitor data between different systems and different companies. They monitor the processes they support, and when they detect a problem or a slow-down, they send alerts to people assigned to handle those issues. Whenever a transaction happens that does not follow one of the simple routine processing rules, the BPM system traps the data related to that transaction and notifies a qualified person.

People will either be able to correct the data so that it fits back into a simple, predefined process, or they will take care of the transactions themselves all the way through. They will have time to do this because they won't be bogged down and worn out doing the routine stuff. This is where they can generate the most value for customers and for the company; this is known as generating agility dividends; and people will do a great job on these tasks, too. Since they are non-routine, they are interesting. They involve thinking, communicating with others, and problem solving. People like doing this kind of work. It's fun. The human brain is more fine-tuned than any computer to do just this kind of work. By automating the mass of rote, routine, and repetitious work, your organization will get great cost efficiencies. By empowering people to handle the non-routine tasks, companies will become very responsive to unique customer needs. It is this blend of efficiency and responsiveness that enables a company to outperform its competition.

Cost savings happen when companies are able to act in a coordinated manner to continually optimize their common and individual business processes and adjust to changing business conditions on a daily basis. These continuous adjustments to changing conditions result in a stream of cost savings generated by optimizing operations to adjust to changes in prices of labor and raw materials and changes in supply and demand for a company's products and services.

Profits are generated by continuous tailoring of products and services to changing customer needs and desires. Products that are tailored to meet demanding customer service requirements are worth more than the commodity versions of those products. This tailoring of products results in sales revenues that are slightly higher than the market average, because customers are willing to pay a few percent more to get those tailored products.

FOUR TECHNOLOGIES ENABLE RESPONSIVE BUSINESS PROCESSES

There are four application technologies that companies can use in various combinations and become very responsive to changing conditions and emerging threats and opportunities:

1. Business process management (BPM)
2. Complex event processing (CEP)
3. Business intelligence (BI)
4. Simulation modeling

BPM is a way for companies to observe productivity in their operations and carry out a continuous, incremental process of improving operational performance. A company starts by mapping out its key processes and defines the steps or work tasks in each process. Then it uses BPM software to collect and display a continuous stream of data that shows the movement of transactions through each step. The BPM software can be used to automate many of the routine tasks, such as moving different kinds of data from one task to another. It can also be set to detect certain error conditions and send automatic alerts to people who need to respond to these conditions quickly.

CEP complements the capabilities of BPM systems. A CEP system can monitor multiple data streams and can do real-time comparisons of data in these data streams to detect predefined patterns in the data that indicate the occurrence of certain events. Companies can define specific event patterns that then trigger the system to make certain responses. Some events may trigger the system to set in motion a set of online calculations and responses that react to those events. Other events may trigger the system to send alerts to people. For instance, a CEP system used by an airline might detect that an airplane is at a departure airport and that a large storm is heading toward that airport. It also detects that a boarding gate at the arrival airport is reserved for that airplane. In these data streams, the system can detect that the airplane's departure will be delayed by the approaching storm and that the time slot reserved for the boarding gate at the arrival airport has to be changed. The system can then make the change itself or it can send an alert to airline staff so they can respond appropriately.

BI systems collect, store, and analyze data. These systems allow people to orient themselves and decide on what actions to take. They collect data from many different sources. Data can be collected from sensors and radio-frequency identification (RFID) devices. Data can be collected by BPM systems or data can be obtained from the many transaction processing systems in a company such as ERP systems, order entry systems, or CRM systems. Once the data is collected, it is stored in a database where people access it as needed. Often the database is updated with new data on a continuous or real-time basis, and summary displays of relevant data are available to people through Web-based dashboards.

When people access the data, they use BI software tools that help them analyze the information and display the results. BI software tools run the gamut from simple spreadsheets and charts to complex multivariable regression analysis and linear programming. The proper mix of BI tools is determined by the needs of the people in a situation and their skill and training levels. The combination of BPM and CEP and BI systems is sometimes referred to as enterprise performance management (EPM).

Simulation modeling software is a category of software that is starting to get increasing attention. Because of the fast pace of change in business, companies are faced with the need to make important decisions more often, and these decisions have significant consequences on company operations and profitability. Companies increasingly need to make decisions about how to best operate in conditions they have not encountered before. Simulation modeling has powerful capabilities for improving the quality of decision making in an organization.

Simulation modeling software allows people to create models of things such as a factory or a supply chain network or a vehicle delivery route. Then they can subject the models to different inputs and different situations and observe what happens. A design that may seem good on paper could very well turn out to have problems that are not apparent until the design is modeled and its performance is simulated under a range of different conditions. It is much faster and cheaper to discover problems through simulations than to find out the hard way through real experience.

Existing transaction systems, such as ERP, order management, accounting, inventory management, delivery scheduling, factory control, and maintenance systems provide a steady stream of data that reflects individual processes in a company or between groups of companies. This data can be monitored through the use of BPM and CEP systems to provide a comprehensive end-to-end picture of the productivity and performance levels in these operating processes. BPM systems can update this picture on a real-time or nearly real-time basis, and show people where the bottlenecks and disruptions are that need their attention.

Once people have identified the bottlenecks and disruptions, they can make use of BI databases and analytical software to investigate the problems and identify their root causes. When root causes are identified, people can design ways to address them. Then, by using simulation systems, they can model potential process changes and see the probable impact of each different change. In this way, people select the most effective changes and implement them with a high level of confidence that they will actually deliver the desired results.

The power of these four technologies is multiplied when they are used together and when they are used on a universally accessible platform such as the cloud. This is because they enable more effective and timely collaboration among companies working together. When these technologies run in the cloud, people in all participating companies can see data and status of operating processes in real-time, and this transparency enables effective and timely brainstorming and problem solving. Companies have the opportunity to collaborate and design extraordinarily responsive business processes to drive their operations, enabling them to continuously adjust their operations to changing and unforeseen developments in information technology.

NOTES

1. Joseph A. Schumpeter, *Capitalism, Socialism and Democracy* (New York: Harper, 1975) [orig. pub. 1942], pp. 82–85.
2. Frank Gens, "Defining 'Cloud Services'—An IDC update," IDC Exchange, (September 30th 2009), http://blogs.idc.com/ie/?p=422.
3. Darryl Plummer, "Experts Define Cloud Computing: Can We Get a Little Definition in our Definitions?" Gartner article, 2009, http://blogs.gartner.com/daryl_plummer/2009/01/27/experts-define-cloud-computing-can-we-get-a-little-definition-in-our-definitions/.

4. Jeff Kaplan, "Simplifying the Term 'Cloud Computing'" Datamation.com blog, (June 25, 2009), http://itmanagement.earthweb.com/netsys/article .php/3826921/Simplifying-the-Term-Cloud-Computing.htm.

5. Frank Enfanto, VP of Worldwide IT Operations, ACI Worldwide, private email correspondence with author (December 22, 2009).

6. Rick Pittard, telephone interview by Michael Hugos, February 10, 2010.

7. *Ibid.*

8. Bechtel Corporation, "Pioneers of the Private Cloud," December 21, 2009, www.alacrastore.com/storecontent/tectrends/177031.

9. *Ibid.*

10. Bernard Golden, articles on private clouds at CIO.com, 2009, www.cio .com.au/tag/Bernard%20Golden.

11. See note 6.

12. Gartner report, January 13, 2010, www.gartner.com/it/page.jsp?id=1278415.

CHAPTER 4

Leading with Green: Expanding the CIO's Role in Eco-Efficient Information Technology Adoption

Randy Betancourt and Alyssa Farrell

I n developing the content for this chapter, the authors conducted a series of interviews with industry experts, practitioners, and consultants. These individuals, drawn from a wide-range of backgrounds and skills, articulated a variety of viewpoints that are woven into this chapter. These contributors include seasoned IT executives, practitioners, and policy experts who all share a common goal: helping the enterprise meet its business requirements for IT performance and availability while profitably achieving enterprise sustainability objectives.[1]

Contributions for this chapter's content were provided via interviews with the following experts: Dr. Daniel Arneman, Greenhouse Gas Specialist for The University of North Carolina at Chapel Hill; Dr. Prajesh Bhattacharya, Data Center Industry Specialist at OSIsoft LLC; Mr. Robert Bonham, Senior IT Director at SAS; Mr. Ray DeCristofaro, Director for Processing Services at The University of North Carolina at Chapel Hill; Mr. Jim Etheridge, Associate Director for Processing Services at The University of North Carolina at Chapel Hill; Ms. Joanna Gordon, Associate Director and Global Leadership Fellow for the World Economic Forum's Information Technology Industry; Mr. Nicholas Kim, Global Leadership Fellow for the World Economic Forum's Information Technology Industry; Mr. Rich Lechner, Vice President of Energy and Environment at IBM; Mr. Jim McAdam, Energy Engineer at The University of North Carolina at Chapel Hill; Mr. Stephen Nunn, Global Practice Lead for Infrastructure Consulting and Green IT for Accenture; Mr. Thomas Spiller, Senior Director of International Programs at SAS; and Mr. Jerry Williams, Sustainability Project Director at SAS.

This chapter goes beyond the public and political rhetoric to address the essential Green IT business propositions and describe successful outcomes of an eco-friendly IT, with insights into how the enterprise competently and deliberately begins such a journey to avoid pitfalls and blind alleys along the way. This chapter does not arrive at a checklist of activities, such as implement virtualization, raising data center temperature, and enforcing PC power management policies—issues which are thoroughly addressed in Chapter 5. This chapter articulates best practices that reinforce the CIO's role as a key executive leader for enterprise sustainability practices. IT know-how and resource management skills are often an under-appreciated enterprise asset as businesses seek to transform into leaner and more productive entities. Each contributor cited three main reasons that CIOs are the obvious executives to drive the Green IT evolution, and in some cases, the business practice revolution involving global sustainability initiatives: (1) broad insights into the enterprise, (2) proficiency in resource management, and (3) deep experiences increasing productivity without significant cost growth.

The first of these reasons relates to the CIO's strategic role inside the enterprise. Best practice CIOs have established a solid reputation for shifting IT from a cost center to a revenue center, and what better opportunity than Green IT initiatives for driving transformative enterprise processes, as businesses emerge from the near economic meltdown of 2007 to 2009? Now more than ever, enterprises have accelerated efforts to rethink the underlying assumptions that drive business strategy and operations. As one of the few executives who have a view into all lines of enterprise business, the CIO can see, analyze, and understand the totality of enterprise business processes. The CEO of one of the largest banks in the United States once stated that he gets more insight into his business operations from the CIO than from the business executives heading the company's various lines of business. His reasons: Business executives have to know their functional specialties; the CIO is responsible for knowing all the enterprise functional businesses and the infrastructure that each uses to operate to achieve strategic goals. The CIO's unique role as an enterprise decision-maker presents tremendous opportunities to the forward-thinking individual! Where's the waste? Where's the latency? Where's the slack? With this broad perspective, the CIO is ideally suited to provide the necessary leadership to identify and enable transformation of dated, wasteful processes into a leaner set of processes. CIOs hold a position of responsibility where these enterprise-wide strategic opportunities carry significant potential for strategic enablement, but they happen infrequently.

This transformative role is widely accepted. In late 2008, The Climate Group conducted research on behalf of the Global eSustainability Initiative (GeSI). The resulting report, "SMART2020: Enabling the Low Carbon Economy in the Information Age," quantifies the direct emissions from information and communication technologies (ICT) and highlights areas where ICT can enable reductions in other sectors of the economy. "While the [IT] sector plans to significantly step up the energy efficiency of its products and services, ICT's largest influence will be by enabling energy efficiencies in other sectors, an opportunity that could deliver carbon savings five times larger than the total emissions from the entire ICT sector in 2020."[2]

The second of these reasons relates to the CIO's skill in developing relevant best practices, such as hardware resource optimization as a case in point. In the mainframe-dominated computing era discussed in Chapter 2, IT established a set of best practices and rigor around driving the efficient utilization of these high-cost, scarce computing resources, known as capacity planning. This discipline required the understanding of resource consumption and how to assign costs and priorities to activities (jobs) in ways that maximized throughput at the best possible costs. Capacity planning is just one of a number of enterprise-wide IT responsibilities for measuring and optimizing resource utilization as part of a more sustainable strategic agenda.

The third of these reasons relates to the CIO's responsibility for some of the most energy-intensive assets owned by the business. Today's data centers have a power density between 50 to 100 watts per square foot. Newer designs call for densities in the range of 600 to 1000 watts per square foot.[3] As the demand for IT resources continues to grow, not only do operational expenditures grow, but pressure is then placed on capital expenditures to fund new data center build outs. Left unchecked, data center energy costs will grow to be the second-highest budget item behind labor costs. CIOs remain under enormous pressure to control costs. And given their experiences over the past decade, where IT budgets have been relatively flat, and demand from the business for compute resources have continued to grow, innovation inside the IT organization has helped to close these gaps.

WHAT IS GREEN IT?

The technology industry definition of Green IT too often depends on any given vendor's latest promotion. Acknowledging that vendors operate in their own economic self-interest, it becomes even more challenging for CIOs to effectively sift though the multitude of promoted benefits when purchasing enterprise hardware, software, and services. Surprisingly, our contributors shared a substantively uniform definition of Green IT. They shared a strong focus on driving continued improvements in energy management, since growing resource demand coupled with volatile energy prices remains a serious economic challenge for CIOs. To help put this into perspective, the Environment Protection Agency estimated the energy consumption of servers and data centers to be at an annual rate of 61 billion kilowatt-hours (kWh) in 2006, which represents 1.5 percent of the total U.S. energy consumption at a cost of $4.5 billion. The federal government's portion of this consumption was 10 percent.[4]

While energy management initiatives and their associated cost and carbon-footprint reduction are a common concern, Green IT encompasses policies relevant to the lifecycle management of enterprise assets, as well as the efficient utilization of existing assets. From the practitioner's perspective, "going green" means identifying best practices that meet growing resource demands and service level agreements (SLAs) through efficiency gains by both improving server utilization rates and throttling demand.

Contributor Stephen Nunn, Accenture's Global Practice Lead for Infrastructure Consulting and Green IT, describes the concepts of Green IT along five dimensions:

1. Driving data center energy efficiencies through virtualization and other practices, which orchestrate provisioning of workloads to appropriate resources. This means effectively measuring and increasing server utilization rates.

2. Promoting more effective policy controls for the desktop environment and reducing print demands.

3. Modifying IT procurement processes to take into account factors such as energy efficiency, tax and other economic incentives, product recycling policies, minimized packaging, and other green criteria.

4. Increasing the silicon-footprint to decrease the carbon-footprint. Example initiatives include mobile workforce policies and video-teleconferencing substitutes for travel. The best practice CIO seeks out opportunities to drive business process efficiencies throughout the enterprise.

5. Delivering shareholder value. If an enterprise has a clear agenda on IT and sustainability that encapsulates the elements the other four dimensions, shareholder value is more secure and likely to increase.

Nunn warns that enterprises that continue to operate without strategies that incorporate integrated Green IT initiatives do so to the detriment of brand and profitability. The CIO needs to define what Green IT means for the enterprise and how Green IT fits into enterprise sustainability initiatives. This is the first step in successfully aligning IT with broader enterprise initiatives to reduce energy consumption and greenhouse gas emissions.

WHO CARES ABOUT GREEN IT?

Chapter contributors and secondary research overwhelmingly confirm the need for executive leadership to establish and sustain Green IT objectives. Without executive-level commitment, Green IT initiatives become a series of tactical measures that drive only short-run benefits. In the case of The University of North Carolina at Chapel Hill, Chancellor Holden Thorp has committed the university to carbon neutrality by 2050. Significantly, the university is utilizing the Office of the Chancellor to provide the leadership to reach this long-term goal. The University has had an active sustainability program since 2001, and in 2006 it began focused efforts to measure carbon emissions.[5] As they execute specific projects to instrument, measure, analyze, and optimize energy across the hundreds of buildings in the university's real-estate portfolio, Greenhouse Gas Specialist Daniel Arneman, Energy Engineer Jim McAdam, and their colleagues see this level of executive support as absolutely essential. Moreover, sustained executive leadership promotes an amplification of stakeholder participation. Arneman and McAdam highlighted the frequency of new ideas for energy reduction and financial savings from a variety of constituents, including students, staff, and faculty. For example, a special project committee on Renewal Energy Policies proposed a bill to add a four dollar per semester fee onto student tuition to fund energy conservation projects. This proposal passed. Not only are the students directly engaged, but they are very likely to carry these attitudes and traits forward into their professional careers as well.

Today's consumers consult a wealth of information sources before making their purchase decisions. Solid evidence suggests that consumer purchase behaviors are beginning to respond to carbon price signals. A 2009 *Financial Times* article by Andrew Edgecliffe–Johnson cited a study of 20,000 people by Havas Media in which, "half of [consumers] are willing to pay a 10 percent premium for sustainably produced goods and services despite the pressures of the economic crisis."[6] To further illustrate how consumer behaviors are altering demand, citizen participation has become a significant driver in holding government agencies accountable for policy directives and regulations. Based in Brussels, Belgium, Thomas Spiller, Senior Director of International Programs at SAS, reports that citizen participation has become a significant driver in holding government agencies accountable for policy directives and regulations. Through a program based in Brussels, Belgium, European Union (EU) citizens have access to a mash-up of maps and real-time feeds for a number of air quality measures. The site allows a real-time, comparative analysis of air quality around the EU.[7] These tools raise citizen consciousness about the impacts and benefits of sustainability efforts.

Regardless of industry, enterprises will come under increasing regulatory scrutiny over Greenhouse Gas (GhG) emissions, further complicated by the myriad of international, governmental, regional, and local regulations and regulatory bodies with oversight responsibilities. EU enterprises are already subject to the Emissions Trading Scheme (ETS). The U.S. House of Representatives passed the American Clean Energy and Security Act (H.R. 2454) on June 26, 2009. In its present form, the Bill contains a series of measures and incentives that mandate major U.S. sources to reduce their carbon admissions 17 percent by 2020 and over 80 percent by 2050, compared to 2005 levels.[8] If carbon allowances were trading today at $50 per ton, this would add $200,000 in additional IT cost for every 1,000 enterprise servers, assuming that the servers in question are energy efficient models less than three years old.

GREEN IT: A QUICKLY MATURING MANAGEMENT DISCIPLINE

Energy conservation and environmental initiatives have become essential elements on the list of CIO responsibilities. This section examines enterprises and CIOs leading green initiatives, with an eye on low-hanging fruit, best practices for measuring energy and carbon, and a glimpse into future innovations that hold tremendous potential.

Leadership

Our panel of expert contributors agreed that an IT organization can be transformed only with clear direction from the CIO. Transformative change means a holistic approach to Green IT—one that integrates planning, purchasing, implementation, usage, maintenance, and disposal. Engagement of employees is critical because new ideas bubble up, and employee support for project implementation becomes more participatory. Individual contributions can reduce IT's impact on the environment, inside and outside the data center, but tremendous efficiencies are gained when all parties are moving towards a common goal.

Is the CIO the lone wolf in helping to green the enterprise? IT often begins green initiatives in a silo, either because its business model can be self-contained or because other executives cannot yet see the value of enterprise-wide participation in a broader sustainability initiative. Prajesh Bhattacharya, Data Center Industry Specialist at OSIsoft LLC, has found that most organizations focus on Green IT as a silo because the IT industry recognized cost savings of energy efficient systems and data center design *before* the sustainability movement hit the boardroom. But some of the more-respected companies in the world, including Cisco, have both a corporate initiative and IT-specific green strategies., Bhattacharya suggests that the CIO and IT organization must inform top management about the benefits of going green.

The CIO continues to play a key leadership role in the enterprise that has already adopted a sustainability initiative, where the CIO participates as a subject matter expert on critical internal councils that drive overall enterprise strategy. Research shows that enterprise sustainability initiatives are often directed by the CEO and managed by a chief operating officer or through an entirely new senior executive, the chief sustainability officer. The relationship between Operations and Information Technology is one of dynamic partnership covering all facilities, mobile assets, and data centers at the heart of the enterprise carbon footprint.

The CIO wears two hats with established green enterprise initiatives: (1) promote supportive enterprise initiatives to measure and manage sustainability; (2) measure and validate the IT organization's performance within all green enterprise initiatives. Accenture's Stephen Nunn shared a story about a data center consolidation project that his team was managing. The driver of consolidation was cost efficiency. However, the company had declared a goal of becoming carbon neutral. In assessing the future impact on energy and carbon, the consolidation project would reduce carbon emissions below projected levels by 56,000 metric tons over a five-year period. This represented a savings of over $1 million at the current value of carbon credits on the market. The CIO delivered an IT project that made business sense and aligned with the corporate goal of carbon neutrality.

C-Suite executive leadership commitment strengthens the CIO's ability to execute a Green IT agenda. From university chancellors who sign a carbon neutrality pledge to Fortune 500 companies who pledge emissions reductions goals, an enterprise commitment to a sustainability agenda is vital for facilitating the appropriate IT investments.

Current Practices

A closer look at successful IT investments reveals some common programs and initiatives that make a solid business case for Green IT, regardless of industry or geography. This low-hanging fruit is often the first focus of Green IT initiatives because the return on investment makes business sense for the CIO, regardless of broader enterprise sustainability initiatives.

Power-saving initiatives present the CIO with abundant opportunities to directly cut energy costs. The best practice CIO encourages the enterprise to purchase low-power hardware whenever possible, and when looking to upgrade, put "power-saving capabilities" on the list of purchase criteria.[9] The inclusion of power-oriented criteria in a formal RFP attracts the attention of vendors, and the best practice CIO asks suppliers to disclose toxic substances used in the manufacturing process to address enterprise liabilities as stakeholders become increasingly concerned about the global rise in e-waste. With the advent of the REACH initiative in Europe, this won't be an unusual information request, and CIOs might find some interesting disparities in otherwise similar IT assets.[10]

Tools such as the Environmental Product Electronic Assessment Tool (EPEAT) from the Green Electronics Council and Energy Star from the U.S. EPA help to provide a centralized database of performance ratings for desktops and servers. Energy Star is releasing new standards that rate the energy efficiency of data centers and storage devices. EPEAT seeks to measure the performance of desktops, notebooks, and monitors against environmental attributes using standards established by the Institute of Electrical and Electronics Engineers (IEEE).

Accenture identified five key areas where IT can have a demonstrable impact on reducing energy consumption and broader corporate green agenda:[11]

1. **End user working practices.** Telework, consolidate shipping, switching off lights, and laptops when not in use

2. **Office environment and equipment.** Energy-efficient equipment, VoIP, double-sided print features

3. **Office infrastructure/data center.** Virtualization, server consolidation, distributed computing

4. **Procurement.** Green supplier selection criteria, asset lifecycle management that includes disposal

5. **Corporate citizenship.** Manage risk and compliance, communicate performance externally, engage employees

Data center floor design can seem like the clash of art and science in the IT underworld. The organization of hot and cold zones is the ultimate match of form and function, resulting in a finely-tuned machine that is energy efficient and meets service level requirements without being over-provisioned. Data center redesigns can yield tremendous savings, particularly when coupled with consolidation and virtualization projects.

Virtualization has an impact on power and cooling requirements because it changes how and when machines are used. IBM reported that the energy savings gained from server and storage virtualization and consolidation can be further maximized if data center managers adjust their power and cooling infrastructure to accommodate the reduced loads. The cycle of initial reduced load followed by load growth should incorporate adjustments to power and cooling, where there are several approaches for efficiently cooling consolidated loads.[12]

SAS Internal Case Study of Innovation and Virtualization

SAS is a leading software supplier for business intelligence and analytics with 2009 revenues of $2.3 billion. Its IT organization, known as Information Systems Division (ISD) supports a wide range of computing infrastructure, including an IBM z9 Enterprise Class mainframe, over 1,000 mid-range UNIX servers (HP, Sun, and IBM), over 5,000 Windows servers, 2,500 virtual servers and approximately 15,000 laptops and desktop devices.

A challenge faced by the business was managing the time-consuming process of demonstrating SAS software to customers and prospects. It was estimated that for every hour of customer-facing presentation time, over 15 hours were consumed in software setup, configuration, and customizations. The estimated cost of each software demonstration to customers was $13,750. In 2005, ISD was given the task of creating a robust, reliable environment available 24/7/365, using industry standard hardware to be utilized by the field support staff for customer-facing software presentations. The environment had to be available to staff operating in over 80 countries worldwide.

In the initial pilot, the virtualized server environment was designed and built to handle up to 50 simultaneous customer-facing presentations. The initial pilot was successful, and the decision was made to move from pilot to production. Moving to production, ISD scaled the environment to meet global demand in 2007. With a production environment, management estimates the cost-per-customer-presentation to have dropped to $5,700. The savings accrue from reduced staff-time on configuration tasks, reduced cooling and energy costs, and a longer laptop hardware refresh cycle, since these devices are no longer part of the software demonstration mix. Asset utilization has increased, and sales support staff costs were reduced by 43 percent.

The Business Case

Experience showed the baseline for virtual machines allocated to a physical server (using IBM System x3950 dual-core 64-bit Xeon Processors MP) to be 11 to 1. Like most IT organizations, ISD decided its risk of failure outweighed the costs of over-provisioning. The production environment was hard-capped at 77 virtual machines. Questions about meeting demand immediately arose. Where are the bottlenecks? And when were the purchases of additional host machines needed?

ISD initiated a capacity plan and collected performance data after the environment moved into production. The capacity plan was developed as a justification for the purchase of additional host machines. ISD decided to focus on performance data drawn from VMware's Virtual Center. Virtual Center was already used to provide real-time environment management for the environment. ISD used a commercially available SAS solution for performance analysis and optimization because it is already in use to meet capacity analysis needs and forecasting workload demands for the entire compute infrastructure.

After collecting measurement data from VMware's Virtual Center over a 30-day period, ISD applied a forecast model, anticipating a pattern suggesting resource constraints. Instead, the analysis showed precisely the opposite. As shown in Exhibit 4.1, there was no discernable pattern suggesting resource constraints, other than that the data shows Wednesday as the most popular day to present customer-facing software demonstrations. The data suggested that ISD actually *increase* the number of virtual machines (VMs) to meet business demands without having to purchase additional physical servers. As a result, ISD avoided the purchase of new server hardware. The number of VMs was increased from 11 to 14 for an increase of 27 percent in capacity without additional expenditures.

This case study demonstrates that despite concerns regarding difficulty and time to implement, an IT organization should first determine if a new design innovation will more efficiently solve a capacity

SAS Remote Access Computing Environment
30-Day Forecast—Peak Virtual Machines

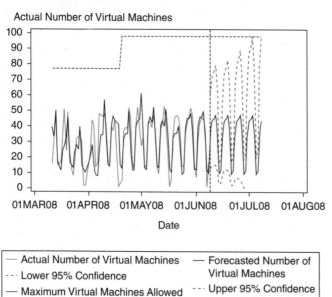

— Actual Number of Virtual Machines	— Forecasted Number of Virtual Machines
--- Lower 95% Confidence	
— Maximum Virtual Machines Allowed	--- Upper 95% Confidence

Exhibit 4.1: 30-Day Forecast for Virtualized Server Demand

problem than simply adding more resources. In this case, virtualizing the environment rather than adding resources not only avoided the need to rebuild the existing presentation portfolio, but also led to a substantial Green IT return on investment (ROI), due to reduced power consumption and data center space. In summary:

- Traditional capacity planning is needed, but combining it with the ability to do real-time analysis and forecasting provides more consumable data for decision-making.

- Being able to defer purchasing additional resources with data to support the decision not only leads to significant business ROI (in the form of dollars and resources not spent for purchasing, installing, and maintaining equipment not needed), but also achieves Green IT goals.

- IT must have good cost information to establish a baseline for comparative analysis.

Measuring Energy and Carbon

Energy consumption and carbon emission measurement practices are related, but not equal, endeavors. Energy consumption is generally measured as the kWh used by a particular stationary or mobile asset. These kWh may be produced by a third-party provider (electric utility) or an on-site power generator, and are typically metered for billing purposes. Most data centers have a power management plan that provides an uninterrupted power supply via battery and generators if the electric supply from the utility should be interrupted. The kWh provided by the batteries and generators may be metered in terms of run-time rather than kWh. An accounting of energy consumption from such sources is therefore an educated estimate.

European countries, Australia, and New Zealand have been some of the first to consider, and in some cases implement, regulations that require enterprises that consume large amounts of power from the public grid to report their consumption and emissions. This is undoubtedly the first step in a reduction scheme that will create incentives to operate more efficiently with less energy. As a result, Stephen Nunn notes that enterprises are starting to become more energy conscious, particularly when reviewing future technology purchases because resource, utility, and petrochemical companies have started their own significant initiatives to measure their customers' baseline energy consumption and evaluate overall carbon footprint.

While it seems straightforward on the surface, the CIO faces major challenges obtaining data when deciding to measure enterprise IT energy consumption. IT assets are scattered around an organization, and even if one starts with the data center—the hub of IT activity—detailed information may not be available. Most IT organizations are just beginning instrumentation of data center assets, which can be an expensive and lengthy process. According to UNC's Director for Processing Services, Ray DeCristofaro, CIOs need to have a strong business case to justify upfront costs for detailed metering in the data center. Furthermore, is the IT organization equipped to handle the data once it is received? SAS Senior IT Director Robert Bonham suggests that domain experts who understand power systems don't have background in analytics, and they will need to acquire these skills. So even if information is gathered, there may be some delay before it can be used for productive decision-making.

Regardless of the upfront costs, contributor Prajesh Bhattacharya emphasizes that a CIO "absolutely should factor in the energy cost as part of the operating cost of the asset. On average, within two years, the cost to run the asset is equal to the initial capital investment." Bonham agrees, but uses a slightly broader cost evaluation methodology that includes a per-square-foot charge for the space used in the data center and the proportionate cooling required. In the end, the CIO will not take the initiative to aggressively reduce the cost of IT energy consumption without alignment or incentives to proactively measure and manage that consumption. Consequently, the CIO should own the budget for power consumed in the data center and be given the authority to keep and reinvest any savings generated from energy consumption initiatives back into the IT organization. The same can be said about the CIO's responsibility for measuring and reducing carbon emissions. As the liability for enterprise carbon emissions increases, ownership should reside with the party responsible for the activities that generate greenhouse gas emissions—in terms of both distribution and information technology—and this requires a better understanding about calculating carbon emissions.

The *carbon footprint* of an IT asset, facility, product, or organization is actually much more than the measurement of carbon dioxide (CO_2) alone. It is the measurement of six greenhouse gases (GHGs) listed in the Kyoto Protocol: carbon dioxide (CO_2); methane (CH_4); nitrous oxide (N_2O); hydrofluorocarbons (HFCs); perfluorocarbons (PFCs); and sulphur hexafluoride (SF_6). An enterprise carbon footprint is expressed numerically as a *carbon equivalent* (CO_2e), which is the universal unit of measurement to indicate the global warming potential (GWP) of each of the six GHGs, expressed in terms of the GWP of one unit of carbon dioxide.[13] A carbon footprint is a numerical value that can be used to compare similar assets within an enterprise. For example, a CIO may evaluate the CO_2e per square foot in a data center in Atlanta, Georgia, with one running in Delhi, India. Aside from kWh consumed, the largest variable in that equation is the source of generated power—the combination of coal-fired plants, nuclear operations, and hydro power or other renewable sources that make up the energy supplied to that facility.

A carbon footprint also has a financial value. As proposed legislation may limit GhG emissions for many companies, enterprises may soon be required to buy the right to emit more than a specified, allowable limit when they cannot find ways to reduce internally, or if those reduction strategies are more costly than the credits available for purchase. *Carbon markets* have been established in many regions of the world, both voluntary and regulatory. The largest market is the European Union's Emissions Trading Scheme (EUETS). The value of a *carbon future* on this market is typically the baseline for most financial models that estimate the carbon cost of an enterprise asset or activity. However, establishing a value for carbon also means being able to assess the impacts of proposed regulations during the lifecycles of various enterprise IT assets. Prajesh Bhattacharya calls this the "political cost of carbon," which refers to the inherent uncertainty that a CIO faces when determining when, if, or for how long the enterprise will have to pay for the right to emit GHGs for IT infrastructure energy consumption. The team at The University of North Carolina has found that carbon footprinting provides a good means to understand broader impact of electricity and fuel, transportation, and waste. While their planning also attempts to account for the future cost of carbon, the legal landscape is unclear. Financial models evaluate their assumed carbon costs under a variety of proposed U.S. legislation.

Most CIOs today are not factoring a shadow cost of carbon into IT procurement decisions, primarily for two reasons: (1) the IT organization is not able to gather trustworthy data, either internally or from the vendor, and (2) the IT organization is not currently charged for carbon emissions. Bob Bonham at SAS indicated that what IT managers need are the standards for measuring the emissions associated with IT assets so that they can start to include that information in procurement evaluation processes.

To resolve this market uncertainty, enterprises will need to participate and support the legislative development process. A clear decision on carbon regulation is needed to minimize confusion about carbon pricing, and the price signal will force CIOs and their enterprises to make different decisions and develop new strategies, based on new environmental mandates and emissions criteria. Today's visionary enterprises are already making significant investments that pay off with internal efficiencies, but also by generating new revenue. In fact, GE's "Ecomagination" business generated a green revenue stream topping $17 billion in 2008, growing at an astounding 21 percent.[14]

Future Innovations

Beyond product-level innovations, enterprises and their IT organizations may seek transformative change that radically alters processes and structures to deliver high-quality services with minimal impact on the environment. Along with transformative change, CIOs have adopted new performance measures such as Power Usage Effectiveness (PUE). PUE is a ratio that compares the total power used by a data center (or any IT facility) to the power consumed by its IT equipment. It is a measure of efficiency, so lower ratios indicate higher performance per kilowatt consumed.

In early 2010, Hewlett-Packard (HP) announced the opening of a new data center that takes advantage of innovative technologies to reduce energy and water consumption.[15] As the first ever wind-cooled data center, the operation leverages its location in blustery northeast England to draw in external air through giant intake fans, then filter out any dust and contaminants before circulating it around the server racks. Back-up chillers stand ready to assist for the average 20 hours each year that the external temperate exceeds 75 degrees Fahrenheit. HP has estimated that the extra cost for the natural cooling and backup chillers is about 6 percent above normal building expenses, which will be recouped in under two years due to the anticipated power savings.

The center boasts several other environmentally friendly practices, including a rainwater capture system that can be used to increase the humidity as needed, and low-power requirements due to light-colored server racks. Since lighter colors reflect, the data center designers discovered they could reduce lighting by 40 percent with no impact on visibility. All of these practices combine to make the HP facility perform at an amazingly low PUE of 1.2 percent, meaning that for every 1.2 watts of electricity consumed, 1 watt goes towards powering the IT equipment and the minimal remainder provides the power for cooling and other facility needs.

There are also substantive examples of IT innovations in public applications that can improve our environmental quality. In partnership with the European Environment Agency, Microsoft built a two-way communication platform called Eye on Earth to merge scientific information about water and air quality with an individual's experience at the street level (see Exhibit 4.2). Users enter their location, and the system returns the official measurements of air pollution in the user's area. Users can contribute to the rating by submitting remarks and their own rating of the air or water quality. This combination of government-led research and social media can have tremendous impact when city planners are evaluating bus routes or traffic planning. This innovative project involves cities in sustainable decision

Eye on Earth recorded 53 user ratings for this location in Milan, Italy. Local observations disagreed with the "official" rating of "Very Good," Instead reporting that the air was "Dirty," "Smelly," and "Irritating."

Exhibit 4.2: Microsoft's Interactive Environmental Quality Application

Source: *www.eyeonearth.eu/.*

making and makes it relevant through the contributions of its citizenship.

IT applications can also ensure that an enterprise spends its resources wisely by reducing fuel, water, and waste, which each have environmental as well as financial benefits. One example of using analytics to achieve optimal outcomes is Waitrose Grocery in the United Kingdom. Waitrose is an employee-owned company synonymous with quality and variety. They use modeling and predictive analytics from SAS for accurate demand forecasting, reducing stockholding by 8 percent and wastage by 4 percent.[16] Controlling costs is critical in the highly competitive retail market, and innovative IT solutions can help deliver that necessary edge.

COMMON CHALLENGES PRESENTED BY GREEN

The relative immaturity of the Green IT business space is a testament to the significant challenges that enterprises face when planning and executing IT strategies with environmental considerations. Implementing any new technology within an existing infrastructure or modifying service level agreements is no small task. Green IT initiatives challenge the status quo of "business as usual," and it takes courageous CIO leadership, backed by other C-Suite executives, to make this transformation.

Our expert contributors focused on the challenges in these five areas:

1. Inability to access data

2. Lack of internal domain expertise

3. Complex vendor relationships

4. Constantly evolving standards, or lack thereof

5. Building a financially sound business case

"We must have those figures somewhere!" Evaluating energy and carbon consumption requires actual data, or enough information to make relevant allocations from other data sources. One of the most significant challenges many enterprise IT organizations face is to identify if the necessary data exists and, if it does, who owns it. Prajesh

Bhattacharya described this important step as "navigating the organizational maze." Projects will fail if existing monitoring systems and data owners are not identified and incorporated into the plan.

Once the owner is identified, CIOs may find it surprising that their colleagues are reluctant to share their data about electricity and fuel consumption. While "data hoarders" are not unfamiliar corporate enemies, the dynamics of gathering data for environmental measurement is a unique situation because the data providers are not sure how their information will be used. Will it constrain them in the future? Will they look bad in comparison to other parts of the business? This uncertainty can compound natural aversion to sharing data across organizational silos. In many cases, the data simply may not be available due to lack of monitoring systems in place. The CIO must weigh the cost of implementing such a system with the data management efficiencies and analytical decision support that it will provide.

"Is this really the right approach?" While power and fuel constraints are felt today in many developing economies, the last time that North America and Central Europe were concerned about energy availability was in the 1970s. The workforce that reengineered assembly lines, rationed oil and gas, and streamlined transportation logistics in response to these pressures has mostly retired. Since that time, we have had decades of unbridled growth in computing demand, leading to a focus on delivering services to businesses at any cost, with ill-considered risks. As a result, enterprises and their IT organizations lack the necessary skill set to validate ROI assumptions for important sustainability investment decisions. Financial accountants are retooling their professional experience to focus on carbon accounting, including an understanding of the legislative proposals that would establish a price on emitting greenhouse gases. Operations managers are expanding the scope of data they regularly monitor and manage to include data sources for energy and periodic consumption. As Robert Bonham stated, "There is no substitute for hands-on experience." If IT organizations lack such internal experience, the CIO must look for opportunities to partner with a trusted domain expert or consulting organization on any project such that knowledge transfer is a key outcome.

"But I thought you said that . . ." The image of "going green in the data center" has been tarnished by the perception that Green IT is a ploy by hardware vendors to drive a refresh regime into client accounts by positioning more energy efficient hardware. Vendors don't support this approach any more than CIOs, but it sure makes for catchy advertising and is a relatively simple ROI calculation. While hardware efficiency is one component of a larger sustainable strategy, the benefits of replacing existing hardware must be evaluated alongside other initiatives, such as asset lifecycle management, reuse, and recycling. This is where the vendor relationships can get complex. CIOs must work collaboratively with vendors to develop programs that reduce energy consumption and stay true to their objectives, even if that means new performance-based contracting vehicles or going to other reference sites to see the technology in action.

Sometimes vendors bring new ideas to the table and challenge the conventional wisdom held by CIOs and IT Directors. The University of North Carolina recently raised the data center temperature by 14 degrees after learning that newer hardware can tolerate this environment. The reduction in energy demand has resulted in measurable cost savings. However, the temperature change has become the staff's scapegoat when hardware fails. The IT Director and vendor have worked together to demonstrate that the failures are unrelated to the change in data center temperature.

Contributor Stephen Nunn insisted that CIOs "move away from all this hardware hype and look across the organization at how IT resources are consumed today." There are natural opportunities to use existing IT capabilities that optimize process manufacturing jobs or improve transportation routing in the distribution channel—all of which can have a larger net effect on reducing the enterprise carbon footprint than an "IT for IT" project.

"Which number is our baseline?" There must be a common language around measurement standards and protocols for enterprises to learn from each other. Multinational enterprises are also challenged to respond to country-specific reporting guidelines, which may or may not be based on internationally agreed-upon frameworks. Nicholas Kim, Global Leadership Fellow for the World Economic Forum's Information Technology Industry, shared that there are roughly 343 different protocols just for Smart Grids in the United States. That seems counterintuitive for a program whose mission is to streamline and improve the efficiency of energy delivery systems. Kim's colleague, Associate Director and Global Leadership Fellow Joanna Gordon agreed, adding "in the absence of standards, how do you measure the benefits received? Just because a new IT project increases the energy consumption, does that mean that the efficiencies gained through reductions in shipping and travel are not valuable? IT has a distinct opportunity to establish standards that allow for the comparison of various outcomes and behavioral changes."

"Let's reduce the guesswork and get some real ROI." A generational shift in our workforce is changing the way CIOs approach the provisioning of information and communication technology and services. As discussed in every chapter of this book, the ecological and marketplace values of a younger generation have pushed senior executives to think differently about eco-efficiency and using technology in new ways, and the anticipated economic benefits will push the C-Suite to adopt new eco-efficient practices. According to IBM's Vice President of Energy and Environment Jim Lechner, for every dollar saved in IT energy reduction efforts, there can be five to eight dollars saved in additional benefits. For example, in the case of virtualization, additional savings accrue to the organization beyond reducing energy costs, such as lower software licensing costs or reductions in labor costs.

With the exception of a few scientifically-oriented research institutions, enterprises today must address the financial business case associated with any new project or investment. But how do CIOs assess the options, weigh the various benefits, project anticipated outcomes, and communicate all of this in layman's terms to other C-Suite colleagues? This is a significant challenge, particularly in the emerging area of environmentally friendly programs. There are five steps we have identified to assist a CIO in building an appropriate business case for investment in sustainable information technologies:

1. Know where you are today.

2. Establish (and communicate) a hurdle rate.

3. Assign resources and engage employees.

4. Validate vendor claims (and still discount).

5. Model short term *and* long-term gains.

As SAS Sustainability Project Director Jerry Williams can attest, it is very important to know enterprise energy consumption *before* starting to quantify improvements. A project that promises to deliver a 75 percent reduction in energy consumption for a specific IT asset sounds like a no-brainer. Industry experts often estimate that the cost of energy for an IT asset over the course of its lifecycle equals the upfront cost of the capital investment. But what if that asset accounts for less than 5 percent of the IT energy footprint? It would be more prudent to look at projects that can shave 10 percent off the IT organization's highest energy consumers. Unless CIOs know what drives current energy consumption, they cannot target reductions in areas that make the most financial sense for the business.

Energy consumption is a quantitative value well suited to Web-based dashboard technology, which encourages more frequent tracking and communication of information throughout the organization. All too often, the individuals who pay the energy bill want to track the dollars to budget but not the consumption of KwH or the business value derived from the IT application. A current project underway at the Poste Italiane Group is breaking down energy information silos.[17] Poste Italiane uses software from SAS to analyze energy efficiency in over 250 facilities, including those with the highest energy consumption, such as data processing centers, executive centers and the largest branches. Their analysis has identified best practices, which when implemented, led to immediate reduction in energy consumption and a total 7 percent reduction in CO_2 emissions. Future developments involve correcting operation and maintenance behaviors for the systems and indirectly for the buildings.

The next opportunity for a CIO is to establish performance objectives and acceptable ranges of internal rate of return, then communicate these objectives and rates to the rest of the enterprise. Members of the Energy Services and IT Production Operations teams at The University of North Carolina reinforced the importance of communicating this specific information. They argued that staff members take the initiative to submit qualified suggestions that have a high chance of delivering results and being supported in the enterprise when they understand the characteristics of a project that meets funding requirements.

Appropriate resources must be assigned to gather and analyze information for sustainable business cases. An enterprise benefits tremendously by appointing someone as the lead contact for green development. This person is responsible for researching available options and becomes a trusted advisor within the enterprise. There are so many opportunities for matching grant funds, reductions in tax liability, or public-private partnerships. With a dedicated resource, these agents have the initiative to research potential funding sources that might propel some projects within the internal rate of return. Funding for environmentally-related initiatives is a dynamic and quickly evolving market.

In addition to naming a green lead, Jerry Williams advises that the enterprise never move ahead with green initiatives unless employees are on board. "There are passions tied to the environment that are kin to politics and religion." Establishing employee engagement at the grassroots level reinforces support from the executive boardroom. If a CIO fosters participation from employees at every level of the enterprise, employees become aware of new opportunities, recommend cost-conscious solutions, and know that their ideas will actually get heard.

Next, the CIO must validate the anticipated benefits of the proposed technology. There are multiple paths to this validation, from site visits to custom tests run by the vendor. Prajesh Bhattacharya recommends using the most realistic data available to build the ROI model. CIOs who have monitored data about asset-level consumption from a production site can use this data to predict the performance of the proposed equipment. This is most practical for larger items like pumps, chillers, air handling units, UPS, and those items which have asset level monitoring. For smaller assets like servers and PCs, Dr. Bhattacharya suggests running them in a test environment and gathering data to see how they behave, as opposed to trusting the information on the product label. Even with these tests, Jerry Williams recommends discounting the figures by as much as 50 percent: If a project passes the financial hurdle rate at 50 percent performance, then a CIO can feel confident about moving forward.

Stephen Nunn reminded us that improving the energy efficiency and environmental impact of IT operations is a long-term strategic approach to optimizing the CIO's green agenda. Many short-term tactical activities, such as desktop virtualization and distributed computing pay immediate benefits. However, they also support a holistic sustainability program for the organization—one that pays off in terms of reduced costs and carbon emissions. As governments increasingly drive low-carbon solutions into the IT industry, Nunn counsels enterprises to invest in internal efficiency programs, so that they have fewer liabilities for carbon emissions in the future. Once enterprises become financially liable for greenhouse gas emissions, the internal hurdle rate for projects (and rate of implementation) will change dramatically.

ROLE OF PUBLIC POLICY

The development and implementation of environmental policies have a direct impact on how CIOs adopt green practices and promote the efficient use of IT throughout the enterprise. In particular, local regulations can create new opportunities for investing in green technologies by making the financial business justification more favorable. The CIO should develop a working relationship with government affairs or public policy experts in the enterprise if public policy is a new management knowledge area. This chapter's expert contributors reinforced the need for the CIO to understand environmental regulations for four reasons:

1. Prepare for any reporting requirements.
2. Take advantage of qualified tax incentives.
3. Capitalize on new market opportunities for products and services.
4. Provide feedback that improves and refines legislation.

Reporting requirements affect enterprises above thresholds established by the country of operation. In the United States, facilities that exceed 25,000 metric tons (MT) each year of Scope 1 greenhouse gas emissions face regulatory reporting.[18] This is estimated to affect over 13,000 facilities. In the United Kingdom, companies whose electricity consumption exceeded 6,000 megawatt-hours (MWh) during 2008 are required to participate in the CRC Energy Efficiency Scheme (formerly known as the Carbon Reduction Commitment). It operates as a cap-and-trade mechanism, providing a financial incentive to reduce energy use by putting a price on carbon emissions from energy use.[19] As a significant consumer of energy, CIOs are suddenly in the spotlight in these regulated entities.

While regulation may place a reporting burden on enterprises, it may also open new doors for reduced tax liabilities and new markets for products and services. Investments in building control systems, low-energy equipment, renewable energy installations, and alternative fuel products can all qualify for rebate programs and other financial incentives that significantly shorten a project's payback period. If an enterprise, such as a university or government agency, cannot take advantage of tax reduction benefits, some grant-based programs provide matching funds. Last but not least, look for opportunities to partner with utility providers. They face the direct carbon management regulations discussed earlier and therefore have incentives to work with large electricity consumers to cap demand. Some utilities find it more cost effective to invest in energy-efficient technologies than to build a new power plant. Rich Lechner estimates 800 different incentives programs designed to encourage energy efficiency and sustainable practices in the United States alone.

New regulations also create opportunities for emerging markets and solutions. Government can play a significant role in establishing the right environment that fosters investment. Germany's renewable energy market is a well-known example of regulation that created the stimulus for new business investments. Tom Spiller described how economic incentives created the wind and solar energy industries, which were nonexistent prior to the establishment of favorable policies. Now Germany is the world leader in alternative energy production, and their citizens have developed skills and competencies in a distinct business area which can be leveraged for companies around the world.

CIOs should remain educated regarding legislative developments to provide input that advances the aim of enterprise *and* environmental stewardship. With advice from internal government affairs, CIOs should identify a process by which they can stay informed. One way is through local or national trade associations. Most associations have policy committees that monitor various proposed regulations and their impact on membership. CIOs can often follow policy perspectives through the association Web site or in-person meetings.

ROLE OF THE CIO

In May 2003, Nicholas Carr authored an article in the *Harvard Business Review* with the provocative title, "IT Doesn't Matter."[20] He makes the case that information technology has evolved into a commodity similar to the way previous technology revolutions produced innovations such as steam power, railroads, and electrification. In the early stages, these innovations produced competitive advantage. Over time, fewer competitive advantages are afforded to the enterprise that continues to use new IT spending as a competitive advantage. Carr cites research from a 2002 study produced by the consulting firm Alinean. "[It compared the] IT expenditures and the financial results of 7,500 large U.S. companies and discovered that the top performers tended to be among the most tightfisted. The 25 companies that delivered the highest economic returns, for example, spent on average just 0.8 percent of their revenues on IT, while the typical company spent 3.7 percent." His most relevant conclusion is about the ways that CIO's role has evolved toward the continuous improvement of financial returns from existing IT assets.

Since 2002, the business and economic challenges for the CIO have only increased. Not only do CIOs manage more complex infrastructures, but given the capital-intensive nature of these assets, CIOs are under increasing pressure to improve returns to the enterprise. Analyst and research firms widely cite inefficient returns from IT investments. For example, one consultancy estimates the average data center facilities utilization at 56 percent owing to the traditional practice of over-provisioning. Even worse is the estimate for average server utilization at 6 percent. In a 2007 joint study with the Uptime Institute,

McKinsey reports that, "Data center facilities spending (CapEx and OpEx) is a large, quickly growing and very inefficient portion of the total IT budget in many technology intensive industries, such as financial services and telecommunications. Some intensive data center users will face meaningfully reduced profitability if current trends continue."[21] The challenges do not end there. For many industries, data centers are one of the largest sources of GHG emissions, and the likelihood of regulatory scrutiny is steadily increasing.

Apart from the impact that man-made activities have on the environment, a robust sustainability agenda provides the opportunity to bring measurable enterprise efficiencies. These increased efficiencies translate into real economic savings and reductions in material consumption. CIOs only have to think about their own enterprise business processes, how and when they were established, and whether they have been sufficiently and recently examined for efficiency improvements. For example, consider a simple commodity, such as road salt used for de-icing highways. For over 50 years, the New York City Department of Transportation has used truck-mounted snow plows as a means to disperse de-icing salts on the Brooklyn Bridge. The city applies salt for obvious safety benefits in a trade-off with the significant corrosion of the iron and steel superstructure. In 1998, the city spent $33.4 million replacing the lower suspended road-deck due to the corrosive effects of repeated salt application.[22] The city also decided that it would "optimize" the de-icing process. A traditional process improvement would have been to accelerate the scheduled purchase of the truck fleet to opt for increased fuel economy. Reasonable, but this would have likely delivered marginal benefits at best. Alternatively, the city began a project to automate delivery of liquid potassium acetate, an effective substitute de-icing compound, to the roadbed during this repair effort. The city installed pipes on both sides of the roadway and is able to remotely activate spraying equipment through a set of nozzles placed near the roadbed. In a series of tests over three winter seasons, the city showed a 61 percent cost reduction by utilizing this automated method over the traditional use of manned trucks. These cost savings do not include the benefits associated with the superstructure no longer subjected to salt corrosion and the resulting increases in duty-cycles.

What do de-icing bridges and IT have in common? According to IBM's Rich Lechner, IT tools and best practices can be used to make improvements not only in the data center environment, but bring efficiency and sustainability practices to all sorts of environments. He states, "[a]s the world becomes increasingly instrumented and interconnected, the definition of where IT ends and where the physical infrastructure begins will become increasingly blurred." Not surprisingly, Lechner believes that the "Green IT" label casts the CIO's enterprise role too narrowly. He believes it is better to think in terms of "Green Infrastructure," arguing that the scope of CIO responsibilities in today's global environment extends well beyond improving the efficiencies of data centers and the computing infrastructure: It extends to warehouses, factories, vehicle fleets, and office buildings, to name a few. CIOs also have a responsibility to help the enterprise improve its sustainability efforts by harnessing technology and best practices for non-infrastructure areas such as manufacturing processes, optimizing distribution networks, improving methods for the way people work, product design, and product lifecycle management. Viewed in this light, CIOs have new opportunities to bring innovative and management skills for delivering new value to the enterprise. Driving out costs will continue to be high on CIO agendas; however, development and execution of a comprehensive energy management plan, well beyond just the data center, means delivering leadership and driving innovation. Nicholas Kim summarizes by saying, "[t]his is a way for CIOs to re-demonstrate their importance and value to the organization."

There remains no doubt that even in the budget-constrained world of IT, executive leadership must drive the broader enterprise sustainability agenda. There are numerous IT opportunities for the CIO to reduce capital and operating expenses, immediately and into the future. The same is true within the broader business of the enterprise. While some Green IT projects may require upfront capital investment costing more than non-green alternatives (purchasing more energy-efficient hardware or introducing a mobile workforce policy), other initiatives like PC power management and duplex printing come at no cost at all aside from a time investment. Coupled with government or utility-sponsored incentive programs that encourage

Agenda Items	Areas Impacted
Work with board to develop the enterprise Social Responsibility Agenda	CEO, COO, CFO
Develop CSR plans and measurements	COO, CFO
Establish enterprise sustainability workgroup	Executive leadership from all divisions
Work with executives to align incentives	VP of Corporate Real Estate, Facilities Management, VP of Procurement
Review IT design and architecture	CFO, IT organization
Business process outsourcing	CEO, COO, CFO
Mobile workforce policy development	CEO, COO, HR
Enterprise energy management plan	COO, VP of Enterprise Real Estate
Implement data center energy efficiencies	IT organization
Direct global energy management policies	IT organization, VP of Enterprise Real Estate, Facilities Management
Understand/respond to regulatory impacts	CEO, VP of Public Affairs
Publish resource consumption metrics	Inter-Enterprise, Extra-Enterprise
Leverage public/private financial incentives	CFO, VP of Public Affairs

Exhibit 4.3: Emerging CIO Leadership Roles for Enterprise Sustainability Goals

sustainability practices, Green IT projects start to become even more financially attractive.

For example, in December 2008 under its Non-Residential New Construction Program, Pacific Gas & Electric awarded its largest rebate ever: $1,427,477 to NetApp. NetApp received the rebate as a result of their state-of-the-art new data center design. The utility estimates an annual energy savings of $1,178,000 and a CO_2 reduction of 3,391 tons.[23]

Exhibit 4.3 lists critical areas where best practice CIOs fulfill their emerging roles in providing leadership for enterprise sustainability goals. These agenda items point to a number of new CIO skill sets. Perhaps even more challenging is the CIO's role in driving changes in existing business practices. As an example, Rich Lechner observes that few IT organizations attempt to throttle IT resource demand from the business. Like a factory working overtime to produce more widgets (and thus more top-line revenue), it would seem counterintuitive to suggest reducing output. But like many optimization problems, once the data becomes available for analysis, it may turn out that producing fewer widgets and alternatively re-allocating the input resources to manufacturing gizmos may be more profitable. IT must make all the costs for IT resource demands transparent to achieve cost control. This

Resource	Location
American Society of Heating, Refrigerating and Air-Conditioning Engineers	www.ashrae.org/members/
The Data Center Pulse	datacenterpulse.org/
Uptime Institute	www.uptimeinstitute.org/
The Green Grid	www.thegreengrid.org/
Data Centre Specialist Group	http://dcsg.bcs.org/
IBM	www.ibm.com/green
Accenture	www.accenture.com/Global/Technology/Technology_Consulting/Shaping-the-Green-Agenda.htm
HP Green Business Technology Initiative	http://h20338.www2.hp.com/enterprise/us/en/technologies/green-business-overview.html
EU Emission Trading System	http://ec.europa.eu/environment/climat/emission/index_en.htm
U.S. Environmental Protection Agency ENERGY STAR Program	www.energystar.gov/ia/partners/prod_development/downloads/EPA_Datacenter_Report_Congress_Final1.pdf
Conceptualizing 'Green' IT and Data Center Power and Cooling Issues	Gartner Research ID Number G00150322, September 7, 2007
U.S. Data Centers: The Calm Before the Storm	Gartner Research ID Number G00151687, September 23, 2007
Managing the company's carbon footprint: The emerging role of ICT—Economist Intelligence Unit	http://graphics.eiu.com/upload/ATandT_Cisco.pdf
Silicon Valley Leadership Group	http://svlg.org/
Smart 2020 Report	www.smart2020.org/
Federal Energy Management Program	www1.eere.energy.gov/femp/index.html
European Community Regulation on Chemicals and Their Safe Use (REACH)	http://ec.europa.eu/environment/chemicals/reach/reach_intro.htm
Google Efficient Computing	www.google.com/corporate/green/datacenters/
EPEAT IEEE 1680 standard	www.epeat.net/
Allocating Data Center Energy Costs and Carbon to IT Users	www.apcmedia.com/salestools/NRAN-7WVU54_R0_EN.pdf

Exhibit 4.4: CIO Resources

does not mean IT must implement chargeback processes, but enterprise employees need to know the fully-burdened IT costs. Transparency and rigor for understanding and measuring all IT resource costs determines if the organization is a leader or a laggard. To help CIOs meet these challenges, Exhibit 4.4 lists the CIO consultation resources.

RISKS AND COMMON MISTAKES TO AVOID

The main risk for the enterprise CIO and Green IT initiatives is not taking the appropriate, timely actions. Enterprises have less flexibility in devising optimal solutions if they allow regulatory events to drive energy management policies. By delaying efforts to tackle these issues now, CIOs risk that other critical future projects will be crowded out or delayed while the unprepared enterprise responds to regulatory mandates. Rich Lechner warns that there are an estimated

59 jurisdictions around the globe with various carbon reduction schemes. Our expert panel of contributors makes the case that efforts to implement energy, water, and carbon management policies go well beyond meeting simple regulatory reporting requirements. Green IT initiatives offer enterprises opportunities to create new value for customers, shareholders, and employees.

While each IT project has its own set of financial risks, a broader financial risk is not taking advantage of tax benefits and other incentives offered by governments and energy providers. For example, the American Recovery and Reinvestment Act of 2009 offers U.S. businesses numerous tax incentives for eligible projects that meet measurable improvements in energy efficiencies. Many utilities offer financial incentives to businesses that are able to shift energy demands to non-peak hours. Some IT organizations can achieve this by shifting "batch-windows" onto processors in those time zones where non-peak load pricing is in effect. Another risk noted by our contributors is insufficient domain expertise for energy or carbon abatement projects. These gaps include inadequate understanding of necessary resource data and how this data should be analyzed and presented. As previously discussed, a lack of enterprise instrumentation forces repeated manual efforts to acquire such data. This makes data collection expensive. Unreliable data is worse than no data at all; it leads to incorrect decision-making and projects that degrade or make processes sub-optimal.

IT faces serious challenges, both near and long term, when it comes to data collection. Just meeting current business demands, data volume growth is nearly exponential, and collection management practices clearly unsustainable. The Chinese firm Li and Fung, which specializes in retail supply chain optimization, was carrying 100 gigabytes of data daily in its network. Today that volume is 10 times greater.[24] Paradoxically, the increased instrumentation and resulting data from enterprise devices used to measure resource consumption will only add to the deluge. To cope, IT will need to improve its tiered storage strategy, relying more heavily on virtualized storage. In addition to improving utilization of storage assets, the cost growth rate for storage becomes another driver for capturing the fully loaded costs of compute resources and reflects these costs to the enterprise through a chargeback regime. Even if the IT organization deploys a plan to actually chargeback through inter-company transfers, enterprise employees need a detailed understanding of the financial implications of their IT resourcing decisions to help manage demand. Nearly every IT organization has a server virtualization project completed or underway. Initial virtualization efforts provide increases in asset utilization; the risk remains that asset utilization remains suboptimal without a rigorous capacity planning effort to continue to increase utilization rates.

SUMMARY

Enterprises and their IT organizations in all industries face pressure to measure and report performance on key environmental programs. The CIO plays a significant role in delivering accurate enterprise information, as well as managing the carbon footprint of IT operations. The CIO can also proactively identify opportunities to apply information technology and reduce emissions in other areas of the business. While this might increase the silicon footprint, Stephen Nunn believes these practices can significantly reduce an overall carbon footprint.

Leadership must come from the top. The CIO plays a crucial executive role in driving change within an enterprise. Efforts to improve environmental performance are strengthened when the CIO's green strategy is aligned with objectives articulated by the CEO and other top executives. Without a broader enterprise sustainability initiative, the CIO has the expertise and responsibility to initiate a cross-organizational program. The rapid maturity of Green IT practices has exposed the common challenges faced by both vendors and end-users. It is therefore imperative that CIOs provide the resources and time to develop a business case for green investments that verifies anticipated savings and considers available incentives.

This is not a time to sit idle. Emerging regulations will soon shine a spotlight on areas of risk in the energy management practices of many enterprises and their IT organizations. Significant opportunities exist to immediately drive performance improvements. By being proactive, the CIO will emerge as one of the most important enterprise leaders in the transformation towards a low-carbon economy.

NOTES

1. The authors wish to express their gratitude to the panel of contributors who offered their valuable time and insights.

2. The Climate Group for GeSI, "SMART2020: Enabling the Low Carbon Economy in the Information Age," 2008, www.smart2020.org/publications/.

3. Neil Rasmussen, "Guidelines for Specification of Data Center Power Density," White Paper #120, 2005, www.apcmedia.com/salestools/NRAN -69ANM9_R0_EN.pdf.

4. U.S. Environmental Protection Agency, ENERGY STAR Program, "Report to Congress on Server and Data Center Energy Efficiency, Public Law 109-431," August 2, 2007, www.energystar.gov/.../EPA_Datacenter _Report_Congress_Final1.pdf.

5. The University of North Carolina at Chapel Hill, 2009 Climate Action Plan, at www.climate.unc.edu/portfolio/cap2009.

6. Andrew Edgecliffe-Johnson, "'Greenwash' Hype Fails to Sway Skeptical Consumers," *Financial Times*, May 1, 2009, http://74.125.95.132/search? q=cache:ayY_0GReysMJ:search.ft.com/search%3FqueryText%3D %2522social%2520marketing%2522+financial+times+may+1+ 2009+Andrew+Edgecliffe%E2%80%93Johnson&cd=1&hl=en&ct= clnk&gl=us.

7. www.airqualitynow.eu/comparing_city_details.php?brussels.

8. The American Clean Energy and Security Act (H.R. 2454), Committee on Energy and Commerce, http://energycommerce.house.gov/index.php ?option=com_content&view=article&id=1633&catid=155&Itemid=55.

9. Tiffany Maleshefski, "5 Steps to Green IT" eWeek, October 12, 2007, www.eweek.com/c/a/IT-Infrastructure/5-Steps-to-Green-IT/.

10. REACH Regulation gives industry greater responsibility to manage the risks from chemicals and to provide safety information on the substances. Manufacturers and importers will be required to gather information on the properties of their chemical substances, which will allow their safe handling, and to register the information in a central database run by the European Chemicals Agency (ECHA) in Helsinki, http://ec.europa.eu/ environment/chemicals/reach/reach_intro.htm.

11. Stephen Nunn, "How IT can contribute to the environmental agenda across and beyond the business," Accenture, 2007, www.scribd.com/doc/ 16272402/Green-IT-Beyond-the-Data-Center.

12. Tom Brey, "Impact of Virtualization on Data Center Physical Infras-tructure," IBM Operations Work Group, January 27, 2010, www .thegreengrid.org/.../EffectsofVirtualizationonDataCenterPhysical Infrastructure.ashx?.

13. See "The Greenhouse Gas Protocol: Corporate Accounting and Reporting Standard, Revised edition," April, 2004, www.ghgprotocol.org/standards/publications.

14. "GE Ecomagination Revenue Grows 21% to $17B," *Environmental Leader*, May 27, 2009, www.environmentalleader.com/2009/05/27/ge-ecomagination-revenue-grows-21-to-17b/.

15. Jeremy Kirk, "HP Opens First Ever Wind-Cooled Data Center," *InfoWorld*, February 10, 2010, www.infoworld.com/d/green-it/hp-opens-first-ever-wind-cooled-data-center-831.

16. "Waitrose Improves Stockholding, Reduces Waste," www.sas.com/success/Waitrose.html.

17. "Poste Italiane Group: A Handful of Data, a Lot of Energy Savings, www.sas.com/success/poste.html.

18. Scope 1 emissions are also known as "Direct GhG emissions." They are emissions from sources that are owned or controlled by the reporting company. They are primarily the result of power generation, transportation, and biological or chemical processes. Scope 1 emissions do not include purchased electricity.

19. "CRC Energy Efficiency Scheme," http://www.decc.gov.uk/en/content/cms/what_we_do/lc_uk/crc/crc.aspx.

20. Nicholas Carr, "IT Doesn't Matter," *Harvard Business Review*, May 2003, pages 41–49.

21. McKinsey & Company, "Revolutionizing Data Center Efficiency," May 7, 2008, www.mckinsey.com/clientservice/bto/pointofview/revolutionizing.asp.

22. Brandon L. Ward, Project Manager, "Evaluation of a Fixed Anti-Icing Spray Technology (FAST) System," 2002, New York City Department of Transportation, Division of Bridges, ops.fhwa.dot.gov/Weather/best_practices/NYCDOTanti-icingSys.pdf.

23. PG&E for Data Center Energy Efficiency, "NetApp Receives $1.4 Million Rebate," www.netapp.com/us/company/news/news-rel-20081208.html.

24. "The Data Deluge," *The Economist*, London, Feb 27, 2010, Vol. 394, Issue 8671, pg. 11.

CHAPTER 5

Sustainability, Technology, and Economic Pragmatism: A View into the Future

Jonathan Hujsak

SUSTAINABILITY

Once it was familiar only in the lexicon of bioscience professionals, but now CIOs have increasingly come to understand, embrace, and employ the principles inherent in this word—*sustainability*—to realize strategically renewable IT systems capable of operational diversity and healthy productivity over the long term. Sustainability is defined as:

1. The ability to sustain something.

2. (ecology) a means of configuring communities, systems, and human activity so that cultures, their members, and their

economies are able to meet their needs and reach their greatest potential in the present, while preserving resources, biodiversity and natural ecosystems, planning and acting for the ability to maintain these ideals for future generations.

Sustainability is one of the most misunderstood topics in today's media, often considered to be anti-business and anti-technology, and frequently associated with phrases like "green anarchism," "social ecology," and "eco-socialism." It's widely believed that sustainability negatively impacts the bottom line, lowers standard of living, reduces enterprise agility, and strangles innovation. Nothing could be farther from the truth. Sustainability in practice is not much different from familiar cost reduction and efficiency moves, and has much in common with Business Process Reengineering (BPR). Sustainability improvements are grounded in economic pragmatism and often turn cost centers into profit centers by reusing resources and consolidating business processes. These improvements apply not only to businesses of all shapes and sizes, but to society in general, regardless of culture, industrialization, or geography. We all live in a closed system (the Earth) and therefore we all share a finite set of resources for which there are no replacements.

Unless the world becomes more sustainable, the forces of globalization will eventually exhaust all known resources and industrialized society as we know it with its globally distributed supply chains will simply grind to a halt. Millennia of human progress will be suddenly reversed in a chaotic, violent process of deglobalization. If we can reach a state of sustainable equilibrium, however, we can ensure that resources, natural or man-made, are carefully managed to preserve the delicate balance within our sealed biosphere. We can ensure that future generations will inherit a world even richer than before, make room for additional population growth, support the advancement of both undeveloped and developing nations, increase our standard of living, and literally, "have our cake and eat it too." Information technology has long been a historical driver of globalization, and in the future it must play a pivotal role in achieving the global sustainability now needed, because the reach of human influence and our species' ability to radically alter our planetary ecosystem demands immediate agency and foresighted stewardship. By the same token, the role of the CIO will become ever more important in the global enterprises that survive and thrive in this highly integrated, globalized, sustainable world of the future.

Information technology (IT) organizations are the distributed *neural network* of the global, enterprise organism that now reaches the most remote regions of the world, providing these areas with unprecedented connectivity to sophisticated information, trading, and financial systems. The scope and scale of global enterprise IT operations are growing at an exponential rate, as Ray Kurzweil's monumental work, *The Singularity is Near*, illustrates with its exhaustive collection of technology trend lines.[1] As these trends indicate, information technology will be one of the most pivotal elements in the global enterprise, not just for the sustainability improvements it can provide, but for the transformative influence it will have on the rest of enterprise operations. Those who lead these organizations, CIOs and CTOs, will play an increasingly important role that will soon overshadow many other high-level executive functions.

GLOBALIZATION, DECENTRALIZATION, AND SUSTAINABILITY

Globalization is increasing at a quickening pace, transforming the most remote corners of the world with a flood of technology, finance, information, and cultural memes. The rate at which new products are developed, tested, manufactured, and marketed into this environment is now increasing at an exponential rate, as revealed by Kurzweil's *The Singularity is Near*. In this chaotic, accelerating global market, segments such as mobile computing and communications are experiencing product obsolescence that even overtakes product release. Cell phones are prime examples of this trend and today have product lifecycles of less than a year. Much of this product churn is driven by the wide availability of powerful electronic design and automation (EDA) tools that automate the design of increasingly miniaturized electronics, simulating the final functionality and performance of the product before a prototype is ever built. The end result is a lowering of technology barriers that reduces time to market, drives "feature explosion," and fuels consumer expectations. More and more technologies are becoming commoditized almost instantly under the intense pressure of lowered trade and financial barriers, highly efficient supply chains, improved communications, and a growing number of global competitors. A highly visible example of this effect is the emergence of multiple competitors to the revolutionary Apple iPhone within months of its release.

The Shifting Landscape of IT

Concurrent with the rapid pace of globalization is the explosive growth in offshoring of manufacturing and business processes. The global business process offshoring (BPO) market is currently worth $30 billion, with an upside potential of more than $250 billion. It includes a complex mix of finance, accounting, customer interaction and support, credit card processing and billing, telecomm billing, legal process, and a variety of emerging knowledge services.[2] Information technology offshoring (ITO), which preceded BPO, is moving at an even faster pace (more than 30 percent growth per year) and is currently estimated to be worth over $50 billion worldwide.[3] India now leads the BPO market with an estimated 37 percent market share. Canada follows closely at 27 percent, and then the Philippines at 15 percent. A number of other countries are rapidly gearing up to follow them into the market, including Ireland, Mexico, Central and Eastern European countries, South Africa, and China. Both the ITO and BPO markets are driven by large transnational customers such as Thomson Reuters, Dell, HSBC, American Express, and Citigroup that are reaping substantial benefits including lower costs, increased flexibility, and access to a growing global pool of talent. Keeping up with these rapidly shifting global opportunities will require unprecedented agility from future global IT organizations.

Sustainability, Theory, and Practice

To understand the profound impact that information technology will have in the future and the pivotal role that IT leadership will play, the CIO must first understand sustainability principles, sustainability frameworks, and how all of this fits into enterprise strategic planning. From the literal definition at the beginning of this chapter, dozens of sustainability initiatives have sprung up over the last 20 years or so, providing well-grounded theories, principles, and standards for the enterprise to follow. Several of the most widely known frameworks introduced in this chapter include Carbon Footprint, Ecological Footprint, and The Natural Step. Many references are readily available for the large number of lesser known frameworks not mentioned here. This section provides the essential information that a CIO needs to guide the C-Suite toward a forward-thinking, factually-researched menu of applied enterprise sustainability models and an introduction to the terminology that a best practice CIO requires to understand emerging sustainability research as a basis for ecologically and financially sustainable IT practices that enable enterprise strategy.

Carbon Footprint

One of the best known metrics of sustainability is the Carbon Footprint, a measure of the direct and indirect greenhouse gas (GHG) emissions caused by the enterprise, its services, and its products. Six primary GHG types are defined by the UN Framework Convention on Climate Change Kyoto Protocol that set emission standards for 37 industrialized countries and the European Union. GHGs interfere with the radiation of heat into space as part of the Earth's natural temperature regulation process, contributing to global warming. The atmospheric heating potential of GHGs is measured using the relative Global Warming Potential (GWP) scale, which assigns carbon dioxide the reference value of one.[4] A GHG with a larger value of GWP has a greater impact on global warming. The six greenhouse gases identified by the Kyoto Protocol are:

1. **Carbon dioxide (CO_2)** is a trace gas in the atmosphere (0.038 percent) that is used by plants in the process of photosynthesis to make sugars used in plant respiration and growth. Estimates of the natural lifetime of CO_2 in the atmosphere vary, but generally range up to 100 years.

2. **Methane (CH₄)** is the principal component of natural gas and is eventually oxidized in the atmosphere to produce carbon dioxide and water. It's a very potent GHG with a GWP value of 72. Methane has an estimated atmospheric lifetime of about 12 years.

3. **Nitrous oxide (NO₂)** is a colorless gas with a lightly sweet odor that is a strong oxidizer, with effects not unlike molecular oxygen. It has a GWP of 298 and has long been linked to ozone layer depletion. NO₂ has an estimated atmospheric lifetime of 114 years.

4. **Hydrofluorocarbons (HFCs)** are common compounds used as refrigerants in commercial, industrial, and consumer applications. GWPs for these compounds range from 140 (HFC-152a) to an amazing 11,700 (HFC-23).[5] HFC lifetimes in the atmosphere range up to 260 years.

5. **Perfluorocarbons (PFCs)** have extremely stable chemical structures and are not broken down in the atmosphere like other GHGs, remaining in the atmosphere for several thousand years. Two of the most important PFCs, tetrafluoromethane (CF₄) and hexafluoromethane (C₂F₆), are byproducts of aluminum production and semiconductor manufacturing and have atmospheric lifetimes of 50,000 and 10,000 years, respectively. They have respective estimated GWPs of 6,500 and 9,200.

6. **Sulfur hexafluoride (SF6)** is a colorless, odorless gas widely used in the power industry as a high-voltage dielectric insulator for electrical equipment such as circuit breakers and switchgear. It has an estimated lifetime in the atmosphere of 3,200 years and GWP of 23,900.

Carbon Footprint is a location specific metric that takes into consideration how "clean" the energy sources are in a specific region (i.e., GHG production). The energy portion of the footprint is typically calculated by summing the total direct and indirect fuel consumption of the enterprise facility or activity in the region including fixed assets, transportation, heating and cooling, and other sources and multiplying the total by a regional emissions factor which converts the value to the equivalent mass of CO₂. One gallon of gasoline, for example, is equivalent to 8.7 kg of emitted CO_2. A diesel-powered delivery truck that gets 10 miles per gallon and drives 50,000 miles per year will result in:

$$[(50,000 \text{ miles/year})/(10 \text{ miles/gal})] * (9.95 \text{ kg } CO_2/1\text{-gal})$$
$$= 49,750 \text{ kg} CO_2/\text{year}$$

which converts to 54.83 short tons per year. To put this in perspective, a fleet of 100 such trucks would emit 5,483 short tons of CO_2 per year.

Corrections for non–energy related GHG emissions such as HFCs must be made to this value to get an accurate aggregate value for enterprise Carbon Footprint. According to the Greenhouse Gas Protocol Initiative (www.ghgprotocol.org) Scope 3 Accounting and Reporting Standard, all GHG emissions data must be accounted for and converted to equivalent CO_2 tonnage.[6]

There are three distinct scopes that must be addressed in calculating Carbon Footprint:

Scope 1: Direct emissions from the enterprise facility including electrical generators (emergency and cogeneration systems), boilers, water heaters, gas-powered ovens, kilns, or dryers, or similar equipment, vehicles, and refrigeration systems.

Scope 2: Electrical energy purchased from an external utility or source.

Scope 3: Indirect emissions resulting from your supply chain including purchased materials, delivery vehicles and freight services, employee commuting, employee travel (car rentals, train, airlines), outsourced services, and offshoring.

Ecological Footprint

Carbon Footprint is just one component of the more comprehensive Ecological Footprint, a metric first defined by William Rees at the University of British Columbia in 1992,[7] and codified as a set of standards that apply to national and subnational population groups by the Global Footprint Network Standards Committee.[8] The Ecological Footprint is an estimate of the areal extent of biologically productive land and sea necessary to offset resource consumption and to assimilate any resulting waste. The original nation-level, population-centric approach has been adapted to calculate footprints for a variety of enterprise systems and products. Calculating the footprint for manufactured goods, however, can be explosive and complicated in combination by lack of information about proprietary materials and processes, as demonstrated by Sibylle Frey's analysis of a typical mobile phone.[9]

Closely related to Ecological Footprint is *biocapacity*, an aggregate measure of the production of ecosystems in a specific area, which may include arable land, pasture, forest, ocean, river, or lake. Land or water area is normalized to world average biocapacity equivalents in global hectares, using yield factors (global hectares/hectares [gha/ha]) that take into account the degree to which the local productivity is greater or less than the world average for that usage type. Biocapacity increases with the amount of biologically productive area and with increasing productivity per unit area. The total biocapacity of the world is currently estimated to be in the range of 11.5 to 12.5 billion gha. When the Ecological Footprint of civilization exceeds this value, the world is no longer sustainable. It's estimated that humanity's Ecological Footprint exceeded this value in 1997 by over 30 percent.

One of the standard methods for calculating Ecological Footprint uses a matrix technique not unlike the input-output multiplier method widely used to make economic projections. The highly similar Consumption Land Use Matrix (CLUM) translates row inputs that represent standard categories of consumption to column outputs that represent Ecological Footprint land use types such as crop land, grazing land, or forest. CLUM matrices are generated in several different ways. Process-based CLUMS are created by gathering data that associates land use type to consumption categories, such as the amount of forest land required to produce the wood for manufacturing printer paper used in a billing process. Input-output–based CLUMs are constructed by extending existing physical or monetary input-output tables with Ecological Footprint data. The monetary input-output table, for example, maps an activity to its direct and indirect economic impact on other business sectors of the community. The resulting economic impacts can then be mapped to their respective Ecological Footprints based on land use types.

The Natural Step

One of the most well known and widely applied sustainability frameworks is The Natural Step (TNS), founded by Karl-Henrik Robèrt in Sweden in 1989. TNS is an internationally recognized organization with offices located in Australia, Brazil, Canada, Israel, Japan, New Zealand, South Africa, Sweden, United Kingdom, and the United States. It's been successfully applied across a wide variety of industries, including real estate, metals, appliances, utilities, food, retail, apparel, fast food, healthcare, paints, chemicals, furniture, and more. TNS has been adopted and successfully used by over 100 major companies including Bank of America, McDonald's, Nike, Interface, Starbucks, Home Depot, and Ikea.

TNS represents a systems approach to sustainability analysis and is based on four fundamental Principles of Sustainability.[10]

1. "Prevent the progressive buildup of substances extracted from the Earth's crust." For example, mining, extracting, and refining of the naturally occurring and highly toxic element mercury from cinnabar ore and preventing its subsequent accumulation in our environment through sustainable, lossless reuse.

2. "Prevent the progressive buildup of chemicals and compounds produced by society." For example, avoiding the buildup of highly toxic man-made compounds in the environment such as dioxins, PCBs and DDT, by using non-toxic, sustainable alternatives.

3. "Prevent progressive physical degradation and destruction of nature and natural processes." Examples include sustainable harvesting and replanting of forest regions, avoiding depletion of soil nutrients by using sustainable agriculture practices, and preserving fisheries and diversity of species through sustainable commercial fishing practices.

4. "Promote conditions that empower people's capacity to meet their basic human needs (for example, safe working conditions and sufficient pay to live on)." Other examples include offshoring and outsourcing operations that promote safe working conditions and standard wage levels, which combat the causes of social unrest, violence, and political instability.

The TNS Framework employs a practice of "backcasting," or working backwards, from a desired future state, one of ideal sustainability. In backcasting, you start with a vision of the future, and iteratively plan actions that take you ever closer your future ideal. This is similar to traditional strategic planning methodologies, such as SWOT (Strengths, Weaknesses, Opportunities, and Threats) and SCAN (Strategic Creative Analysis) that begin with a desired end state or objective, identify internal and external factors that are favorable or unfavorable to achieving success, and then plan incremental steps to reach the desired objective. There are now many successful case studies of this process to draw from.

Ashforth Pacific, Inc., is a typical, successful example of the TNS framework that produced a wealth of tangible and intangible benefits. Ashforth Pacific has a total of 55 employees and provides third-party property management, construction, and parking management services to markets throughout the Western United States. The company currently manages over 15 million square feet of office space. By applying the four TNS Principles, Ashforth developed a variety of sustainability programs that focused on energy, water, waste, and toxic materials. Over a five-year period, Ashforth saved a total of $654,000 by reducing energy consumption through adjustments to lighting, heating, and cooling systems throughout its building inventory. They saved over $43,000 annually through several water conservation projects that included sustainable improvements to their landscape irrigation systems. They also instituted a variety of waste reduction programs, including increased emphasis on electronic communication, double-sided copying, use of recycled paper ($15,000 annual savings), recycling of construction materials, and centralization of trash collection.

At the other end of the spectrum is Nike, Inc., with annual revenues of over $18 billion and nearly 800,000 workers in contract factories spread across the world. Nike senior management, led by CEO Phil Knight, began adopting the principles of TNS in 1997. Nike has continued to infuse TNS principles into their product lifecycle, strategic decision process, and employee culture for over ten years. By 2003, Nike manufacturing operations reduced their solvent use by 95 percent by instituting the use of alternative water-based cements, cleaners, and similar materials. The reduction in the use of hazardous chemicals not only improved worker safety, it significantly reduced the environmental impact of Nike manufacturing operations. The resulting annual cost savings on materials alone amounted to nearly $4.5 million in 2003. In another example, Nike introduced improved machine technology for manufacturing its shoeboxes (which were already using recycled materials) in 2008 and realized not only a material savings of 4,000 tons per year, but an additional annual cost savings of $1.6 million. Over the years Nike has increasingly woven the principles of sustainability into its product line and design philosophy, and earned rewards in the form of tangible cost savings and intangible social capital, market positioning, and competitive advantage.

These are just a few examples drawn from a much larger collection of case studies that span the entire spectrum of industries worldwide. They consistently demonstrate not only tangible cost benefits but a broad range of intangible benefits resulting from increased sustainability. The next section narrows this focus to a particular aspect of the enterprise, IT.

FUTURE OPPORTUNITIES FOR IMPROVING GLOBAL IT SUSTAINABILITY

Information technology holds the promise of revolutionary improvements in global enterprise sustainability that will dramatically enhance enterprise agility, increase operational efficiency, and even turn cost centers into profit centers. Until recently, this potential was largely unexplored while basic improvements in material recycling and facility energy efficiency were the primary focus. In the last several years, however, IT's growing impact on the sustainability of a broad spectrum of industries and institutions in commercial, government, and academic sectors has been felt. These improvements have a far-reaching global effect and are driven by advances in data center consolidation, server, storage, desktop, and network virtualization, cloud computing, workforce mobility, ubiquitous computing, energy and environmental management, disaster recovery, information assurance, and physical security. They physically manifest as deferred construction, downsized buildings, reduced floor space, lower energy consumption, savings in heating/cooling, reduced peak electrical usage, co-generation, employee well-being, customer satisfaction, and many other tangible and intangible benefits. IT is now a key enabler of global enterprise sustainability, and its direct and indirect influence will be increasingly felt in all facets of global enterprise operations.

IT server and data center operations account for a significant portion of worldwide energy consumption, and every key sector of the world economy now depends on them. According to the U.S. Environmental Protection Agency, in 2006 over 1.5 percent of the total U.S. energy consumption, shown in Exhibit 5.1, was attributable to data center operations, or over 120 billion kilowatt-hours (kWh) projected for 2011 (see Exhibit 5.2). This amounts to over 61 million kWh of energy consumed with an aggregate value exceeding $4.5 billion. A single enterprise-grade data center consumes enough energy to power 25,000 households.[11] These numbers are projected to double by the year 2011[12] and reflect a doubling of energy consumption since the year 2000. Of the total energy consumption, about 50 percent is currently attributable to power and cooling infrastructure alone. Data center Carbon Footprint, if unchecked, will increase by a factor of four

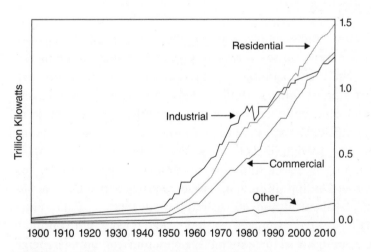

Exhibit 5.1: Total U.S. Energy Consumption by Segment

Source: *EIA.*

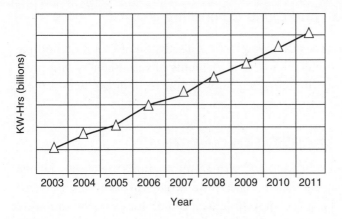

Exhibit 5.2: Annual U.S. Data Center Electricity Usage

by the year 2020. Fortunately, we have the means available to prevent this.

On the commercial side, data center growth is being driven by a number of factors including the growth of global electronic financial transactions, expansion of the Internet, rise of electronic healthcare systems (e.g., a single high-quality digital chest X-ray can consume 20 megabytes or more; a CT scan of a heart can consume 200 megabytes or more), increase in global commerce and services, and the impact of satellite navigation and commercial package tracking services.[13] On the government side, similar expansion is being driven by digital records retention, Internet publishing of government information, growing defense and national security systems, disaster recovery preparations, information security initiatives, and the impact of digital health and safety requirements.

Overall, data centers now account for as much as 25 percent of corporate IT budgets, and operational costs are rising by as much as 20 percent per year. In a recent Sun Microsystems poll, 68 percent of IT managers reported that they were not even responsible for their data center power bills. These numbers will rapidly spiral out of control unless these systems become more sustainable, ultimately resulting in widespread service interruptions due to energy or infrastructure shortages. The solution, however, lies not in curtailing growth, but in embracing an entirely new paradigm of high performance, energy-conserving, and sustainability-enhancing enterprise IT technologies.

Virtualization and Cloud Computing

This section extends the best practices discussion of Cloud Computing in Chapter 3 to include essential elements of sustainability best practices for this rapidly emerging information technology, with a focus on storage and virtualization practices.

Data Center Consolidation and Virtualization

Data center consolidation and virtualization efforts are closely related and have a major impact on enterprise Ecological Footprint. Deferred construction of a single large-scale data center, for example, can offset tens of thousands of gha of Ecological Footprint. When a hundred or more global data centers are consolidated down to just a few, the reduction in footprint can be substantial. New innovations in high-density, modular data centers significantly increase the capacity and utilization of these assets, while considerably reducing operating costs. Relocation of data centers near sources of renewable energy and cooling such as hydroelectric dams further reduces cost and enhances Carbon and Ecological Footprints. Virtualization amplifies this effect by significantly increasing asset utilization levels and reducing overall power consumption and cooling load.

The total Ecological Footprint of a data center is calculated by first enumerating the fixed and recurring resources needed to construct, equip, commission, and operate the facility. Each component and process used in the project must be traced back to the original source. The calculation must account for the amount of biocapacity, or amount of biologically productive land or sea (measured in gha) dedicated to the production of the item and for consumption of any wastes resulting from the use of that item. A cell phone, for example, has an Ecological Footprint of about 32 global square meters. An average PC has a footprint of about 764 global square meters. (CFOs love this stuff).

Most of the waste and inefficiency associated with commercial products results from the basic material processes, energy, and emissions used in their production, not their disposal. For example, every metric ton of gold used to make electrical contacts in a rack server requires 350,000 tons of ore to be mined. One metric ton of platinum

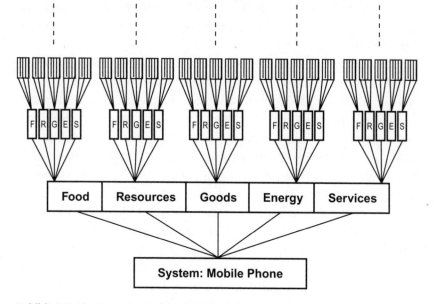

Exhibit 5.3: The Recursive Nature of Calculating Ecological Footprint

requires 950,000 tons of ore. Obviously, recycling materials without loss of value has a huge impact on sustainability when the effects of the entire supply chain are considered. Every pound of aluminum that is recycled, for example, saves 8 pounds of bauxite, 4 pounds of chemical products, and 14 kW of energy. Exhibit 5.3 illustrates the explosive problem of tracing sources of Ecological Footprint from a complex system such as a data center back to their origins. Consequently, few detailed studies have looked at systems more complex than a single cell phone,[14] and even those studies were limited by materials and processes considered proprietary by the manufacturer. Even the most basic first order analysis shows that the footprint of a large, multi-building, enterprise class data center complex can amount to tens of thousands of global acres (>10,000 gha). This value, to make matters worse, does not include the additional impact of powering and cooling the data center, or the impact of staffing the data center to operate it. Obviously every time construction of a data center is avoided, or an existing data center is decommissioned, there is a tremendous reduction in enterprise Ecological and Carbon

Footprint, and an equivalent increase in enterprise sustainability, graphically illustrating the impact of IT on overall enterprise sustainability.

The best practice CIO can be certain of one thing. More and more C-Suite teams are actively managing these issues because shareholder activists have all this information at their fingertips. Robert Stephens warned in Chapter 1 that it is only a matter of time until each and every corporation has its pants pulled down on the Internet. The real blow to enterprise profitability comes when this kind of information is exposed by shareholders to an ignorant executive management team.

Conventional data centers consume about 150 to 300 Watts per square foot power density.[15] These are now starting to be replaced by a new generation of sustainable, modular data centers packaged in integrated "containerized" units that can be installed outdoors with minimal shelter. A single Sun Modular Data Center (MDS), for example, contains 200 kW of IT server capacity in 160 square feet, or 8 times the density of conventional data centers. The integrated closed loop water cooling system used in the MDS is 40 percent more efficient than conventional data center HVAC systems.[16] Power conditioning systems are removed from the MDS container and packaged as external transformer units with power busses extending into the container, further reducing cooling requirements. The similar Hewlett-Packard (HP) POD (Performance Optimized Data Center) is packaged in a 40 foot container and replaces 4,000 square feet of conventional data center space. The POD is 50 percent more power efficient than conventional data center build-outs according to HP and can support loads of 1,800 Watts per square foot, or 27 kW for each of its twenty-two 50U racks. This equates to a Power Usage Effectiveness (PUE) of 1.25 compared to 1.7–2.0 for a conventional facility. A 40-foot POD can house as many as 3,520 computer nodes and is equipped to accept chilled water for cooling. Containerized data centers such as the MDS and POD can be more easily relocated to cooler, higher latitudes, allowing the external atmosphere or adjacent rivers to be used to augment server cooling, saving 10 percent or more in cooling costs, while simultaneously reducing Carbon and Ecological Footprint (i.e., sustainability and economic pragmatism go hand-in-hand).

There are many ongoing examples of major data center consolida-tion to point to at the time of this writing. HP Corporation is currently in the process of consolidating 85 worldwide data centers into just 6 by converting to a virtualized blade server-based infrastructure. This consolidation move will save HP an estimated $1 billion annually and will be phased in over three to four years. Three of the six data centers will be dedicated to disaster recovery. The consolidation effort will be used as a showcase for HP technologies, reaping not only tangible savings from reduced footprint, but a variety of intangible benefits in the form of market positioning, competitive advantage, social capital, and technical discriminators.

Emerson Network Power recently consolidated over 100 data centers worldwide into just four, while reducing high-cost peak energy demand at its main corporate data center by using a 550-panel, 100-kW rooftop solar photovoltaic array.[17] Although powering an entire data center with photovoltaic panels would be quite expensive, a hybrid approach can produce substantial savings through "peak shaving" during times when utilities are forced to buy energy in the expensive spot markets (and pass these costs on to the enterprise). Alternative renewable energy sources can also be employed, in some cases, by utilizing waste from nearby operations as feedstock for anaerobic digesters or gasification systems. The CAPEX associated with a 2.5-MW digester-based generation system today is about $2.5 million, or $2.50 per Watt, about half the installed cost of an equiva-lent solar PV system.

Other "greenfield" data center projects are being driven as much by enterprise growth as by needed improvements in sustainability. Amazon, for example, is building a new $100 million, 116,700 square foot data center complex near the Columbia River in Oregon. The location, scheduled for completion in the third quarter 2010, provides a sustainable answer to the sizeable problem of cooling hundreds of thousands of servers. River water is piped directly into the site after being processed through a water treatment system. Power from the Columbia River hydroelectric sources provides a large-scale renewable energy source to offset its Carbon Footprint.[18] Google recently built a similar 30-acre complex in The Dalles, Oregon, also along the Columbia River.[19] One of the major attractions of this small-town location is the nearby Dalles Dam hydroelectric complex. With an overall length of 8,875 feet and height of 260 feet, the dam hydroelectric complex includes a powerhouse with a total capacity of 1,779 megawatts, ample renewable capacity for the local Google operations. Also making this an ideal location is the local fiber optic hub tied to the coastal PC-1 landing of the 640 Gbps fiber optic network, linking the United States with Japan and Asia.

Similar river-cooled data centers have sprung up 130 miles to the north built by Yahoo and others. In yet another twist on sustainability, Microsoft's new $550 million, 477,000-square foot data center in San Antonio, Texas, uses 602,000 gallons a day of recycled municipal wastewater to cool the facility during peak cooling months. Water cooling, however, is not the only approach to improve data center sustainability. Microsoft's Dublin data center uses the year round cool ambient air found at the higher latitude to eliminate the need for chillers entirely. Waste heat generated from large data center operations can also be used for a variety of sustainable applications, including space heating of buildings, facility hot water pre-heating, industrial heating of local commercial greenhouse operations, and heat for sustainable wastewater treatment (anaerobic digestion).

Server Virtualization

Virtualization (see Exhibit 5.4) typically goes hand-in-hand with data center consolidation, and contributes significantly to enterprise sustainability by increasing asset utilization, reducing energy consumption, and decreasing Ecological Footprint. Server utilization in conventional data centers can be as low as 6 percent, and the same servers can use as much as 74 percent of peak power when idle.[20] By running multiple virtual machines on a single hardware platform, physical server energy consumption can drop as much as 80 percent, while server utilization can increase to as much as 60 to 80 percent. This means that as much as a 15:1 reduction in the number of physical servers is possible with an associated drop in Ecological Footprint (i.e., more than 700 square global meters per server). Blade servers, in particular, can reduce overall energy usage by as much as 35 percent over conventional servers. For each physical

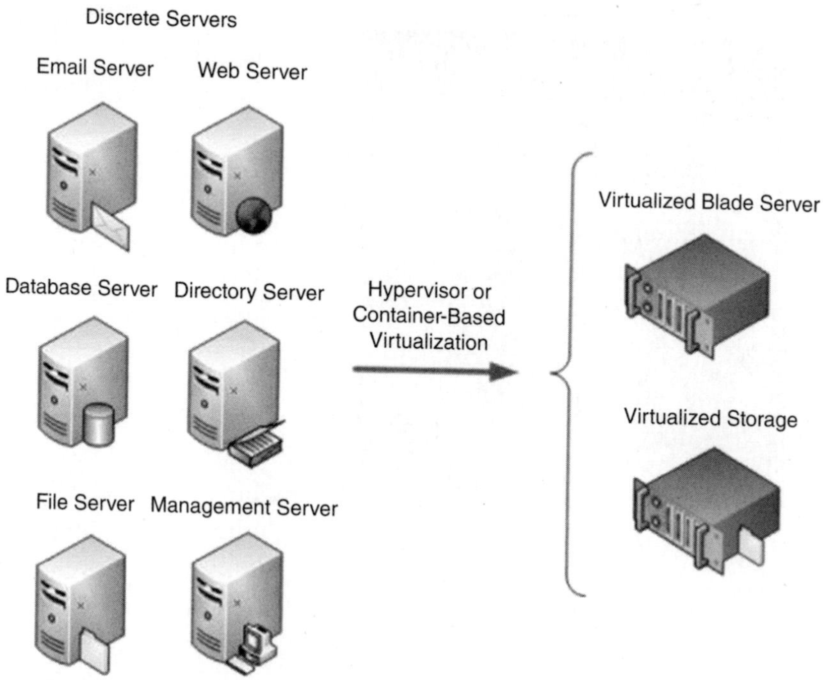

Exhibit 5.4: Consolidation of Server Functions through Virtualization

server that is virtualized, 4 metric tons per year of CO_2 emission are eliminated, an amount equivalent to a gas-guzzling SUV getting 15 mpg being taken off the road.

Resource impacts often manifest in non-intuitive ways. A single Google search, for example, involving several related queries, is estimated to produce about 7g of CO_2. By comparison, boiling a teapot of water costs about 15g. To further put this into perspective, the world IT industry generates as much GHG as all of the world's airlines put together, according to Evan Mills at the Lawrence Berkeley National Laboratory.[21]

Different types of standalone virtualization (as opposed to hosted) can have different impacts on data center sustainability, depending on the nature of the workload. Where applications are CPU bound or cannot run under the same operating system, there is little difference in efficiency between the different virtualization approaches. In cases where applications are IO bound and can run the same kernel and

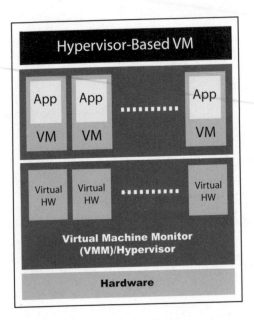

Exhibit 5.5: Hypervisor Virtualization Model

similar operating system versions, however, the differences can be substantial. Hypervisor and container-based virtualization are two of the most common forms and illustrate both ends of the spectrum. At one end (hypervisor), we have VM isolation at the hardware abstraction layer (HAL). At the other end we have VM isolation at the application binary interface (ABI)/system call layer.

In the hypervisor, or full virtualization model (see Exhibit 5.5), applications execute within a virtual machine, which is a complete unmodified operating system image hosted on a fully abstracted hardware layer. The hypervisor, also known as a Virtual Machine Monitor (VMM), runs directly on the base hardware, handling privileged instructions trapped by the individual Virtual Machines (VMs) and rewrites the machine code on-the-fly, a sophisticated technique patented by VMWare that maintains isolation between the VMs preventing exceptions that would otherwise crash the system. Contemporary hypervisors often leverage hardware-assisted virtualization such as Intel VT™ or AMD-V™ to trap privileged calls, removing the need for binary translation and significantly increasing system performance. The VMMs used in virtualization products such as VMWare ESX Server, Citrix XenServer, KVM, and Microsoft Hyper-V are typically built from Linux, Solaris, Microsoft, or custom kernels that leverage these hardware extensions. In theory, any OS that can run native on the actual hardware can run within a VM hosted on a hypervisor platform. In reality, however, specialized device drivers are often unavailable.

Paravirtualization offers a significantly higher performance and more scalable alternative to the hypervisor model by providing an isolated application execution environment with virtual instructions, virtual registers, and a simpler interface to virtual I/O devices (i.e., virtual drivers). This, however, requires the use of customized "virtualization aware" versions of the guest OS as opposed to the "off-the-shelf" version hosted by normal hypervisors. Paravirtualized guest OSs share access to the underlying hardware, eliminating the need for the VMM to trap protected instructions, replace, and rewrite them, thereby increasing efficiency. Experimental paravirtualization systems such as Denali (University of Washington) have demonstrated the ability to host hundreds of simultaneous Lightweight Virtual Machines, compared to 5 to 10 VMs for a conventional hypervisor system such as VMWare ESX.

In container-based virtualization (see Exhibit 5.6), as typified by Solaris Containers, Parallels Virtuozzo, and Linux V-Server, the virtualization environment provides protected application areas, or resource partitions, within a single, shared, OS image, not unlike the practice of mainframes years ago. The partitions provide a complete execution environment for software applications, allowing them to share a root filesystem, system executables, and shared libraries, in effect sharing an instance of the base OS. For this reason, container-based virtualization solutions do not support heterogeneous collections of different hosted OSs as hypervisor systems do. Applications running in a container-based "VM" still see a single, bootable, OS that behaves just like an ordinary, non-virtualized OS, and can be easily migrated from one physical server to another. Elimination of the complex HAL layer, however, significantly reduces the virtualization overhead compared to hypervisor based systems. Benchmarking studies have shown that

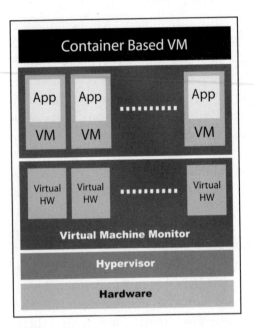

Exhibit 5.6: Container-Based Virtualization Model

container-based systems run close to the performance of unvirtualized systems, with a 1 to 10 percent overhead, depending on operating system and workload. Hypervisor systems, in comparison, often incur overhead as high as 40 percent. Based on overhead alone, the most sustainable solution with the smallest Ecological Footprint would be container-based virtualization for I/O dominated workloads. For large and highly homogeneous enterprise data center operations such as Google or Amazon, there are obvious advantages to using this form of virtualization.

Current trends indicate a continued evolution of lighter weight virtualization layers, in some cases leading to the embedding of "flash" hypervisors directly into the motherboard hardware. These embedded hypervisors will load network bootable VMs from the cloud into local memory and access virtualized disk storage, entirely eliminating the requirement for local disk capacity and associated energy consumption and hardware footprint. This, of course, is just a natural evolution of the diskless node, or hybrid client, which employs a network bootable OS and remote storage.

Choice of virtualization approach is a subtle and complex decision process that involves consideration of cost (recurring and non-recurring), performance, reliability, maintainability, scalability, availability, workload characteristics, security, and ultimately sustainability. In some cases, the cost of porting legacy code to a common OS is simply prohibitive, precluding shared resource approaches such as container-based virtualization. In other cases, reliability concerns dictate maximum isolation between VMs, requiring a robust hypervisor approach. In still other cases, trading performance, efficiency, and cost for isolation is advantageous and can yield significant savings and gains in sustainability and a lowered Ecological Footprint. Virtualization in its many forms and variations is clearly here to stay and will be a key element of cloud computing into the future.

Storage Virtualization

Storage virtualization (see Exhibit 5.7), evolving from today's Network Attached Storage (NAS) and Storage Area Networks (SAN), is yet another approach to hardware consolidation and utilization optimization. This approach is used for "pooling" distributed, heterogeneous storage resources to make them appear as a single, uniform, logical unit of storage. This has the effect of increasing device utilization levels and reducing capacity requirements and subsequent footprint. Typical

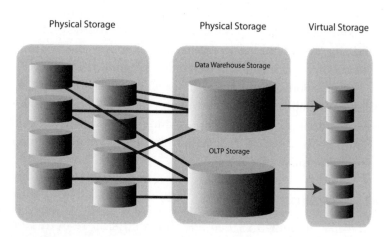

Exhibit 5.7: Storage Virtualization Model

data center environments with widely distributed storage assets can have storage utilization levels as low as 20 percent. By adding storage virtualization, redundant hardware can be eliminated, data center floor space reduced, energy consumption lowered, and cooling requirements reduced. Storage management costs can often be reduced by half or more. Payback periods as short as 12 months have been demonstrated with return on investment (ROI) exceeding 180 percent over a typical three-year period.

Desktop Virtualization

Taking the virtualization paradigm even further, desktop software is transformed into a managed virtualized service and removed from the remote client platform. This natural evolution from remote desktop and network workstation technology allows the user to do more with less by facilitating access to complex enterprise cloud applications with no more than a lightweight Netbook or smartphone platform (e.g., Citrix Nirvana Phone—"desktop in your pocket"). If you combine the newer smartphones with built in MEMs projectors (that can project a 50 inch diagonal image) with flexible, roll-up, Bluetooth keyboards, you get a highly virtualized, high-performance workstation that fits in your pocket. With the current pace of technology, cell phones with 1080p projector performance will be out before you know it. Country-specific internationalizations (e.g., language, legal, contractual, cultural) will be instantly delivered to the desktop, application user interfaces, document editors, and other resources courtesy of the cloud, and adjusted as the GPS tracked worker moves fluidly from country to country. The result is a tremendous increase in workforce mobility and global enterprise agility that will be needed to adapt to the rapid pace of globalization and the opportunities it brings for lowering cost, increasing enterprise performance, and diversifying the supply chain. IT isn't just an automation enabler anymore—it's the key to global enterprise survival.

Network Virtualization

Just as server and storage virtualization map physical resources to logical groups, network virtualization (see Exhibit 5.8) can be used

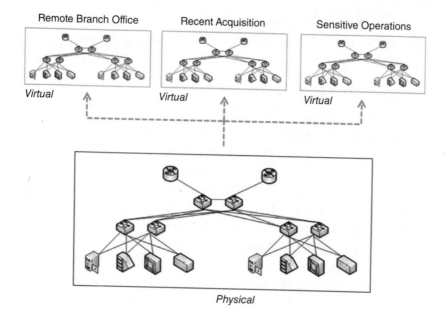

Exhibit 5.8: Network Virtualization Model

to reduce the physical and hence Ecological Footprint of network services, while preserving access control and path isolation. Networks that were formerly physically separated can now be virtualized through Generic Routing Encapsulation (GRE) tunnels or Multiprotocol Label Switching (MPLS) that create separate, virtual networks over a single, physical IP backbone. Routers, switches, and firewalls can be consolidated and virtualized in the same way as servers to support independent logical networks with virtual routing tables and security features, eliminating redundant hardware, increasing utilization, saving energy, and lowering Carbon and Ecological Footprint.

Virtualization as a Sustainability Strategy

From the preceding discussion it's apparent that data center consolidation/virtualization moves require detailed analysis of the planned workload to optimize energy efficiency, reliability, availability, performance, security, and other factors that realize the benefits of sustainability. The end result, however, has proven to be worth the effort, as illustrated by the many compelling case studies that are freely available. The benefits include not just lower operating costs (CAPEX and OPEX), but a host of intangible benefits for both the global enterprise and its host communities.

Cloud Computing, Agility, and Sustainability

Server, storage, and network virtualization are the basic building blocks of cloud computing and enable a potent, sustainable mix of Software as a Service (SaaS), Platform as a Service (PaaS), and Infrastructure as a Service (IaaS). Cloud computing gives global IT organizations unprecedented agility, enabling them to quickly respond to dynamic market conditions, shifting sources of supply and demand and new global opportunities with little or no change to physical, Ecological, or Carbon Footprints. Enhanced supply chain agility is key to reengineering the enterprise to deal with rapidly changing markets while maintaining competitive advantage and preserving barriers to entry. In the future, cloud computing will be instrumental in coping with demanding time-to-market challenges such as those currently found in the mobile phone industry. Given the recent trend in shifting Supply Chain Management (SCM) from vertical integration within the enterprise to horizontal integration with highly dynamic supply chain partners, cloud computing and the agility it provides will be increasingly important. The resulting real-time supply chain communication will improve efficiency, reduce waste, minimize excess inventory, and lower operating costs—all resulting in improvements to enterprise sustainability.

The combination of virtualization and service-oriented architecture (SOA) enables rapid provisioning of resources to the most remote, IT-challenged environments. Best practice CIOs already know that entrepreneurs in developing countries can tap into global SaaS providers with no more than a smartphone, gaining instant, on-demand, pay-as-you-go access to powerful financial and information resources. In the same manner, mobile members of the global enterprise can access enterprise grade applications such as customer relationship management (CRM), enterprise resource planning (ERP), business intelligence (BI), human resources (HR), enterprise performance management (EPM), and computer integrated manufacturing (CIM) with no need for in-country, physical, brick-and-mortar (B&M) presence. Cloud computing facilitates scalable provisioning as a single representative in a foreign location expands to a field office, to a branch office, and ultimately a small division, all without significantly increasing in-country IT footprint.

In cases where on-site IT software customization support is required, PaaS can be leveraged to deliver a virtualized platform with dedicated storage, applications, and development tools from the cloud to users anywhere in the world. From the user's perspective, they have a unique, dedicated development platform that's no different from a local PC. Instead, a lightweight, resource-constrained mobile platform can be used in the remote location. No local IT support personnel are needed—everything is managed remotely in the cloud. An IT "strike" team working remotely for a limited period with an offshore supplier, for example, can implement customized supply chain integration solutions on the spot without the need for a local office, thereby eliminating space, energy, landline connectivity, legal, janitorial, security, and insurance requirements and their logistical intricacies.

For more permanent remote operations that need to support a sophisticated mix of sales, marketing, accounting, engineering, and other functions on-site, an entire scalable virtual data center can be stood up through cloud IaaS. Using a potent combination of server, desktop, storage, application, and network virtualization, a comprehensive, customized, country-specific suite of enterprise functionality including CRM, ERP, HR, payroll, email, Voice over IP (VoIP), collaboration, backup, disaster recovery, and other branch office functions can be rapidly provisioned.

As discussed in previous sections, deferring construction of a physical in-country data center can save upwards of 10,000 gha of Ecological Footprint. On the pragmatic side, IT resource utilization more than quadruples in many cases, the cost of operations drops precipitously, and the end result is a workplace environment better suited to emerging Generation Y workforces, shareholders, stakeholders, and generations to come.

MOBILITY

As a running theme throughout this book, best practice CIOs have become aware that the workplace is undergoing radical change driven by cultural shifts brought by new groups entering the workforce such as Generation Y. These groups have grown up with high-performance personal computers, laptops, and mobile phone technology, all evolving at an exponential rate. The physical changes in the workplace they are affecting have a potentially far-reaching effect on enterprise sustainability, and Ecological and Carbon Footprint.

According to "career doctor" Randall S. Hansen, PhD, this newest crop of workers "has no interest whatsoever in working in a cubicle—not because it is beneath them, but because they feel advances in technology should let them be able to choose to work from home, Starbucks, or anywhere there is a Wi-Fi connection."[22] They are attracted by Results Only Work Environments (ROWE) that encourage workers to "work wherever they want, whenever they want, as long as the work gets done." Generation Y workers are not afraid to challenge the status quo and prize employers that encourage creativity and independent thinking. Employers also are finding that recruiting such employees requires benefits such as flexible work schedules, emphasis on work/life balance, telecommuting, and office environments more akin to college campuses than traditional business interior design. In addition, these new generation workers expect from their IT organizations computing capacity on demand, anywhere, anytime—the hallmark of cloud computing.

Offices of the Future

Generation Y workers prefer "open plan" flexible offices, which emphasize shared, open spaces with few private, dedicated offices. Shared hot-desking stations, touch-down areas, computing islands, and a limited number of enclosed, "private harbor" offices are preferred instead of floors of dedicated, identical cubicles. Strongly resembling college campus environments, these spaces are used by Generation Ys to facilitate shared conversations, rapid-issue solving, intense and open information sharing, and pervasive tacit learning. The flexibility they encourage requires sophisticated, high-bandwidth wireless computing and movable resources and furnishings that can be re-arranged on the fly to support ad hoc task requirements. From a sustainability perspective, open office environments require less space because less area is wasted in corridors and dead spaces. In a sense, open office environments represent a "virtualization" of the physical work environment and in fact produce a highly similar increase in utilization and smaller Ecological Footprint. Less space means less energy to support it and fewer materials consumed in the construction and commissioning of the building.

These changes in office environments are now becoming visible in major corporate settings, and the benefits are becoming visible as well. IBM reports that it is now saving $100 million a year in real estate costs because less office space is needed.[23] The workforce at Accenture, a major management consulting firm, is so mobile that not even the CEO has a dedicated office. The Crayon marketing firm has even gone to the extent of putting its headquarters entirely in cyber-space. Their workers, scattered across multiple cities, rarely meet in the physical world but have routine weekly meetings in their virtual headquarters.

Another benefit of moving from traditional B&M operations to more virtual settings is that talent can easily be recruited from any-where in the world, not just the local geography. Costly relocation packages (often exceeding $100,000 or more) are no longer needed, and the disruptions of home and family associated with relocation can be avoided, increasing employee satisfaction.

Evolving Mobile Computing and Telecommunications

Growing numbers of global enterprise workers in developed and developing countries alike are embracing the mobile computing and communications technologies that reduce or eliminate the need for conventional office space, allow the work to roam with the worker, and directly connect workers with sophisticated international enter-prise financial and information services. These improvements are cre-ating a world-spanning, sustainable fabric of transactions, collaboration, social networking, data sharing, and knowledge management that increasingly blurs the boundaries of the global enterprise, its supply chain, and its customers. In a similar manner, it blurs the boundaries between developed and developing countries, accelerating the process of globalization. This fabric has been compared by a number of authors to a growing, increasingly sophisticated neural network, which will gradually acquire distributed intelligence and cognitive abilities as it evolves and supports its human users.[24]

Evolving smartphones, combined with virtualized SaaS, PaaS, and IaaS services delivered through 4G LTE and WiMax wireless broadband, enable radical changes in mobile workforce capabilities. CIOs everywhere are witnessing business applications formerly requiring fully provisioned desktop workstations now appearing on mobile phones, thanks to mobile desktop virtualization. MEMs based, built-in DLP projectors are appearing in mobile phones such as the Samsung W7900 and currently provide 400x240 resolution on a 50-inch screen. HD projection resolution is, as you might expect, just around the corner. Today, standalone versions of these embedded projectors support 720p resolution and are available off-the-shelf. We'll see 1080p projectors within a year or two. Toss in a roll-up Bluetooth keyboard and mouse, and you have an enterprise workstation with a 50-inch screen that fits in your pocket.

These game changing developments are further fueled by seamless vertical handoffs in mobile communications systems. Vertical handoff refers to automatic handover from one communications medium to another, for example, between a carrier's 3G/4G network and an enterprise wireless Wimax or WiFi network. This is similar to the horizontal handoff we see today as users roam from one cell to another using the same technology, except the implications are far greater. For example, in the future, when a mobile worker engaged in a complex online collaboration session enters a campus building, their multimode handset will seamlessly switch between the external 4G LTE or 802.16m network to the campus building-hosted wireless VoIP system without dropping any of the concurrent voice, video, or data streams or incurring noticeable latency. As the worker enters an office telepresence environment, the mobile multimedia/multimodal session will instantly and seamlessly transfer to the fixed environment, taking advantage of local resources tied in through pervasive computing, all transparently and dynamically configured according to user preferences and enterprise administrative, economic, and security policies.

As we've already seen with today's basic SIP and H.323 VoIP systems, significant cost savings are reaped by simply transferring a call from the external carrier 3G network to the enterprise wireless VoIP system, particularly when the called number is already in the enterprise domain. If the original call was to an external number, considerable savings can still be realized by re-routing an external call through a much lower cost campus landline calling plan. Increasingly widespread roaming between public cellular networks and private VoIP systems will have the effect of reducing the load on public networks, allowing them to do more with less physical infrastructure, conserving limited carrier bandwidth, and reducing their Ecological and Carbon Footprints in the process.

In particular, if we consider the electromagnetic spectrum to be a limited natural resource just like air or water, we have now conserved "electromagnetic footprint" at the same time. The iPhone, which a year after its introduction represents only 3 percent of AT&T's subscriptions, has significantly strained their 3G network,[25] in some cases causing delays of as much as 15 minutes to load applications. It's predicted that sometime in 2010 the number of mobile broadband users will exceed the number of fixed-service users and climb precipitously from there (see Exhibit 5.9). This problem is aggravated by a natural bandwidth resource so strained that carriers

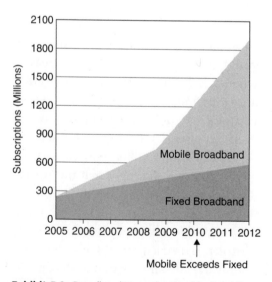

Exhibit 5.9: Broadband Usage by Fixed and Mobile Segments

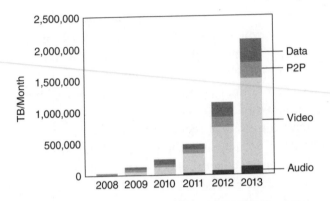

Exhibit 5.10: Projected Growth of Broadband Media Elements

are forced to use a discontinuous patchwork of pieces of spectrum to provision their networks. Exhibit 5.10 shows the projected growth for the different media elements eating up this mobile spectrum. Projections of 4G data rates as high as 1 gbps obviously raise serious sustainability questions considering the limitations in natural electromagnetic spectrum. Extensive use of horizontal and vertical handoff, data compression, cognitive radio, and other emerging technologies for bandwidth conservation will be needed to avoid exhausting this precious natural resource long before the promised benefits are realized.

To really put these developments in perspective, consider that worldwide PCs in use topped 1 billion in 2008 and will surpass 2 billion by 2015, with the majority of this growth coming from BRIC countries (Brazil, Russia, India, and China). These numbers, however, are quickly being overtaken by the proliferation of ever more powerful mobile phones. The first billion cell phones took 20 years to sell, the second billion only four years, and the third billion only two. This is even more significant when you consider that over half the world's population now owns a cell phone.[26] Clearly, PCs are no longer the driver of change in the global workplace. This is true because much of the action is now occurring in developing countries that lack the basic market and utility infrastructure needed for PCs and their networks (e.g., stable power, hardware/software distribution channels, and landline network connectivity.)[27] Mobile phones, however, allow users to easily bypass entire phases of traditional infrastructure development, such as postal services, landline telecommunications, and even road networks that would otherwise take decades to build out. Mobile phones are deployed through vastly simpler distribution networks and support direct access to sophisticated enterprise applications hosted in global clouds. These observations are supported by a recent Forrester survey of emerging markets that shows: (1) a strong correlation between mobile phone adoption and a rise in per capita GDP; and (2) that people in developing countries are spending a higher percentage of their income on cell phones and related equipment than their counterparts in developed countries.[28]

The most basic rural economies can now stand up sophisticated, current generation wireless communication networks in a fraction of the time required for traditional infrastructure. Self-contained, low cost, cellular networks in a box or trailer can be readily obtained from a host of worldwide suppliers that feature built-in gateways to international landline circuits and sophisticated features such as automatic call handoff to in-building VoIP systems. These low-cost cellular solutions are rapidly being deployed in developing countries and supplanting functions that were formerly handled by primitive traditional services that were risky, expensive, and inconvenient. These new mobile services are having profound and far-reaching effects on developing countries that are rapidly improving their standard of living, reducing corruption, and fueling growth of local economies. Automation of business services has in many cases eliminated corruption by removing traditional middlemen illegally profiting from the market.

In India, users can now wire funds to friends and family, using a mobile phone and Visa card, and are now paying bills by text message. Fishing boats in Kerala, southwestern India, are able to phone ahead to retail markets with the details of their catch, stabilizing markets and prices. Text messaging is used to monitor elections in Africa by observers who instantly report evidence of election tampering, reducing political corruption. In economies throughout the third world, mobile phones are now used to manage the distribution of perishable commodities, reducing waste and improving the diets and health of distant cultures. Beyond these local improvements, mobile phones provide a platform for mobilizing and integrating a developing country's citizens directly into the world's financial systems, bypassing complex traditional phases of national financial system evolution.[29]

Telepresence, Teleoperation, and Robotics

Some of the most interesting new developments in the global enterprise have to do with different forms of virtual presence. Simple conference calls and Video Teleconferencing (VTC) sessions are rapidly giving way to more immersive telepresence systems. Even more advanced are teleoperation systems that are being used to extend expert human skills to tasks in remote locations. Fully automated robotic systems are already becoming commonplace in many areas of manufacturing and material handling. These developments are having major impacts such as increased efficiency, better utilization of human and machine capital, lower Ecological and Carbon Footprints, and ultimately improved enterprise bottom line.

Telepresence systems are a significant improvement over their earlier VTC counterparts. VTC equipment was often installed after the fact in non-optimized conference rooms, resulting in poorly lit, heavily shadowed participants on the other end of the connection. Instead of scaled-down, hard-to-resolve, and often dark visual displays, telepresence offers a more integrated, optimized solution where participants are rendered as bright, high resolution, life-size images, imparting a comfortable face-to-face ambiance to the meeting. Telepresence meetings can combine participants from as many as 48 different locations, significantly reducing air travel and ground transportation incurred by employees. A single deferred round-trip cross-country flight for one person, for example, saves over 1600 pounds of CO_2 emissions, to say nothing of the high cost and inconvenience of air travel (i.e., both tangible and intangible benefits are realized). The resulting decrease in the number of air travelers will result in fewer aircraft needed by the airlines, smaller traffic hubs, and so on as you recurse down through the supply chain.

Automotive transportation between different enterprise locations can be reduced, creating additional cost savings (especially when the price of gas may soon rise again above $5 per gallon) and has the same, recursive effect on Ecological Footprint. In the near future, home telecommuters and travelers will have portable telepresence systems that tie back into the enterprise social fabric. Cisco, a leading manufacturer of telepresence systems, uses them extensively in their own operations. They hold about 7,000 meetings a week using telepresence, saving over $300 million annually in travel costs and offsetting several hundred metric tons of annual CO_2 emissions.

Telepresence benefits extend far beyond simple business meetings. Remote medicine applications instantly bring specialists to remote areas that lack sufficient population to justify the cost of local experts. It can be used in teleoperation applications to allow personnel to operate equipment at great distance, or in locations that are extremely hazardous, as commonly done today by NASA in robotic space exploration or by the military in battlefield UAV (unmanned aerial vehicle) operations. In a sense, teleoperation allows us to "virtualize" highly skilled employees, eliminating the need for redundant staffing at different global sites, and maximizing their utilization across the enterprise.

Robotics extends the idea of virtualizing skilled employees one step further, by capturing skills into rudimentary (i.e., typically rule-driven), autonomous machine intelligence, which can be deployed in large scale throughout production line operations, as is now done with robotic assembly systems in automotive plants, largely eliminating human workers. Computer Integrated Manufacturing (CIM) operations integrate robotics into completely automated production operations, tying together design, planning, purchasing, inventory control, and manufacturing. Robots are often combined with multiple machine tools in "flexible manufacturing" cells (FMCs) or flexible manufacturing systems (FMSs) that are used as building blocks for production lines. These cells can be quickly reconfigured and adapted to different tasks, in effect virtualizing physical manufacturing capabilities, all controlled through CIM. FMCs and FMSs significantly raise the utilization of manufacturing assets and provide enhanced agility to respond to rapidly changing market demands.

Looming world food shortages resulting from climate change–driven desertification, water shortages, and weather anomalies will mandate even larger scale, highly efficient, and increasingly robotic megafarm operations. Already, large-scale farming efforts utilize agricultural equipment automatically guided by Global Positioning System (GPS) satellite data fused with airborne remote sensing based maps of crop conditions.[30] Soon, this equipment will no longer have a human in the cab and will be fully autonomous and monitored from a remote command center, with control of hundreds of square miles of crop production. Robotic operations will be driven by large, complex data sets that will have evolved from today's Precision Farming Data Sets (PFDS) and Precision Agriculture Data Sets (PADS) that combine spatial, navigation, agronomy, and other data layers to support operations such as seeding, fertilizing, weeding, and harvesting. Sophisticated agricultural analytics driven by vast, high-dimensional spatial data warehouses will be used to compare and predict variety performance based on characteristics such as soil type, fertility level, PH, and other current and historical factors. These data sets will be provisioned and delivered through virtualized cloud resources managed by teams that may live and work on another continent.

Both autonomous and teleoperated robotics will significantly change the future enterprise while reducing its Ecological Footprint. Many business units in the future will operate with limited or no human presence. This trend will impact many different industries including agriculture, construction, mining, prospecting, offshore oil drilling and production, medicine, manufacturing, and education. These robotic systems will take over both mundane and dangerous tasks, allowing the enterprise to function with greatly enhanced safety and significantly reduced human overhead. The integration of such machine intelligence into the global enterprise poses a significant challenge for future IT leadership, and entails taking on additional responsibilities that will blur the distinction between manufacturing, production, service delivery, and traditional IT.

UBIQUITY: PERVASIVE COMPUTING, UBIQUITOUS SENSORS, AND AD HOC COMMUNICATIONS

Pervasive and ubiquitous sensing, computing, and communications will dominate the global enterprise of the future. Nanotechnology-enabled MEM sensors are already diffusing throughout the enterprise, sensing force, shock, vibration, location, temperature, chemistry, and other environmental conditions. In the future they will record, preprocess, analyze, and transmit their data findings into the enterprise cloud for processing. Ordinary office equipment, such as printers, will evolve beyond today's rudimentary and reactive self-diagnostics to employ fully predictive maintenance management, supplies requisitioning, load balancing, and cost optimization. Instead of operating as isolated units, they will form self-organizing peer networks for load balancing, resource optimization, fault recovery, and cost effectiveness.

Today's radio-frequency identification (RFID) devices will soon be superseded by new generations of active, intelligent devices that harvest kinetic, electromagnetic, acoustic, or thermal energy from their surroundings to power their electronics. These "always on" devices will constantly feed information into the cloud to support real-time tracking, decision support, quality analysis, and cost optimization. They will drive revolutionary improvements in efficiency and resource utilization that are felt throughout all levels and reaches of the global enterprise.

Future RFID sensors that detect vibration, temperature, and chemical spectra will identify equipment maintenance issues before they become critical. The historical data they produce will drive warehouse analytics that produce highly optimized maintenance and procurement strategies, prolonging the lifetime of equipment and thereby avoiding needless unsustainable waste that might otherwise wind up in landfills. The low cost of these sensors will allow them to permeate through every corner of the enterprise, and the eventual adoption of the 16 octet IPV6 address space with its 2^{128} possible addresses will allow each sensor to have its own unique IP address, much as we assign unique MAC addresses to network interface cards (NICs) today.

Evolving tracking devices based on nanotechnology and molecular electronics will rapidly supersede today's rudimentary hybrid polymer tags. They will be a composite of extremely low power microcontrollers, MEM sensors, GPS navigation, ad hoc networking devices, near field multiband communications transceivers, and sophisticated energy harvesters. These devices will continue to perform their traditional package tracking functions but will extend their reach to other unpowered applications such as asset tracking and location, physical security, hazard detection, material inventory, and safety functions.

As packages move between different shippers and transshipment points, their RFID devices will opportunistically reach out for wireless network access points and report back to the cloud with current status. To reach access points they will build ad hoc, self-organizing near-field networks with other packages in the vicinity to eventually reach a package within range of a wireless network leading to the Internet. Packages within range will advertise the resource on the ad hoc network, helping to build and propagate routing information for other packages. Patents, for example, have already been issued covering this specific capability (e.g., U.S. Patent 7126470—Wireless adhoc RFID tracking system).

Interesting scenarios immediately come to mind. A package containing hazardous material could periodically upload into the cloud data reports on physical handling (mechanical shock), orientation, and chemical spectra (leaking chemicals). If one or more of these parameters drifted out of tolerance, virtual assets would autonomously be allocated in the cloud to perform multi-sensor fusion on the data, looking at events in the recent history. If a potential safety hazard is detected, both the company and the shipper would be immediately alerted and provided with the package location and other relevant data. Similar scenarios are possible for fragile or perishable goods. Criminal diversion of high value items could also activate sophisticated tracking and locating functions that invoke law enforcement action.

Looking farther into the future, other examples of ambient computing in the workplace begin to emerge. Ambient computing leverages intelligent agents and ad hoc networks in the enterprise to tie together distributed sensors and processors that track people, machinery, vehicles, tools, buildings, environmental conditions, and other aspects of the work environment. Where today's rudimentary sensors detect someone entering a work area and switching on the lights, tomorrow's ambient computing environments will continuously adapt the work environment to maximize worker comfort, efficiency, and safety.[31] Ambient agents will use eye tracking and gaze analysis to sense where the user's attention is focused. They will notice that the user has missed an urgent on-screen alert, an important change in a graph, or a recalculation in a spreadsheet and discreetly bring it to their attention, or simply fix the problem depending on the user's profile and preferences. Agents will be used to track users in safety-critical, high-liability tasks such as air traffic control, heavy equipment operation, or hazardous manufacturing operations to prevent accidents caused by distraction, fatigue, and other causes. They will detect and assess signs of discomfort, fatigue, stress, or anxiety, and adjust the environment to make the person more comfortable or alert supervision if safety becomes an issue.

Ambient computing agents will need the ability to reason with highly dynamic, uncertain, and ambiguous contextual information. Reasoning will be distributed and include aspects of biomimetic emergent intelligence. Ambient computing lies at the nexus of artificial intelligence, cognitive science, human factors analysis, psychology, neuroscience, and biomedical science, and is often augmented by a number of different AI disciplines such as case-based, probabilistic, spatial, and temporal reasoning. Agents will have different levels of sociability and perception, and may communicate with varying semantics according to the situation. They will need robust reasoning abilities capable of dealing with imperfect descriptions of context that will result from the inevitable failures in communication paths and sensor nodes.

ENERGY: SMART BUILDINGS, RENEWABLES, AND CAMPUS SUSTAINABILITY

Buildings are the largest consumers of energy in the United States (40 percent) and consume 72 percent of all electricity generated. They produce 39 percent of total U.S. CO_2 emissions and consume $572 billion in annual operating costs. The cement alone that goes into their construction accounts for an additional 5 to 8 percent of all CO_2 emissions. The production of one ton of cement from Calcium Carbonate (limestone), for example, produces roughly an equivalent ton of CO_2 from the high-temperature rotary cement kiln. The magnitude of the problem is in the numbers: 130 million tons of cement is used in the construction of buildings each year in the United States (2.3 billion tons globally). The National Science and Technology Council has established the Net Zero Energy High Performance Green Buildings

R&D agenda to address this growing problem. The objective of this agenda is to. develop technologies that will result in buildings that produce as much energy as they consume, hence, "Net Zero Energy," while significantly reducing greenhouse gas emissions. Another objective of the council is the reduction of building water consumption by 50 percent to approximately 50 gal/day/person through conservation, recycling, and rainwater harvesting.

Buildings today are a far cry from the static structures of the past. They now incorporate sophisticated controls for HVAC, lighting, energy conservation, air quality, safety, security, and maintainability. While many of these systems today have limited integration with enterprise information systems, they are rapidly evolving sophisticated analytics and reporting capabilities that will soon support global real-time building management and optimization analytics and interface to traditional executive Decision Support Systems (DSS) and Executive Information Systems (EIS). The benefits will include higher energy efficiency, improved asset utilization, consolidation of physical floor space, and lower Ecological and Carbon Footprint.

Data warehouse–driven analytics that integrate sophisticated fault prediction diagnostic capabilities now tie directly into building automation systems. These applications analyze patterns of building energy usage over time and identify patterns of faults in electrical and mechanical systems that over time cause a gradual drop in efficiency. These accumulating minor faults typically account for a 17 percent drop in building energy efficiency over a two-year period.[32] Given an average electricity cost of $2 per square foot, this loss can quickly become significant. Scientific Conservation, makers of the SaaS application SCIWatch, recently saved one Santa Clara, California building $126,000 in annual energy costs, as well as an additional $93,000 in energy rebates through advanced building analytics. Similar solutions are being adopted by well-established enterprises such as Harley Davidson, Neiman Marcus, and Santa Clara County, California.

Larger scale Enterprise Energy Management Software (EEMS) solutions consolidate data from the entire enterprise real estate portfolio into a real-time data warehouse managed by an Energy Network Operations Center (ENOC). This center supervises lower-level control systems and building automation systems and provides a variety of remote services including building diagnostics, monitoring, control, continuous monitoring-based commissioning, efficiency analysis, energy usage optimization, demand response program participation, energy cost allocation, budgeting and forecasting, utility accounting, performance measurement and verification, and data trending. A single shopping mall in San Diego, California, for example, saved over $400,000 in energy costs over a three-year period by instituting real-time enterprise energy management.[33]

PHYSICAL SECURITY AND INFORMATION ASSURANCE

Just as the future of commerce is the transnational enterprise, the future of crime and terrorism is one of stateless, transnational organizations. These organizations pose one of the greatest threats to the sustainability of global enterprises. Industrial infrastructure is a tempting high value target for these organizations, particularly in cases where catastrophic environmental damage and loss of life would result from an attack. In the future, these attacks will not resemble military assaults. They will be initiated from across the globe in cyberspace with perhaps occasional on-site infiltration to compromise systems not directly connected to the outside world. Such infiltrations already take place by malicious hackers that use social engineering attacks to gain physical access to compromise networks and network devices, remove data, and manipulate security and badging systems. The next generation of terrorist attacks will focus on gaining control of low-level process control and automation systems that can be used to manipulate physical systems such as chemical process plants, nuclear reactors, natural gas pipelines, electrical grids, and other vital infrastructure that can be used to produce catastrophic effects.

December 3, 2009 was the 25th anniversary of the Bhopal disaster, which eventually took the lives of over 25,000 people when the Union Carbide plant in Bhopal released an estimated 42 tons of methyl isocyanate into the atmosphere. Adverse effects have been identified in over 170,000 survivors. Documents seized in recent years from Middle Eastern terrorist groups have confirmed that similar U.S. chemical plants have been identified as targets, particularly those with highly toxic chemicals that are located in close proximity to high-density population areas.[34] According to the Environmental Protection Agency (EPA), there are 125 plants in the United States alone capable of inflicting at least one million casualties and another 3,000 plants capable of inflicting at least 10,000 casualties. Reports have emerged of an undisclosed study by the Army surgeon general that estimates potential terrorist attacks against toxic chemical plants in the United States currently threaten 2.4 million people. Other reports exist of a plant in New Jersey with sufficient hydrogen chloride on site (100,000 pounds) to potentially kill 7.3 million people within a radius of 14 miles, including much of New York City. Official assurances that adequate fences and security guards have been put in place since 9/11 ignore the fact that the attack will most likely occur in cyberspace and will be delivered from the other side of the globe without terrorists ever stepping on U.S. soil.

There are over 470,000 miles of oil and gas transmission pipelines in the United States, with a high concentration along the heavily populated East Coast. Pipeline control and safety systems are vulnerable to a variety of cyber-attack vectors. Security exploits in industrial automation equipment can go unaddressed for years, as compared to the near real-time patch rate of PC operating systems. Complicating matters, the attack may not be direct. An indirect cyber attack on an adjacent electrical or telecommunications grid can produce the same end result potentially resulting in a pipeline breach and large-scale oil spill or gas explosion. Serious disruption of dependent downstream systems such as power plants, aircraft, transportation networks, military bases, and heating will also occur, adding to the collateral damage. Outside of the United States terrorists frequently target pipelines. The Occidental Petroleum Caño Limón pipeline has been bombed 950 times by terrorists since 1986 resulting in over $2.5 billion in revenue loss. A thwarted Al Qaeda attack in Saudi Arabia in 2002 would have disrupted 6 percent of the world's oil supply, creating an environmental catastrophe. Federal authorities report that Middle Eastern hackers have extensively penetrated U.S. energy infrastructure going back as far as 2001.

Even the destruction of buildings such as the World Trade Center has a serious impact on the environment. In that case, hundreds of tons of asbestos were disbursed into the environment that during construction had been used in a slurry mixture of cement and sprayed throughout the building as insulation. Hundreds of first responders to the attack have been diagnosed with cancer traceable to the uncontrolled demolition and combustion of the building structures.

Given the enormous environmental risks and potential economic losses involved, future global enterprises will need to operate sophisticated intelligence gathering, analysis, forecasting, and response centers to protect global assets from potential attack. Closely resembling government around-the-clock counter-terrorism "watch desks," these centers will leverage cloud computing to facilitate data ingest, processing, analysis, correlation, and alert generation from a vast number of sensors and systems distributed throughout the global enterprise. Information sources will include building security systems, energy monitoring systems, SCADA control systems, automation systems, manufacturing information systems, building automation systems, plant monitoring, and incursion detection systems (e.g., video monitoring, motion detection, acoustics, thermal), "open source" news information, employee reports and debriefings, and assessments from external security contractors. This information will be "fused" to provide enterprise management with real-time 24/7 global "situational awareness" in the form of a "common enterprise operating picture" that globally summarizes remote plant status, security alerts, stability assessments of foreign countries, travel advisories, attacks on similar targets, and known threat profiles (e.g., terrorists, insurgencies, criminal groups, corrupt government groups).

Next generation global enterprise security command centers will evolve from today's site specific centers that handle medical emergencies, HAZMAT response, plant monitoring, and physical security control. Already we're seeing the adoption of some of these capabilities in global customer support centers such as Dell's Enterprise Command Centers (ECC), which was patterned after crisis response centers designed for 9/11 scale incidents. What's required next is the adoption of collection, data analysis, reporting, and alerting practices that have been successfully employed by government and law enforcement agencies for gathering data and producing predictive intelligence. If global enterprises, particularly their IT organizations, fail to stand up to these global security capabilities, the results will be grave.

As graphically illustrated by the examples in this section, the potential for massive loss of life, catastrophic environmental damage, and incalculable financial loss is quite real and growing. In February 2010, when leaders of the U.S. Intelligence Community were asked by Congress, "What is the likelihood of another terrorist-attempted attack on the U.S. homeland in the next three to six months? High or low?" Referring to another 9/11 scale incident they replied, "An attempted attack, the priority is certain." Consider also that ongoing conflicts in different parts of the world have produced an entire generation of battle-hardened foreign fighters that will no doubt be looking to inflict damage on global enterprise targets of opportunity far into the future.

INTEGRATING SUSTAINABILITY INTO STRATEGIC PLANNING

The key to achieving sustainability in the global enterprise is tight integration with mainstream enterprise strategic planning. If sustainability planning is relegated to out-of-band processes and isolated staffs, the many tangible (e.g., cost) and intangible benefits simply won't be realized. This is complicated by the fact that for the majority of sustainability frameworks there is a gap between theory and actionable tools and artifacts, requiring organizations to develop ad hoc extensions to their existing processes and tools. While this has not held back initiatives such as TNS, much more could be accomplished by a sustainability framework based on broadly accepted strategic planning methodologies that are scalable and integrate easily with existing strategic planning tools and processes. Fortunately a new sustainability planning framework has emerged that is based on a solid foundation derived from balanced scorecard and strategy map methodologies that are widely used by organizations around the world.

Strategic planning in many global organizations includes the use of strategy maps describing the corporate strategy, and different versions of scorecards to measure strategic performance.[35] Organizations are embedded in all sorts of detailed tactical scorecards that give them enormous amounts of data to interpret. It is difficult to discern the true strategic forest from this mass of tree detail. *Strategy maps* are an important tool for describing the strategy, and *balanced scorecards* are important tools for measuring and managing movement in the desired direction. Drs. Robert Kaplan and David Norton developed the balanced scorecard (BSC) approach as a result of an early project on performance management (PM).[36]

Their early publishing took hold within a PM audience, even though they were promoting what became a particularly effective approach toward strategic management. Hence the legacy of their early work has been that BSC is synonymous in many circles with PM. That linkage includes a burdensome legacy of cascading performance objectives through the chain of command, job families, and functional aspects of the organizational structure. PM cascades of individual objectives are logically guaranteed to yield sub-optimal strategic performance. Such cascades are almost guaranteed to reinforce functional silos, thereby impeding authentic strategic alignment.

Operational measurement and ensuing operationally-oriented scorecards have been used for decades, arising from various management technologies, including total quality management, statistical process control, and business process re-engineering. Balanced scorecards stimulate a more comprehensive approach to *strategic performance* in the context of increasing shareholder value by enabling consideration of both short- and long-term, the financial and nonfinancial, quantitative and qualitative. Comprehensive enterprise perspectives are the explicit intent behind the use of the term "balance" in this approach. Predictably, many so-called balanced scorecards are oriented heavily toward quarterly financial results to hit annual executive bonus targets. As a logical consequence of demanding financial markets, what some enterprises pass off as balanced scorecards are short on balance. As a logical consequence of objective cascades within corporate PM systems (rather than authentic strategic cascades through a strategy execution system), performance scorecard alignment with enterprise strategy is almost guaranteed to be sub-optimal.

Strategy maps are one-page graphic illustrations of strategic objectives. This management tool has proven to be enormously useful for clarifying and communicating strategy throughout the entire enterprise. Risk management is normally not meaningfully included in corporate strategy maps, if it is included at all. The financial meltdown was a result, in part, of PM incentives that were completely out of balance with a strategy that should have included longer-term consideration of financial risk. The root cause of this problem could be debated, but dysfunctional PM design is a good bet for being included in the final diagnosis.

Corporate risk analysis for the global enterprise in the twenty-first century requires consideration of climate change impacts, their geographic variability, intensity, likelihood, and rate of change. This requires a modification of the traditional corporate scorecards and strategy map, as well as the process by which these tools are initially deployed and then used within a twenty-first century corporate governance system.

Recently, a new sustainability planning framework, the Comprehensive Framework for Resilient Sustainability[37] (CFRS), has emerged based on the strategy execution and PM methodology described above that has been used by business, industry, and government and validated throughout the world for decades.[38] CFRS was developed by Dr. Irv Beiman, who has authored numerous articles and two books on strategy execution, and serves as a virtual advisor from Shanghai, China. Dr. Beiman has spent over 15 years in the Far East helping China to develop more efficient, strategic, and risk-sensitive operating models for the twenty-first century.

According to Dr. Beiman, the CFRS framework integrates the three key domains of strategy execution, sustainability, and resilience. The CFRS methodology is unique in its ability to enable the description, measurement, management, and adjustment of strategy execution for resilient sustainability at five distinct stakeholder levels:[39]

L1: Global

L2: Regional/National

L3: Organizational

L4: Cities and Communities

L5: Individuals and Families

In the context of CIO and CTO influences, this discussion focuses on L3: Organizational stakeholder level, which applies to the global business enterprise. The CFRS L3 strategy map template enables enterprises to design a path toward their own resilient sustainability. The L3 objectives are generally consistent with the output from the 2009 COP15 United Nations Climate Change Conference—the Copenhagen Accord. To the extent there is sufficient alignment leading to sufficient results across national borders and organizational boundaries, the CFRS will mitigate the serious concerns raised by the Copenhagen Diagnosis.

CFRS takes strategy maps and balanced scorecards to a more authentic strategic level by enabling risk management for the global enterprise. CFRS leverages these tools to drive the execution of risk-sensitive strategy from headquarters level down to the lowest levels of the organization. The process begins with a basic reformulation of the enterprise strategy and business model to encompass the tangible and intangible benefits and objectives of resilient sustainability. The output from this process is the CFRS L3 strategy map. Exhibit 5.11 is a generic template for an organization's resilient sustainability (RS), a one-page graphic template for designing the corporate/enterprise RS strategy. Areas for strategic objective setting are identified for three layers of outcomes, plus two critical additional layers, *enablers* and *drivers*. These five layers of objective setting for an organization's resilient sustainability are called *strategic* perspectives:

1. Resilience Outcomes
2. Organizational Outcomes
3. Stakeholder Outcomes
4. Sustainability Drivers
5. Learning and Growth Enablers

The design process runs from the top to the bottom of the map, while the execution and causality process runs from the bottom to the top. Directional arrows clarify strategic hypotheses about how to achieve key outcomes. The corporate/enterprise strategy map objectives are further clarified via measures, targets, and initiatives. Objectives clarify what is desired or intended, and measures clarify movement in the desired direction. Initiatives are defined projects that are resourced (time, people, equipment, space, funding, as requested

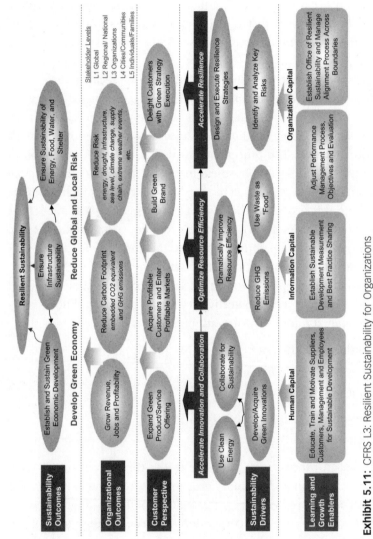

Sustainability Outcomes

Resilient Sustainability

Establish and Sustain Green Economic Development

Ensure Infrastructure Sustainability

Ensure Sustainability of Energy, Food, Water, and Shelter

Develop Green Economy

Reduce Global and Local Risk

Organizational Outcomes

Grow Revenue, Jobs and Profitability

Reduce Carbon Footprint *embedded CO2 equivalent and GHG emissions*

Reduce Risk *energy, drought, infrastructure, sea level, climate change, supply chain, extreme weather events, etc.*

Customer Perspective

Expand Green Product/Service Offering

Acquire Profitable Customers and Enter Profitable Markets

Build Green Brand

Delight Customers with Green Strategy Execution

Stakeholder Levels
L1 Global
L2 Regional/ National
L3 Organizations
L4 Cities/Communities
L5 Individuals/Families

Accelerate Innovation and Collaboration

Optimize Resource Efficiency

Accelerate Resilience

Sustainability Drivers

Use Clean Energy

Develop/Acquire Green Innovations

Collaborate for Sustainability

Dramatically Improve Resource Efficiency

Reduce GHG Emissions

Use Waste as "Food"

Design and Execute Resilience Strategies

Identify and Analyze Key Risks

Learning and Growth Enablers

Human Capital

Educate, Train and Motivate Suppliers, Customers, Management and Employees for Sustainable Development

Information Capital

Establish Sustainable Development Measurement and Best Practice Sharing

Organization Capital

Adjust Performance Management Process, Objectives and Evaluation

Establish Office of Resilient Sustainability and Manage Alignment Process Across Boundaries

Exhibit 5.11: CFRS L3: Resilient Sustainability for Organizations

Copyright © Irv Beiman, 2009. All Rights Reserved.

and approved). Initiatives take place over a planned time line. They are normally focused on achieving a specific strategic objective, although they may impact multiple such objectives. By definition, if an objective is in a strategy map, it is strategic.

This information can be organized in various ways through the illustration of different RS scorecard views. A strategic balanced scorecard for resilient sustainability should not be confused with an operational dashboard, which is normally tactically oriented toward such measurement areas as timeliness, efficiency, quality, and velocity rather than execution of the enterprise strategy in all its aspects. Just as there are levels of RS from global (L1) to organizational (L3) and cities (L4), there are levels of deployment for the CFRS through an enterprise for the purpose of strategy execution. The strategic planning process can be adjusted to include a cascade of the corporate/enterprise strategy map and balanced scorecard objectives down to the next meaningful level of the organizational structure. This often includes strategic business units or product divisions and shared services or functional departments as a next step. The cascading process can be continued in subsequent steps through multiple layers of the organizational structure, eventually reaching individual employees. Vertical alignment from the top to the bottom of the enterprise structure can be achieved during this cascading process. Note that an RS cascade does *not* take place through the PM system. Instead, it takes place through the structure of organizational units, with each *individual's* PM linked to that individual's unit RS scorecard. This is accomplished by the individual and manager examining their unit scorecard and selecting those objectives that individual can enable or otherwise support, then choosing simple metrics or performance outcomes consistent with enabling those particular objectives.

Along with vertical alignment, it is important to also improve horizontal alignment across organizational units during the cascading process. Horizontal misalignments between organizational units are a common cause of flawed strategy execution. This is a particularly salient issue for an organization's resilient sustainability. Every enterprise's RS will benefit from dramatic improvements in resource efficiency across all units. This requires more than the usual operational improvements in work flow and supply chain management arising from business process re-engineering or exceptional improvements arising from significant innovations. It is often the case that intangible misalignments remain among strategy, policy, budgeting, and HR practices. These intangible misalignments can be a continuing source of strategic sub-optimization. Horizontal alignment adjustments during the cascading process can be focused on designing strategic adjustments that create solutions to such issues. Validation of these solutions can be accomplished during the RS governance process.

Strategic governance is focused on the strategic plan. The current status of rationally identified risk issues calls for consideration of risks that are identified at a high generic level by current resilient sustainability templates. These templates enable RS to be folded into the strategic planning process in a systematic and transparent manner. Some enterprise planning processes use a bottom-up process for building investment and profitability plans, with lower levels submitting their investment and funding requests to higher levels for approval. With some enterprises, this can be a back-and-forth iterative process involving a degree of negotiation. Strategy maps, objective targets, and initiative funding requests/approvals create significant improvements throughout the entire enterprise in clarity about the strategy and how to execute it. This enables a rational consideration of strategic budgeting, rather than the more typical iterative changes in operating budgets.

Enterprise governance for RS involves multiple operational aspects, including periodic review meetings, establishing linkages of the RS strategy with budgeting, and HR practices, as well as the establishment of an office of resilient sustainability. The RS office is tasked with creating the necessary enterprise-wide focus on resilient sustainability, organizing the strategic resources, coordinating across unit boundaries, and driving the RS strategy execution process. The RS office mission includes achieving vertical and horizontal alignment for resilient sustainability across all organizational units. To carry out its critical mission, the RS office requires the support and involvement of the CEO and top leadership team. RS office staff work with the CIO and staff to ensure valid and timely data collection of both quantitative and qualitative information related to executing the organization's RS strategy. This information is presented during review meetings for analysis, decision making, planning of corrective actions, and subsequent review of results.

Classic business strategy has been focused on growth, profitability, and branding, with little to no attention paid to risk management. The economic meltdown has put financial risk management on corporate radar screens, but establishing resilient sustainability requires a broader, longer term, and more comprehensive approach toward risk management. Resilient sustainability will continue to be a moving target, mercurial in its status, which will continue to evolve as our biosphere evolves. This requires an ongoing strategic examination of how to achieve resilient, sustainable business success amidst dynamically changing conditions for climate and the global economy, as well as infrastructure, energy, food, and water. For example, water shortages will increasingly affect cost and the regulatory environment for that precious resource. Global changes in country-level national security concern for jobs, infrastructure, food, energy, and water are already beginning to affect country-level government policies differently, based on each government's concerns. Governments will face increasing pressure to impose regulations that directly affect current and future business strategy, creating both opportunity and risk for national and transnational organizations.

The *driver* and *enabler* perspectives of the L3 RS template enable global and national enterprises to manage risk while optimizing resource consumption, building brand, and moving toward more resilient and sustainable business success. The *Learning and Growth* perspective forms the foundation of the strategy map by enabling the four other strategic perspectives. This perspective focuses on arenas of intangible objective settings for human, information, and organizational capital.

Human capital objectives capture sustainability education, training and motivation targets for suppliers, customers, management, and employees. In the context of the current discussion, IT competencies in data center consolidation, virtualization, and cloud computing would be emphasized as objectives to drive *Improve Resource Efficiency* objectives in the next higher perspective.

Information Capital objectives capture elements of sustainability measurement and best practices sharing. These elements would include the establishment of metrics for measuring progress in sustainability, such as Ecological Footprint and Carbon Footprint. These can be used to evaluate progress in higher-level perspectives and their respective objectives, such as *Reduce GHG Emissions*. Techniques for evaluating Ecological Footprint, for example, are complex and enterprise specific, requiring unique metrics and methodologies for computing them to be developed. As enterprise resource efficiency improves, best practices evolve and are captured and reused, accumulating intellectual capital in the process.

Organizational Capital objectives capture elements of the EPM process, its adjustment, and the establishment of new organizational elements to support resilient sustainability. Together they capture fundamental cultural change necessary to institute resilient enterprise sustainability.

Above Learning and Growth, the *Sustainability Drivers* perspective identifies the key sustainability processes, risks, and strategies the enterprise must excel at to continue improving how it adds value for its customers and shareholders. Three strategic themes are identified for operational focus: (1) accelerate innovation and collaboration; (2) optimize resource efficiency; and (3) accelerate resilience strategy formulation and execution. These themes clarify generic strategic priorities for the CIO and IT staff, subject to further revisions and refinement by the CEO and top team. Critical to this perspective is the development and/or acquisition of sustainable innovations. Collaboration across organizational boundaries can be used to accelerate the deployment and commercialization of these innovations. Organizational ecosystems of multiple previously disconnected enterprises are being created for commercialization of new sets of products and services. These organizational ecosystems are creating new requirements for integration across organizational boundaries.

Optimizing resource efficiency is a twenty-first century view of the older cost management theme of improving operational efficiency. This strategic theme has the potential to stimulate significant step change improvements in long-term costs that will flow from the acquisition and development of sustainable innovations. Short-term CAPEX may rise, but longer-term OPEX should drop, relative to the increases forecasted for energy cost spirals. Accomplishing the acquisition and development of sustainable innovations will require the enabling support and technical guidance of the CIO, CTO, and staff. The ongoing need to reduce GHG emissions, combined with the principle of "using waste as food," can lead to significant improvements in resource efficiency. Accelerating the formulation and execution of RS strategy will require access to a wider range of information content delivered from a wider variety of information sources. The CIO's strategic role in this is crucial: to raise the IT organization's level of support to that of enabling the formulation and execution of RS strategy. This may require an adjustment of budgeted resources so that transactional and operational needs are still met, while expanding information resources for clarifying and executing the organization's strategy for resilient sustainability.

Alignment is key to maximizing the tangible and intangible returns from sustainability initiatives. Scrap material from one business unit or enterprise, for example, can be used to fuel a sustainable solution in another business unit or enterprise. CO_2, a potent greenhouse gas, is produced in enormous quantities by industrial processes, such as lime calcining or cement production. In some cases as much CO_2 is produced (by mass) as the product itself. The accepted industry practice is to simply vent CO_2 to the atmosphere after removing particulate matter. This potent GHG, however, has many useful and valuable industrial applications. It's a critical nutrient for algae growth, for example, and represents the primary cost driver in the algae biofuel production process. CO_2 is also used to pressurize pneumatic control systems, decaffeinate coffee, produce urea and other chemicals, and as a lasing medium in high power industrial laser systems. In a recent compelling example, flue gas from coal plants, which has a high CO^2 content, has been combined with fly ash and brine to produce an entirely new form of concrete that completely sequesters the carbon dioxide in a biomimetic process similar to coral formation in the ocean.[40] Information technology is key to creating knowledge alignment within and across enterprises to promote the identification of such opportunities and facilitate cross-boundary collaboration and information sharing that leads to sustainable material reuse.

The *Customer Perspective* objective template embodies the value proposition offered to customers and reflects the associated customer expectations. According to Jenny Dawkins, head of corporate responsibility research at Ipsos MORI Reputation Center, an organization with over 40 years experience in enterprise reputation management, "Our research shows that as of September [2008], three-quarters of the public say it is more important for a company to be responsible in tough economic times."[41] In addition, she states "Also, the level of ethical purchasing has continued to rise year-on-year, so there is now an onus on companies to continue to behave responsibly in line with consumer expectations, while also delivering at affordable prices." As discussed in preceding sections, deliberate sustainability improvements can achieve these results without adverse financial impacts. Information technology has the ability to create not just cost savings that translate to more affordable products and services, but intangible social capital that adds to the value proposition. For example, when Emerson Electric consolidated 100 data centers into just four, they saved hundreds of thousands of gha of Ecological Footprint and a tremendous amount of GHG emissions. At the same time, they earned a substantial amount of social capital that was used to improve market positioning and competitive advantage in a world where corporate environmental responsibility is expected by a growing majority of consumers.

The *Organizational Outcomes* perspective captures both traditional and nontraditional objectives. The traditional ones for any enterprise are revenue growth, profitability, increased shareholder value, and a growing, thriving organization that creates new jobs. Less traditional are sustainability objectives such as lower Ecological and Carbon Footprints, reduced GHG emissions, and a more robust, resilient enterprise. The purpose is to create a global enterprise and its associated organizational ecosystem that can survive the rippling effects of climate change, extreme weather events, rising sea levels, and unstable infrastructure, as well as drought, desertification, and melting permafrost. Unprecedented evolution of the biosphere is creating significant changes in the supply-demand equations for energy, food, water, and raw material commodities. The probability of dynamic supply-demand imbalances must be factored into the global enterprise's strategic planning process. The CFRS enables the enhanced approach to planning that is required for creating the global enterprise's resilient sustainability.

The top perspective in the L3 RS strategy map pulls critical objectives from the top perspective of L1 Global and L2 Regional/National RS strategy maps. The top perspective template identifies three primary arenas that are *not influenceable* by a single global enterprise (although Wal-Mart may be an exception). Each organization, however, should keep these primary arenas on its radar screen for monitoring and subsequent adjustment of lower-level objectives the enterprise can more directly control. The three primary RS arenas have powerful potential to directly impact global and local enterprises. To the extent that global and national *green economies* flourish, climate change impacts are likely to be less severe. To the extent the resilient sustainability of local, national, and international infrastructure is significantly improved, there will be fewer and less severe disruptions in local, national, and global supply chains. To the extent that local, national, and international supplies of food, energy, water, and shelter are better established, these areas are less likely to negatively impact the business environment, markets, supply chain partners, and direct customers of the global enterprise.

Information technology, as shown by the examples in previous sections, has a tremendous impact on the global enterprise not only as a direct source of resilient sustainability, but also as a key enabler of other technologies, groups, and processes that indirectly promote sustainability. The CIO role will clearly be pivotal in driving this transformative process. To gain optimum benefit from the use of the CFRS and its associated methodology, it is critical to establish vertical and horizontal alignment of objectives and incentives across the enterprise. CFRS facilitates this by extending the traditional uses of balanced scorecards and strategy maps to provide a multi-level framework and set of actionable tools for integrating sustainability planning with traditional strategic planning activities. More importantly, CFRS crosses the chasm between high-level sustainability theories, such as

TNS and actionable enterprise strategic planning, leading to a standard, open, cross-domain set of scalable sustainability planning tools, frameworks, and methodologies.

THE FUTURE LIES BEFORE US

The global IT organization and its leadership can have a profound effect on enterprise sustainability by making the right choices, beginning with the strategic planning process. Well-grounded planning frameworks such as CFRS are critical to propagating these changes across and down through the enterprise, while carefully maintaining organizational alignment. As we formulate our strategic objectives we are faced with critical choices, some leading to increased sustainability and others not. If both tangible and intangible benefits are considered, game-changing improvements are possible in enterprise sustainability as well as operating efficiency, global agility, market positioning, and competitive advantage. These changes, however, do not stop at the enterprise boundary but diffuse across supply chain elements as we've seen, accruing benefits along the way. They contribute to a growing wave of globalization that opens new markets, creates new supply chain opportunities, and opens doors to new and unexpected sources of intellectual capital and innovation.

In *The Singularity is Near*, Ray Kurzweil revealed profound and accelerating trends in technology growth that we are now experiencing throughout the developed world. More rapid, however, is the assimilation of this technology in developing countries and the resulting changes in their cultures, economies, and ecosystems. Mobile technology, IT consolidation, and cloud computing are key drivers that are enabling these countries to leapfrog over entire phases of unsustainable industrialization and infrastructure development that older, developed countries have already passed through. These emerging countries are not burdened by heavy foundations of inefficient, large footprint (Ecological and Carbon), and slowly depreciating, unsustainable substratum. They can simply "plug into" the developed world's infrastructure through the global compute cloud and ascend directly from rural, agrarian economies to futuristic, sustainable, knowledge-driven city states. The underlying trends can already be seen today in the rapid migration from rural areas to growing megacities. Asia will have at least 10 hypercities with at least 20 million residents each by the year 2025, according to the Far Eastern Economic Review. Examples include Shanghai (27 million), Mumbai (33 million), Karachi (26.5 million), Dhaka (25 million) and Lagos (25 million+).[42] More importantly, this change represents a more fundamental evolution of the global city-state, distinct from the nation state construct that has dominated global diplomacy and commerce in the past. It also means that if the singularity hypothesis is true, its most profound effects may not be in the developed world, but in the rise of these developing global city states. Keeping up with this spiraling change and the inestimable opportunities it presents will require of the global enterprise unprecedented "virtual agility" as well as "resilient sustainability"—a considerable challenge for today's global CIO.

As the future unfolds, the CIO of tomorrow will have to bridge and master many formerly "stovepiped" organizational responsibilities, skills, and talents that will rapidly lead to an ascendancy of the CIO position in the organizational hierarchy. The technology already exists to make this global transition and adapt the enterprise to the quickening pace. As information technology rapidly morphs, the human dimension must also be addressed to ensure organizational change, maintain enterprise alignment, reinforce relevant incentives, and enhance shareholder value. Solutions exist here as well, such as the CFRS framework, based on tried-and-true methodologies proven throughout the world. The only remaining ingredient necessary for this dramatic transformation is visionary CIO leadership. In the words of the author Alan Cohen:

> It takes a lot of courage to release the familiar and seemingly secure, to embrace the new. But there is no real security in what is no longer meaningful. There is more security in the adventurous and exciting, for in movement there is life, and in change there is power.[43]

NOTES

1. Raymond Kurzweil, *The Singularity is Near* (New York, NY: Penguin Group, 2005).

2. "Global Trends in Business Process Offshoring (BPO)," Everest Global Incorporated, July 10, 2008, www.dti.gov.za/BPO/presentations/Globaltrends.pdf.

3. *Ibid.*

4. *United Nations Environment Programme,* "Climate Change 2001: Working Group I: The Scientific Basis – 6.12 Global Warming Potentials," 2003, www.grida.no/publications/other/ipcc_tar/?src=/climate/ipcc_tar/wg1/247.htm

5. U.S. Environmental Protection Agency, "High Global Warming Potential (GWP) Gases," October 19, 2006, www.epa.gov/highgwp/scientific.html.

6. World Resource Institute, *GHG Protocol Corporate Accounting Standard and Reporting Standard,* (Washington, D.C.: World Resources Institute & World Business Council for Sustainable Development, 2009).

7. William E. Rees, "Ecological Footprints and Appropriated Carrying Capacity: What Urban Economics Leaves Out," *Environment and Urbanisation,* 4(2), 1992, pages 121–130.

8. Global Footprint Network, *Ecological Footprint Standards, 2009,* (Oakland, CA: Global Footprint Network, 2009).

9. Sibylle D. Frey, David J. Harrison, and Eric H. Billett, "Ecological Footprint Analysis Applied to Mobile Phones, *Journal of Industrial Ecology,* 10(1-2), 2006, pages 199–216.

10. Naturalstep.org, "The Four System Conditions," 2010, www.naturalstep.org/the-system-conditions.

11. VSM News Staff, "Virtualization Software from Wyse Technology Delivers Breakthrough Data Center Consolidation," *Virtual Strategy Magazine,* 2009, www.virtual-strategy.com/.

12. Christian Dawson, "The Environmental Benefits of Virtualization," *The Virtualization Journal,* 1(3), 2009, http://virtualization.sys-con.com.

13. U.S. Environmental Protection Agency, "Report to Congress on Server and Data Center Energy Efficiency Public Law," 2007, pages 109–431.

14. See note 10.

15. Sun Microsystems, "Data Center optimization: Three Key Strategies," White Paper, 2009, http://whitepapers.techrepublic.com.com/abstract.aspx?docid=1621377

16. *Ibid.*

17. Jack Pouchet, "Using the Sun to Power Data Centers," *Consulting-Specifying Engineer,* December 2009, pages 16–19.

18. Richard Cockle, "Data Center Being Built on Columbia River," *Oregon News,* November 7, 2008, www.oregonlive.com/news/oregonian/index.ssf?/base/news/1226028328133040.xml&coll=7.

19. John Foley, "Photo Gallery: Google's Scenic Oregon Data Center," *Information Week*, October 19, 2009, www.informationweek.com/news/hardware/utility_ondemand/showArticle.jhtml?articleID=220600963.

20. IBM, "The Green Data Center," 2008 White Paper, www-03.ibm.com/systems/greendc/.

21. Jonathan Leake and Richard Woods, "Revealed: the Environmental Impact of Google Searches," *The Sunday Times*, January 11, 2009, http://technology.timesonline.co.uk/tol/news/tech_and_web/article 5489134.ece.

22. Kellyanne Conway, "Generation 'Y Do I Have to Work from the Office?'" November 3, 2009, www.workshifting.com/2009/11/generation-y-do-i-have-to-work-from-the-office.html.

23. Betsy Stark, "The Future of the Workplace: No Office, Headquarters in Cyberspace," ABC News, Aug. 27, 2007, http://abcnews.go.com/WN/story?id=3521725&page=1.

24. Robert Wright, *Nonzero: The Logic of Human Destiny* (New York: Vintage Books, 2001). Also see note 1.

25. Galen Gruman, *PCWorld*, January 13, 2010, www.pcworld.com/article/186855-2/4g_mobile_services_perpetuate_3gs_big_flaws.html. Retrieved from http://bit.ly/9ZmDIB.

26. Kas Kalba, "The Adoption of Mobile Phones in Emerging Markets: Global Diffusion and the Rural Challenge," *International Journal of Communication 2*, 2008, http://ijoc.org/ojs/index.php/ijoc/article/viewFile/216/179.

27. Clive Longbottom, "The Perfect Device for the Developing World is Not the PC," *ICT for Development*, August 27, 2009, www.comminit.com/en/node/307998/307.

28. Simon Yates, "Worldwide PC Adoption Forecast, 2007 to 2015," *Market Research Professional*, (Cambridge: Forrester Research, Inc., 2007).

29. Elizabeth Littlefield, "At an m-bank Near You," *Finance & Development*, September 1, 2009, pages 49-50, www.imf.org/external/pubs/ft/fandd/2009/09/index.htm.

30. Hemhanshu Pota, Ray Eaton, and Jayantha Katupitiya, "Agricultural Robotics: A Streamlined Approach to Realization of Autonomous Farming," *Industrial and Information Systems*, August 9, 2007.

31. Tibor Bosse, Mark Hoogendoorn, and Michael Klein, "A Generic Architecture for Human-Aware Ambient Computing," *Agent-Based Ubiquitous Computing*, E. Mangina, J. Carbo, and J. Molina (Eds.), (Hackensack, NJ: World Scientific Books, 2009), pages 41–71.

32. Ariel Schwatrz, "SCIWatch Brings Energy Efficiency to Building Automation," *Fast Company*, February 30, 2009, www.fastcompany.com/welcome.html?destination=www.fastcompany.com/blog/ariel-schwartz/

sustainability/sciwatch-brings-energy-efficiency-building-automation.

33. John Mcintosh, "Enterprise Energy Management Systems Reduce HVAC Energy Use and Costs," *California Green Solutions*, February 19, 2008, www.californiagreensolutions.com/cgi-bin/gt/tpl.h,content=1753.

34. Joe Kamalick, "US Chemical Plants Still Targets of Interest for Terrorists." *ICIS News*, June 29, 2009, www.icis.com/Articles/2009/06/29/9228412/US-chemical-plants-still-targets-of-interest-for-terrorists.html.

35. Robert S. Kaplan and David P. Norton, *Strategy Maps: Converting Intangible Assets into Tangible Outcomes* (Cambridge: Harvard Business School Press, 2004).

36. Robert S. Kaplan and David P. Norton, *The Balanced Scorecard: Translating Strategy into Action* (Cambridge: Harvard Business School Press, 1996).

37. Irv Beiman, "The Comprehensive Framework for Resilient Sustainability: A Wake-Up Call to Action for Cities (Part 1)," *Cost Management*, Jan/Feb, 2010; and Irv Beiman, "The Comprehensive Framework for Resilient Sustainability: A Wake-Up Call to Action for Cities (Part 2)," *Cost Management*, Mar/Apr, 2010.

38. Irv Beiman, "Balancing Economic and Environmental Sustainability: A Modest Proposal (Part 1)", *Cost Management*, May/June, 2008; and Irv Beiman, "Balancing Economic and Environmental Sustainability: A Modest Proposal (Part 2)", *Cost Management*, September/October, 2008.

39. See notes 37 and 38 or all ongoing references to CFRS.

40. MIT Symposium, "Sequestering CO2 in the Built Environment," March 23rd 2009, http://web.mit.edu/mitei/docs/reports/calera-sequestering.pdf.

41. Jenny Dawkins, "Getting the Green Light—International Expectations of Climate Change," 2009, www.ipsosmori.com/Assets/Docs/Publications/Core%20Newsletter%20Summer%202009/Getting%20the%20Green%20Light.pdf.

42. http://hypercities.com/.

43. www.brainyquote.com/quotes/quotes/a/alancohen188584.html.

CHAPTER 6

How to Measure and Manage Customer Value and Customer Profitability

Gary Cokins

Measuring and managing customer profitability is increasingly important to any commercial company. The CIO can be a bridge between enterprise finance, marketing, and sales functions. The profitability measurement concepts described here integrate with other topics in this book. As examples, with social networking information companies can assess which types of customers are financially attractive to retain, grow, win back, or acquire. With performance management (PM) scorecards it can monitor how well its sales and marketing teams are accomplishing its customer profitability targets. With environmental impact, it can determine which types of customers are disproportionately consuming greenhouse gas emissions to serve them. IT can foster organizational transformation in this era of the "new normal."

THE RISING NEED TO FOCUS ON CUSTOMERS

While Wall Street continues to suffer from a mentality focused on short-term financial goals, common sense has always suggested the direct link between customer relationship management, sales, and profitability as long-term strategies. This section analyzes the growing art of customer-focused shareholder wealth creation through measurement of sales and marketing return on investment.

Shareholder Wealth Creation Is More than Just Growing Sales

In 2005, Best Buy stunned the business media by formally announcing that they were focusing their marketing and sales efforts to attract and grow those types of customers who were more likely to generate profits for Best Buy. This implied they would pay little or no attention to the types of customers who infrequently shopped in their stores or minimally purchased goods, or only discounted items. Some of Best Buy's competitors immediately pounced on this in an attempt to embarrass Best Buy and broadcast to the marketplace that they would cater to everyone. That reactive maneuver by competitors was a short-lived marketing campaign, and Best Buy held its ground and continued to earn above-industry average profits. Best Buy was simply pursuing what many organizations have intuitively sensed and some have actually measured—there are certain types of customers who are more profitable today and more valuable in the future with long-term potential.

Best Buy was acknowledging a shift in business thinking. It is no longer just about increasing sales but more appropriately increasing sales *profitably*. In short, measuring gross margin profitability on sales from products and standard-service lines is not the only metric to monitor. It is important to additionally acknowledge and distinguish the cost-to-serve between high demanding and low-demanding types of customers to get a full picture of where a business is making or losing money. Accountants refer to this as computing fully-loaded costs. This obvious but often neglected reality is well described by two Columbia University professors:

Most salespeople manage for short-term revenues
(regardless of profits) . . . With an increasingly
sophisticated customer base that wants lower prices,
greater service, and more control; this strategy most often
results in declining profit margins and commoditization.

Increasingly, buying power and market influence is being
concentrated in an ever-smaller number of strategic
customers. Hence, going forward, we believe that
companies will have to think beyond short-term revenue
and profitability of today. They will have to take the long
view and manage their strategic customer relationships as
assets. They will attempt to maximize the net present
value (NPV) of future profit streams from these
customers, thus shifting to the enhancement of long-term
Customer Relationship Capital.[1]

Companies must improve in several areas when it comes to strat-
egizing, measuring, and acting on customer value. Organic growth,
by focusing on existing customers, should be viewed as sustaining
strategy, and understanding customer value is the key to organic
growth. But this is not easily achieved because at the strategy level,
many companies remain focused on "product-out" rather than
"customer-in." If the strategic focus is to sell as many products as
possible, customers get swamped by irrelevant marketing and sales
offers, and they are subjected to poor experiences. It is very difficult
to acquire, grow, or retain profitable customers in that kind of
environment.

To further complicate matters, the CIO is tasked with the challenge
of satisfying two somewhat disparate views and perspectives of their
organization—the information technology (IT) stakeholders and the
business management leaders. Of course, there is overlap, and some
would argue these two views are one and the same. Regardless of the
outcome of that debate, the CIO function is challenged today to deliver
well beyond just maintaining and improving reliable transaction-
based information systems and including effective decision support as
well—which some refer to as business intelligence. In this chapter, we
will address the evolving relationship between an enterprise's CFO
and the chief marketing officer (CMO). The CIO's role is to service
both functions as the bridge between them is strengthened.

How to Measure the Return on Investment on Sales and Marketing

Estimating the return on investment (ROI) on purchasing equipment is near science. In contrast, determining the ROI on some marketing programs may be considered more of an art than science. Thus, a large part of the marketing budget is typically based on faith that it will somehow grow the business. There is a very old rumored quote from a company president stating, "I am certain that half the money I am spending in advertising is wasted. The trouble is, I do not know which half." This expresses a valid concern—and it applies to the many marketing programs in addition to general advertising. Marketing spends money in certain areas, and the company hopes for return. Was that brochure we just mailed a waste of time and money, or did it actually influence someone to purchase? No one in senior management seems to question that sales, marketing, and advertising is something the company must spend money on—but how much money? How much is too much? Where is the highest payback to focus and where to avoid?

Companies are extremely vigilant about *all* spending. They exercise draconian actions, such as layoffs, to right-size their cost structure. The budget expenditures for sales and marketing should be subject to the same intense examination of the COO and CFO as any other spending programs.

The ROI on marketing, and *each* marketing program or campaign, must be better projected—not with fuzzy math but by using modern analytical techniques, fact-based logic, and financial data. After all, in the absence of facts, anyone's opinion is a good one. (And the biggest opinion usually wins! And that opinion is usually one's supervisor or the supervisor of that supervisor.) The CIO function can aid the chief marketing officer (CMO) here. Many marketing functions rely on imperfect metrics, anecdotes, and history that may have been a result of unusual occurrences unlikely to be repeated.

I am not arguing to slash all marketing budgets by exposing them as a waste. In fact, I mean just the opposite. The marketing spend is critical—but treat it as a preciously scarce resource to be aimed at generating the highest long-term profits. This means the need for answering questions like, "Which type of customer is attractive to newly acquire, retain, or win back? And which types are not? How much should we spend attracting, retaining, or recovering them?" Some firms have already enacted programs in these areas to begin trying to answer these questions. More must do this.

Although the marketing and sales functions clearly see the links between increasing customer satisfaction and generating higher revenues, the accountants have traditionally focused on encouraging cost reduction as a road to higher profits. A way for investors, shareholders, and a management team to think about measuring a company's promise for long-term *economic value* growth performance is to measure its customers. Although today the CFO's managerial accounting planning and control systems typically focus on operations management, the CFO is now shifting his or her assistance to the CMO and sales director—and the benefits can be substantial.

The Perfect Storm is Creating Turbulence for Marketing Management

In the last ten years, five major forces have converged placing immense pressure on companies, particularly on business-to-consumer (B2C) ones:

1. **Customer retention.** It is generally more expensive to acquire a new customer than to retain an existing one—and satisfied existing customers are not only likely to buy more but also "spread the word" to others like a referral service. Hence there is an increasing focus on customer satisfaction. The trend in emphasis is toward growing existing customers and making them loyal rather than a focus on acquiring new ones. This has resulted in loyalty programs and other frequency points programs growing in popularity.

2. **A shift in the source for competitive advantage.** In the past, companies focused on building products and selling them to every potential prospect. But many products or service lines are one-size-fits-all, and are managed like a commodity. To complicate matters, product development management methods (PDM) have matured and accelerate quick me-too copying of

new products or service lines by competitors. Consequently, as products and service lines become commodities, where competitors offer comparable ones, then the importance of service rises. There is an unarguable shift from product-driven differentiation towards service-based differentiation. That is, as differentiation from product advantages is reduced or neutralized, the customer relationship grows in importance. This trend has given rise to many marketing organizations focusing on segment, service, and channel programs, as opposed to traditional product-focused initiatives. Business strategists all agree that differentiation is a key to competitive advantage. This was a main revelation in Michael Porter's seminal book published in 1998, *Competitive Advantage*, which launched strategic planning as an essential company function.[2]

3. **"One-to-one" marketing.** Technology is being hailed as an enabler to: (1) identify customer segments, and (2) tailor marketing offers and service propositions to individual customers (or segments). There is now a shift from mass marketing products a seller believes it can sell to a much better understanding of each customer's unique preferences and what they can afford. Spray-and-pray marketing campaigns waste spending needlessly. Companies may even need to better understand their customer's customer. Traditional marketing measures like market share and sales growth are being expanded to more reflective measures of marketing performance, such as additional products and services sold to existing customers. There is frequent reference to "share of customer wallet." Customer lifetime value, to be discussed later, is a trendy new indicator for customer economic value. In short, the message is that companies must now continuously seek ways to engage in more content-relevant communications and interactions with their customers. Each interaction is an opportunity to gain knowledge about customer preferences—and to strengthen the relationship.

4. **expanded product diversity, variation, and customization.** As product and service lines proliferate, such as new colors or sizes, it results in complexity. As a result, more indirect

expenses (i.e., overhead costs) are needed to manage the complexity; and therefore indirect expenses are increasing at a relatively faster rate than direct expenses. With indirect expenses growing as a component of an organization's cost structure, managerial accounting practices typically require enhancing. (Many costing systems arbitrarily allocate overhead to products based on broad-brush averages, such as product sales or direct labor hours; so they do not reflect each product's unique consumption of indirect expenses. Activity-based costing (ABC) is now accepted as the method that resolves this. ABC traces and assigns costs based on cause-and-effect relationships (Appendix 6A describes a basic outline of ABC). This does not mean that an increase in overhead costs is a bad thing. It simply means that a company is required to invest and spend more on expanded product offerings and services to increase its customers' satisfaction.

5. **Power shift to customers.** The Internet is shifting power—irreversibly—from sellers to buyers. Thanks to the Internet, consumers and purchasing agents can more efficiently explore more shopping options and they can more easily educate themselves. Customers have an abundance of options; and now they can get information about products or services that interest them in a much shorter amount of time than what today appears as the antiquated ways of the past. The customer is in control more than ever before. Consequently, from a supplier's perspective, customer retention becomes even more critical, and treating customers as "a lifetime stream of revenues" becomes paramount. This shift in power from sellers to buyers is placing relentless pressure on suppliers. Supplier shakeouts and consolidations are constant.

The combination and convergence of these five forces means that suppliers must pay much more attention to its customers. The implication is clear. Profit growth for suppliers and service providers will come from building intimate relationships with customers, and from providing more products and services to one's *existing* customer base. Earning, not just buying, customer loyalty is now mandatory. But how much should a company spend in marketing to retain customers, and which type of customers should it spend more on? Few organizations can answer these questions.

When it comes to measuring the overall marketing function, many companies miss the ROI mark. They do not have meaningful, consistent, and reliable marketing performance metrics. Worse yet, in an attempt to build customer loyalty, they continue to deploy blanket mass-marketing strategies rather than differentiate (i.e., segment) their customers based on cross-sell and up-sell opportunities. Good customer intelligence systems help organizations make smarter decisions faster. A workflow or business process without the ability to measure, analyze, and improve its effectiveness simply perpetuates a problem. A good customer relationship management (CRM) system allows end-to-end functionality from sales lead management to order tracking—potentially seamlessly. Exhibit 6.1 illustrates key components for measuring the performance of marketing with examples of performance metrics.

The top half of this decomposition tree focuses on customer value management, which is the topic of this chapter. The lower half

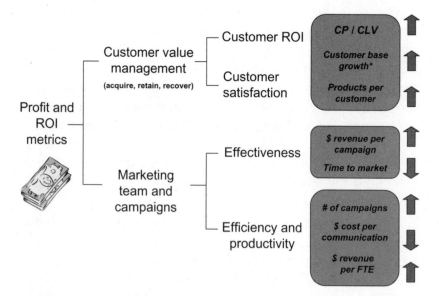

Exhibit 6.1: Marketing Metrics Decomposition Tree

describes the effectiveness and productivity of the marketing function itself, and one of its tools of the trade—marketing campaigns. The CFO should help the CMO measure both. This chapter digs deeper into the two key financial measures for customer valuation management: customer profitability and customer lifetime value (CLV). The following section places customer relationship management into a broad framework and context.

A FOUNDATION FOR CUSTOMER PORTFOLIO MANAGEMENT

As with any other changing element of enterprise strategy, the executive team needs a clear-headed perspective to understand the ways that customer behaviors drive or undermine enterprise profitability. This section presents a rational framework for viewing customer management from the perspective of realigning the enterprise around customers rather than products or services. This becomes the foundation for subsequent development of integrated customer analytics.

Focusing, but Not Obsessing on the Customer

The focus in this part of the chapter is customer portfolio management to reward the company's shareholders. To create higher shareholder wealth, a company must continuously analyze its customer portfolio in innovative ways to discover new profitable revenue growth opportunities. The CIO becomes critical because data typically resides in multiple and disparate databases. A business strategy to realize revenue and profit opportunities will generally pursue the following objectives:

- Identify, understand, and address your best (and worst) customers.
- Target and sell existing products and services to existing customers.
- Target new prospective customers with similar profiles as your most valuable existing customers.

- Develop compelling new product and standard service line offerings, price schemes, and marketing programs for the entire customer portfolio.

- Retain and maximize the share of wallet for profitable customers as well as those who have a high probability of becoming profitable, hence more "valuable," in the future.

A company must possess a number of core capabilities in order to accomplish these objectives. Exhibit 6.2 illustrates how these begin by constructing a foundation of customer information that is a 360-degree perspective with the capacity to reach customers on a one-to-one basis via effective marketing delivery systems. Let's explore these capabilities in more detail.

Single View of the Customer

Companies often have difficulty accessing, consolidating, and analyzing the necessary customer data that exists across their various business systems. This issue is exacerbated with time as the number of

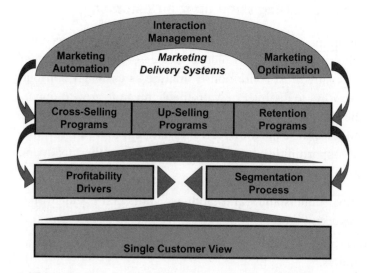

Exhibit 6.2: A Foundation for Customer Portfolio Management

systems and discrete customer databases expands. Becoming customer-centric requires a view of data that involves no walls. For example, a bank should ideally consolidate its information into a single database rather than keep its credit card data in one silo, its bank account data in another, and its mortgage data in yet another. A "single view" of the customer must be created—a view that consolidates relevant and accurate data related to a single customer across different organizations, databases, and operational systems.

Understanding Customer Value and Profitability Drivers

Meaningful transactional and descriptive customer data coupled with the right analytic processes and software provided by the CIO can prove or refute theories about which customers are most valuable to serve and retain and which are not. Understanding customer value and profitability using activity-based costing methods helps define value and profitability segments and their profitability drivers. It also provides clues on how to improve costs-to-serve (and therefore, profitability) in the future. Whether your cost accounting approach is limited in scope to only assign product, standard service line, and distribution costs to customers, or beyond that scope also fully allocates all other costs and capital, identifying customer profitability drivers is a necessary dimension to understanding and segmenting the customer base. These approaches also identify the less profitable (and in some cases unprofitable) customers and provide alternative strategies for how to unlock value hidden in customers as assets.

Meaningful Customer Segmentation Schemes

A customer-centric approach segments the customer base in multiple ways. As an example for a bank, it isn't enough to simply know the ages of customers and say, "We'll market IRAs to the 40-year-olds" or to simply know the total assets a customer holds with the bank and in which accounts. Customer segmentation is much more granular. Continuing with the bank example, it means knowing which customers respond to email marketing efforts or mailers, whether they move money in and out of their accounts and how often, or whether they prefer carrying debt on a home equity line versus a credit card. It means packaging all of this data into a single view of the customer that can be updated in real-time. It is useful, almost essential, to know what the customer is doing today, not only what she did six months ago, and to be able forecast her future behavior based on predictive models. Each industry has its own examples of customer behavior. However, they all typically involve a substantially greater depth of understanding customers than their relatively simplistic monitoring today.

Many organizations primarily segment their customers by the classic "recency, frequency, and monetary spend (RFM)" metrics, by demographics, and by the products and service lines that their customers purchase. In the advanced analytics organizations, these segmentation approaches are viewed as rudimentary, and they do not necessarily relate to customers' future needs or likely behaviors. Without more effective customer segmentation with respect to current needs and/or likely future behavior, companies have difficulty executing successful strategies for improving their profitability—current and long-term—from existing and future customers with new products and standard service lines or increased marketing campaigns. A deficient segmentation scheme may also negatively impact customer loyalty and ultimately increase costs by mismatching product/pricing offers and appropriate customer segments.

Incorporating robust segmentation schemes helps identify movement between segments of specific customers (based on changes in needs and/or behavior) and pinpoints the emergence of new and distinct segments over time. Exhibit 6.3 illustrates the traditional view of how a company may attempt to shift a customer "up to a higher" customer category. In contrast, Exhibit 6.4 illustrates how geo-demographic segments of customers can be shifted across attitudinal and behavioral dimensions.

More sophisticated schemes of segmenting customers by meaningful dimensions, including transaction and mix volumes, demographic, geographic, attitudinal, behavioral, and profitability, yield distinct and manageable groups for targeted activities and differentiated services. Programs such as marketing campaigns tailored for specific offerings or deals have much higher success rates over time due to greater customer response.

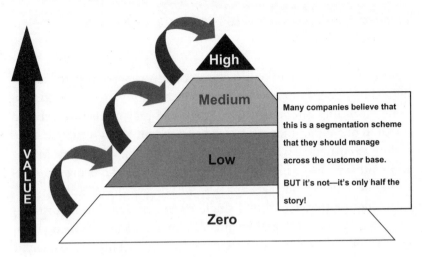

Many companies believe that this is a segmentation scheme that they should manage across the customer base.

BUT it's not—it's only half the story!

Exhibit 6.3: The Customer Value Pyramid

Attitudinal/Behavioral Dimension

Geo-Demographic Dimension	Conservative simple outlook	Sophisticated but safe	Sophisticated high risk / high reward outlook	Unsophisticated high risk outlook
Young/Single				
Young Family				
Older Family				
Empty Nester				
Retired				

Exhibit 6.4: A Segmentation Matrix

Targeted and Appropriate Cross-Selling, Up-Selling, and Retention Programs

Undisciplined mass marketing efforts can cost more than the incremental revenues from new business they bring in. That is, the ROI on some marketing can be negative. Spray-and-pray marketing to broad undifferentiated segments of customers is out. They can also be a turnoff to customers whose mailboxes are bursting with offers. Microsegmenting is in—with the smallest micro-segment being an individual or a household.

Using the foundation of a single customer view, an understanding of customer value and profitability drivers, and a refined customer segmentation scheme, a company can use sophisticated analytic software to predict "what next?" for individual customers. Analytic software allows a company to build predictive models based on customer segment characteristics and outcomes (i.e., demonstrated behaviors), and then apply those models to other customers to determine which customers are good candidates for similar cross-selling and up-selling offers, as well as which customers may be at risk of leaving—either defecting to competitors or no longer purchasing products or services. The CIO must provide users with tools to facilitate these types of models based on an understanding of their uses.

Market basket analysis allows an organization to predict likely candidate customers for cross-sell opportunities given historical data on products and service lines previously purchased by customers, as well as customer demographics, purchase patterns, and other telling variables. Continuing with a bank example, one can identify the purchase stream path certain customers take starting from simple checking and savings accounts upward to more profitable automobile loans and home mortgages. Market basket analysis can lead to insights and potential inputs to predictive models and clusters to identify with greater confidence cross- and up-sell opportunities.

This kind of analysis helps companies understand product affinities by looking for an association between the purchasing of one product or standard service line and another. This association can be detected if two products or services are sold at the same time or even if there is a time lag between purchases. Either way, organizations can identify cross-sell and up-sell patterns, then create models to predict this behavior with more certainty. These models can then be identified to aid targeted marketing campaigns aimed at increasing customer value.

To be clear, market basket analysis and predictive modeling differ in that market basket analysis is more exploratory for learning, whereas predictive modeling applies scoring of customers that enables rule-based decisions for actions.

Retaining profitable and potentially profitable customers is a top priority. Analytics like these examples can be used in a similar way to identify which customers are likely to leave and why—information that can then be used to target effective customer care and retention programs to ensure that the best customers remain with the organization. This ability to predict which customers are likely to defect to competitors—and address the drivers before they become issues—can be a critical competitive differentiator.

Effective Marketing Delivery Systems

After a company understands its customer profitability and their drivers and develops risk-mitigating actions and programs appropriate to serve their segment characteristics, then they need to apply an array of effective marketing mechanisms to deliver the right offer to the right customer, at the right time, at the right cost. Fortunately, there are commercial software providers that with solutions to accomplish just those objectives for the CIO to evaluate in concert with IT organization's customers:

- **Marketing automation software** helps companies plan, automate, execute and measure marketing campaigns. Advanced analytic software integrates with the "single view" customer database, as well as the processes and analytics used to assess customer value and profitability, to develop segments and appropriate cross-sell, up-sell, and retention programs.

- **Interaction management software** enables marketers to immediately respond to changes in individual customer behavior, to execute real-time cross-sell, up-sell, and retention strategies. Sophisticated algorithms can track and recognize changes in individual customer behavior and create real-time triggers and alerts that enable businesses to take instant action. For example, upon an inbound customer phone call to a call center, the customer service representative can follow rule-based instructions to offer deals or make offers to entice the customer to purchase more.

- **Marketing optimization software** helps companies model and assess the cost/benefit tradeoffs of increasingly sophisticated and frequent customer communications. It can provide insight on how marketing constraints affect profitability and can recommend the best assignment of offers to customers to maximize profitability (or some other objective) given defined constraints. Though many of these software offerings are fairly new, the best ones integrate with marketing automation software to ensure a closed-loop marketing delivery system.

The use of real-time customer behavior to improve customer retention and increase cross-sell and up-sell revenue gives companies an opportunity to take a major step toward one-to-one customer communications. Best practices CIOs increasingly take advantage of technology's ability to provide real-time data.

Realigning the Organization around Customers Rather than Products

Even when armed with fresh customer insight, companies fall short if this knowledge does not become a central part of the organization's everyday work activities and priorities. Where are companies dropping the organizational ball? It starts with managing the customer experience. For example, in a bank, from relationship managers and call center representatives to segment managers and ATM machines, the bank must deliver a positive and consistent experience to high-value and high-growth customers. In doing so, the entire organization works together to increase customer value, loyalty, and profit. The majority of companies continue to organize around product groups or lines-of-business rather than customer groups. Such organizational misalignments create poor customer experiences with real financial impacts.

Organizational realignment around customer value cannot happen without technology. Fortunately, technology has matured to the point where it can collect and distribute the customer intelligence needed to keep employees focused on building customer value. When a breakdown does occur, it is because technology is not tied to a focused strategy of acquiring, retaining, and growing the right customers. The CIO can help correct this. Technology cannot do its job if the lines-of-business are working independently with separate solutions and business rules. Technology's role is to integrate data, processes, and people to gain a single view of customers. The best approach is to deploy a suite of solutions that deliver analytics based on rigorous data management. A single technology platform is the organizational back-bone for rolling out business rules on how to identify and treat high-value and high-growth customers. In CIO jargon, some refer to this platform as a unified meta-data repository. CIOs must be moving their IT infrastructures so their applications and analytics can access data this way.

Ownership, accountability, and performance measures are another important piece of the puzzle. It must happen at the management level and the customer-facing level. This is where the strategy maps and balanced scorecards discussed in Chapter 2 fit in. Once the company has accurate customer value scores and tracking mechanisms in hand, managers can establish the strategy, processes, and policies for increasing that value and managing the customer experience. It is then up to customer-facing teams to coordinate to implement management's strategic intent and directives. The company is now in a position to incent, reward, and assess performance based on changes in customer value. Rather than traditional volume-based benchmarks, such as sales, companies can ask "how much has the profitability of the customers under your watch changed?"

Realignment around customers involves balancing a product-driven environment with manageable steps to make better use of customer insight. By mapping the experiences of customers across channels and at each stage of the customer lifecycle, a company gets a clearer picture of where the gaps in execution are taking place. It can then identify which organizational capabilities it must improve upon to close the gaps, including people, processes, infrastructure, and culture. The final step is to prioritize the needed capabilities and draw action plans for achieving results in a manageable time frame.

Preparing for Customer Analytics Integration

Executives must evaluate their company's ability to proactively manage its customer portfolio. They should ask some of these questions:

- Can we build a single view of our customers using all available data sources? How quickly can we merge an acquired firm's data into ours? And with what level of data integrity?

- Do we understand the profitability (and drivers) of our existing customers? Are we more product-centric than customer-centric in our understanding of profitability?

- How do we create and target customer segments? Is each defined segment distinct and manageable?

- If we acquired a company today, could we rapidly determine which of our customers might be interested in a unique product offering of the acquired company? Likewise, how long would it take to tailor a pitch to our new customers about products we currently offer? How would we identify those desirable customers who are at greatest risk of leaving?

- Can we create high-volume, opt-in email campaigns that provide a highly personalized communication with compelling response rates?

- Can our managers and customer service reps access customer profiles on their desktops, allowing for smarter customer interactions?

Affirmative answers to these questions and the ability to execute customer-centric strategies can mean the difference between meeting or disappointing the expectations of shareholders and owners.

Customer value insight drives success. Measuring and acting on customer value is proven to deliver higher profitability, organic growth, and competitive advantage. But the *why* behind customer value is not the problem. It is the *how* that gets overlooked. The result is that most companies have not captured the substantial benefits from more loyal and profitable customer relationships. At least not *yet*.

By refocusing customer strategy, retooling measurement mechanics with aid from the CIO function, and taking steps to realign the organization around customers, companies unlock the vast profit potential of the customer asset. They retain and grow existing customers and acquire new high-potential customers that drive the greatest amount of profit today and in the future. Lasting competitive advantage is not far behind.

DISTINGUISHING HIGH FROM LOW ECONOMIC CUSTOMER VALUE

An undeniable premise lies at the heart of this entire chapter: customer-related costs matter, and this section explores the spectrum of enterprise customers in terms of their economic value. Executive teams that define, identify, and distinguish high- and low-value customers can develop corresponding cost management and customer relationship strategies to maximize enterprise profitability.

Why Do Customer-Related Costs Matter?

Increasing shareholder wealth comes down to three areas: costs, potential customer value, and customer needs. When companies do not sufficiently understand these three areas, they end up placing customers into the wrong value buckets. This ripples out to sub-optimal managerial decisions, the misallocation of marketing and sales resources, and the familiar outcomes of lower profits, slower growth, and no competitive advantage. The CIO function plays an important role merging these three areas.

"The only value your company will ever create is the value that comes from customers—the ones you have now and the ones you will have in the future," state Don Peppers and Martha Rogers, Ph.D., in their most recent book, *Return on Customer*[SM]. "To remain competitive, you must figure out how to keep your customers longer, grow them into bigger customers, make them more profitable, and serve them more efficiently." Over time, enterprise value goes up because the company is maximizing its Return on Customer[SM].[3]

Increasing the profitability of each customer, not simply products and service lines, is a way to sustain long-term *economic value* growth for the enterprise and its investors. How many customers does it have? How much profit is it earning from each customer (or at least each customer segment) today and in the future? What kind of new customers are being added and what is the growth rate of additions? How and why are customers migrating through segments over time?

As a result of varying customer demands for different levels of service, the *cost-to-serve* component of each customer's profit contribution requires measurement and visibility. As widely varying customization and tailoring for individuals becomes widespread, how will companies distinguish their profitable customers from their unprofitable ones? In a sense, it is these customers who are partners selected to grow the supplier's business and wealth creation. Companies now need financial measures for how resource expenses are uniquely consumed, *below the gross margin line* for product costs, by each *diverse* customer.

The problem, however, is that managerial accounting systems of most companies concentrate on product or service line costs (which are often flawed and misleading by arbitrary broad-average based cost allocations) because regulatory financial accounting rules (i.e., GAAP) require compliance. But when it comes to the below the gross margin line expenses, such as distribution channels, sales, and marketing, the accounting rules require these expenses to be recognized during the month period in which they were incurred; they cannot be capitalized and stored in the balance sheet as inventoriable product costs can. Accountants refer to these as *period costs*. But classifying expenses that way is for *external* financial accounting for banks, investors, and regulatory agencies. The discussion here focuses on *internal* managerial accounting to support the analysis and decision making of managers and employee teams. The accountants must begin applying the same costing principles for product costing, typically based on ABC principles, to types of channels and types of customers, so that there is visibility to all traceable and assignable costs. Otherwise, the company has no clue where it is making and losing money.

Today, services are increasingly being added to products, and unique services are being tailored for individual customers. ABC data is essential to validate and prioritize the financial merits of *which* services to add, and for *which* customers.

All Customers Are Not Created Equal

There is an unchallenged belief that focusing solely on increasing sales dollars eventually leads companies to depressed profitability. I support this belief. What matters is a mind-shift from pursuing increased sales volume at any cost to pursuing *profitable* sales volume.

Some customers may purchase a mix of mainly low-margin products and service lines. After adding the "costs-to-serve," such as phone calls for customer service, transactions exclusively in high-cost channels or special delivery requirements, these customers may be unprofitable. Other customers who purchase a mix of relatively high-margin products may demand so much in extra services that they also could potentially be unprofitable. How does one properly measure customer profitability? How does one migrate unprofitable customers to profitability or de-select them and eventually "urge them out"? After the less profitable customers are identified, how can they be managed towards higher profitability? How can profiles of existing highly profitable customers be applied to attract new customers with similar characteristics? If each customer's *value* is not known, then the company is likely misallocating resources by under-serving the more valuable customers, and vice-versa.

To answer these questions, the company must first properly measure its level of customer profitability (or at least segments of customers).

To be competitive, a company must know its sources of profit and understand its cost structure. The CIO and IT organization must provide systems to facilitate this understanding. For outright unprofitable customers, a company should explore passive options of substantially raising prices or surcharging its customers for the extra services. In most cases, this establishes a "market-driven" value proposition between the company and the customer, resulting in either a profitable customer or intentional customer attrition by terminating the relationship. Remember, sending an unprofitable customer to your competitor isn't a bad thing. For profitable customers, increased profit margins can be accomplished by doing the following:

- Manage each customer's costs-to-serve to a lower level.
- Improve and streamline customer facing processes, including adding self-service models where possible.
- Establish a surcharge for or re-price expensive cost-to-serve activities.
- Reduce services; focus first on labor intensive ones that add the least value yet cost the most.
- Introduce new products and service lines.
- Raise prices.
- Abandon products or service lines.
- Improve and streamline internal business processes.
- Offer the customer profit-positive service level options with varying prices.
- Increase investments on activities that a customer shows a preference for.
- Up-sell or cross-sell the customer's purchase mix toward richer, higher-margin products and service lines.
- Discount prices to gain more business with low cost-to-serve customers.

But to accomplish these actions, a company first needs fact-based data about its profits and costs. With this, management will have reliable cost information that can be used to build solid business cases for actions instead of relying on potentially risky intuition or hunches or, worse yet, flawed and misleading cost data.

Focusing on the most valuable and most "growable" customers in the short and long term can have a large impact on the bottom line. However, many marketing retention and acquisition programs indiscriminately address the entire base rather than effectively center on the more profitable customer segments. Having a way to value different types of customers is powerful for developing customer-centric strategies and subsequently determining what level of priority and effort to engage each customer segment.

Should We Pursue the Most Profitable or the Most Valuable Customers?

The goal of marketing is to not only identify potential new customers, but to reach out to *existing customers* through cross-selling (e.g., when I sell you golf clubs, I try to sell you a golf glove) and up-selling (e.g., when I sell you a boat, I sell you an extended warranty option with it). Maximize the value of the relationships the company already has. This is referred to as "organic" growth.

Metrics to evaluate customers might include retention (loyalty) rates, attrition rates, churn propensity, and the marketing standard metrics trio of a customer's purchase history: the customer's RFM. Indirect considerations can include a customer's referral propensity to recruit new customers. Of course, there is a myriad of other socio-demographic (e.g., age, income level, gender) and attitudinal variables that marketers analyze about their customers to understand their tastes and preferences. Analytical tools are becoming essential for marketers to formulate tailored marketing campaigns to the customer segments defined by their analysis. The CIO and IT organization must increasingly provide effective analytic tools for its user community for purposes like this.

Exhibit 6.5 illustrates that just knowing the existing level of profitability for a customer may not always be sufficient. For some kinds of existing customers, such as a young promising dentist or imminent university graduate, their potential future profit as a customer is sizable. However, their current level of profitability does not reveal this. In contrast, for an established dentist near retirement, she may currently be a very profitable customer, but her longer-term value will not be substantial. Therefore, the future potential of a customer, measured along the horizontal axis of Exhibit 6.5, should also be considered. Each quadrant in Exhibit 6.5 suggests different types of actions and treatments to take towards a type of customer to improve profitability.

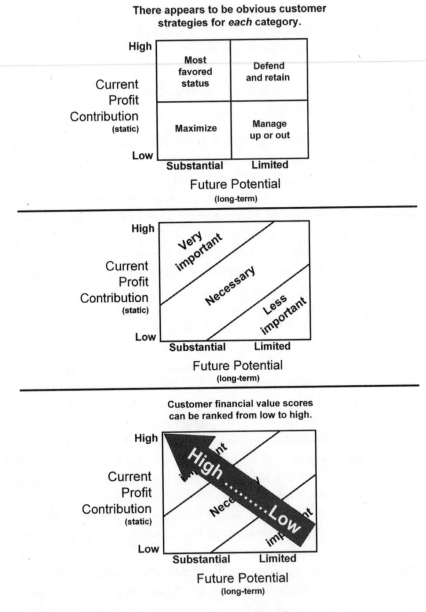

Exhibit 6.5: Current vs. Long-Term Potential Customer Value

Exhibit 6.5 also displays how the customer data points can be rank-ordered into a single customer financial value score based on each customer's distance from the upper-left corner, where the most valuable customers are located. The challenge is to determine the profit return on spending opportunities in order to shift customers to the upper-left corner to increase shareholder wealth.

The more advanced-analytic organizations have become competent in measuring current period customer profitability—the vertical axis of Exhibit 6.5. The ABC methodology and its supporting technology provide the capability to trace and assign the unique consumption of cost that customers, channels, services, and products draw on the organization's resource expenses—their salaries, supplies, and so on. CIOs whose CFO has yet to pursue ABC need to investigate if the CFO's reason for not pursuing ABC is justified or simply due to the fear of too much extra work or some other misconception. Later this chapter discusses the challenge of locating customers along the horizontal axis—measuring the long-term potential financial value of a customer.

Knowing where customers are goes to the heart of customer relationship management systems. Decisions should be made considering the more valuable customers, not just the currently more profitable customers. These examples involve balancing current customer satisfaction with shareholder and owner wealth creation demands—and both involve tradeoffs among short-term and long-term decisions:

■ *Achieving customer satisfaction and intimacy*—Gaining customer loyalty is more than offering "bribes" with perpetual discounts. Loyalty must be earned, not bought.

■ So-called "loyalty" programs are typically just frequency programs lacking intimacy.

■ *Increasing the company's profitability*—How do we apportion our marketing spend between customer retention and new customer acquisition or recovery (i.e., win-backs)?

The sales and marketing functions increasingly require more financial information for trade-off analysis. Measuring customer lifetime value is an important source for financial information.

MEASURING CUSTOMER LIFETIME VALUE

Long-term sustainability is a constant theme throughout this book, and CIOs want to make sure that their executive teams look at the value of a customer from a lifetime perspective. This section reinforces the importance of the ways that customers influence profitability as a part of an equation that includes products and services. This section examines and presents methods for calculating the lifetime value of enterprise customers, both new and existing.

Customer Lifetime Value: Viewing Customers as an Investment

To consider the future profit potential of customers, marketing and sales functions have begun exploring an equation called *customer lifetime value* (CLV) that treats each customer (or segment) as an investment instrument—similar to an individual stock in a portfolio. There can be winners and losers. Since changes in customer behavior are usually not volatile, CLV can be useful to understand profit momentum. Unlike financial statement reporting, CLV measures are not interrupted by "one-time charges" and other short-term but substantial financial statement surprises. CLV links customer revenues to organizational profits. They should never be assumed to always go in the same direction because, as mentioned earlier, high-maintenance customers can be unprofitable regardless of their sales volume.

CLV is a forward-looking view of wealth creation. CLV can be defined as the net present value of the likely future net positive cash flow stream from an individual customer. This involves multiperiod discounted cash flow (DCF) investment evaluation math, not just a single period. This math gets trickier than measuring historical customer profitability levels, because the company needs to consider factors other than what happened in the past month, quarter, or year. CLV also considers the probability of losing some customers. By using DCF math, companies can equate the future stream of net positive cash flow (which are indirectly profits) into a single cash amount (i.e., the *expected value*) of profit stated in today's money.

One appeal of CLV is that it focuses on the customer as the influencer of a company's profitability rather than only the products and service lines that are purchased (although they are included in the CLV equation). Another appeal of CLV is it can also be applied to evaluate which *new* customers, not just *existing* ones, to target and attract through marketing campaigns, and more importantly, to determine how much the firm can afford to spend on acquiring new customers based on their CLV.

CLV synthesizes current level of customer profitability, future potential, and attrition probabilities at the level of an individual customer or household. Customers can exercise their rights to switch to from one supplier or service provider to another. A good example is in the telecommunications industry—cell phones in particular—where annual churn rates can be 30% of the customer base and the relative cost to acquire a new customer can be multiples of the cost to retain an existing one. Predictions of customer attrition are critical because that event terminates any further stream of revenues and associated costs. Industries such as in telecommunications and banking are becoming increasingly competent at developing survival curve models to predict attrition.

CLV can be implemented in multiple ways. It can be used as a customer segmentation tool to segment customer value. It can also be used to segment customers by their churn behavior (i.e., likelihood of terminating being a customer). CLV can also be used to measure marketing campaign effectiveness. For existing customers, CLV can help companies develop customer loyalty and treatment strategies to maximize customer economic value for the company's shareholders. For newly acquired customers, CLV can help companies develop strategies to grow the right type of customer.[4]

Exhibit 6.6 illustrates some of the tactical actions mentioned earlier that a company may take to lift the profitability of a customer relative to the customer's current expected lifecycle.

Exhibit 6.7 illustrates ten revenue and cost elements that determine the CLV of a customer segment over its lifetime. Ideally, the marketers tailor marketing campaigns and differentiated services and offers to assure this planned CLV of each segment is realized. Understanding the CLV of existing customers allows creating profiles,

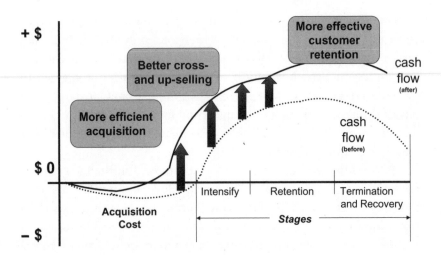

Exhibit 6.6: Leveraging Customer Lifecycles

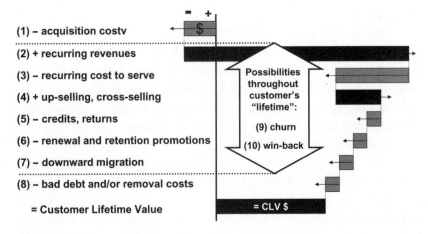

Exhibit 6.7: Determinants of CLV

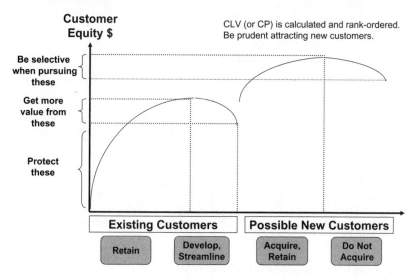

Exhibit 6.8: CLV Value Creation

based on characteristics of customer segments, to attract similar types of new customers.

Exhibit 6.8 displays the cumulative CLV of all existing customers and potentially newly acquired ones. The exhibit illustrates actions and priorities reflecting decisions made for the ten elements in Exhibit 6.7. All customer segments should be managed for higher value, but the strategies will differ depending on the segment. The graph line is rank ordered from the highest to lowest CLV customer. The most valuable customer segments should be protected—their retention being a high priority. Earning their loyalty is critical. Growing value from valuable customers comes next. The less valuable customer segments should be managed for higher returns. For new sales prospects, marketing can allocate appropriate budget to acquisition programs to attract customers with "clone" characteristics to valuable existing customers. The marketing budget spending should focus on higher payback rather than on potentially unprofitable sales prospects. In effect, just like a factory, work to achieve the highest profit yield for each incremental amount of spending in sales and marketing.

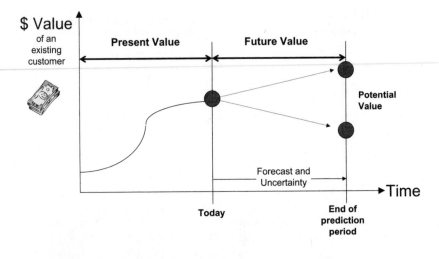

Exhibit 6.9: CLV Depends on Predictions

Copyright © 2006 SAS Institute Inc. (gary.cokins@sas.com). All rights reserved.

Exhibit 6.9 illustrates that calculating CLV involves assumptions and forecasts with uncertainty. Even with customers segmented, forecasting models can be quite sensitive to assumptions. For example, how long will an active customer continue the relationship? How much and when will an active customer spend? If a customer is inactive, is it temporary or did they switch to a competitor? If so, what and how much are they purchasing from a competitor? They may spend $100 with you, but $500 with your competitor. For these last two questions, a company only sees its own data, not external data, forcing it to make assumptions about the missing data. But that simply means you need to gain more competency in statistical forecasting. It is inevitable that to truly manage performance, a shift in competencies will be from control to planning.

Customer Lifetime Value: Investment Analysis Math

Customer value management (CVM) is becoming a buzzword among marketers and is based on CLV math. CVM is an acquisition and customer retention management approach geared to economic value creation for shareholders. As mentioned earlier, a challenging task is

$$CE = \sum CLV \text{ \$ existing customers} + \sum CLV \text{ \$ new customers}$$

> **Where CLV is "the net present value of the likely future profit stream from an individual customer."***

$$CLV \text{ \$} = (-\text{acquisition cost}) + \sum (\text{monthly \$ margin})$$

adjusted for probable number of years of retention

* Peppers and Rogers Web site glossary

Exhibit 6.10: Customer Equity Involves Math

Copyright © 2006 SAS Institute Inc. (gary.cokins@sas.com). All rights reserved.

to locate customers along the horizontal axis in Exhibit 6.5—measuring the long-term potential financial value of a customer. This requires a mindset change to begin viewing a customer as an investment.

Similar to managing equity stocks in an investment portfolio, some types of customers may be big winners while others disappoint. In accounting and finance, evaluating investments requires calculating future streams of revenues and their associated costs. In contrast to calculating the profit from the past month, quarter, or year—a descriptive view—calculating projected financial returns involves DCF math that considers both the timing of future cash inflows and outflows as well as the cost of capital. If the financial interest rate is 10 percent, then $1.10 a year from now equates to $1.00 today. Exhibit 6.10 displays an equation for computing a customer's value score as being the sum of the CLVs for both existing and future customers.

Challenges with Using CLV Math

There are some questions, challenges, and difficulties involved with computing CLV. For example, the CLV equation works assuming that the start time for measuring begins with today. Given this, do you need to go back in time and determine what historical acquisition cost was for existing customers? And how would you derive that amount?

Or alternatively, should you treat past acquisition costs as a sunk cost? Also, how should you assign retention-related expenses? How many periods into the future should be used, since CLV is a discounted cash flow investment calculation, not a past period static one? The resolution to the confusion here is solved when you recognize there are different assumptions based on different questions.

The DCF of a customer's future purchases net of the costs to service the customer is synonymous with CLV. Calculating the DCF of a customer is not as complicated as one may imagine. Although Exhibit 6.11, an example of a DCF equation for measuring future customer value, may initially appear highly theoretical and intimidating, Exhibit 6.12 recasts key elements of the equation into a more comfortable spreadsheet view. The equations basically quantify the price less cost for the expected purchased volume of each product or standard service line less the cost-to-serve (including the cost-to-maintain). These costs are calculated for each customer (or more manageable for each customer segment), and then factored for probabilities.

In CLV calculations, the difficulty with determining the length of the proper planning horizon can be resolved by simply limiting it to only a few years—perhaps just three to five years. With DCF's "net present value," the impact of time on the "expected value" diminishes quickly.

$$CLV^k = \sum_{t=0}^{t=T} \frac{E_t^k - A_t^k}{(1+i_t)^t} = \overbrace{\left(E_0^k - A_0^k\right)}^{\text{Present Value}} + \overbrace{\frac{E_1^k - A_1^k}{(1+i_1)^1} + \frac{E_2^k - A_2^k}{(1+i_2)^2} + ... + \frac{E_T^k - A_T^k}{(1+i_T)^T}}^{\text{Future Value}}$$

CLV^k = Customer Lifetime Value of a customer k
E_t = revenue from a customer k
A_t = expenses for a customer k
k = customer k
t = time period ($t=0, 1, 2, ...$)
$(t=0)$ = today
T = predicted duration of a customer's relationship
i = interest rate

Exhibit 6.11: Calculation of a CLV Can Be Complex!!

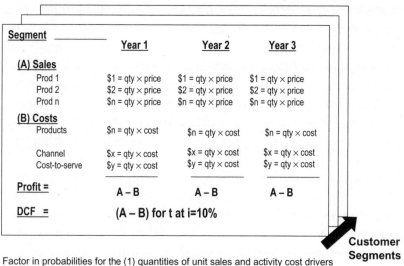

Segment	Year 1	Year 2	Year 3
(A) Sales			
Prod 1	$1 = qty × price	$1 = qty × price	$1 = qty × price
Prod 2	$2 = qty × price	$2 = qty × price	$2 = qty × price
Prod n	$n = qty × price	$n = qty × price	$n = qty × price
(B) Costs			
Products	$n = qty × cost	$n = qty × cost	$n = qty × cost
Channel	$x = qty × cost	$x = qty × cost	$x = qty × cost
Cost-to-serve	$y = qty × cost	$y = qty × cost	$y = qty × cost
Profit =	A – B	A – B	A – B
DCF =	(A – B) for t at i=10%		

Customer Segments

Factor in probabilities for the (1) quantities of unit sales and activity cost drivers for each segment and year, (2) churn date, (3) credit events, (4) etc. ... and calculate and sum!

Exhibit 6.12: Is CLV Math Really That Difficult?

I would not endorse starting off with elaborate CLV equations as in Exhibit 6.11. An organization can begin with simpler equations, using computer modeling, and use estimates for some of the elements in Exhibit 6.7. The benefits will be more in the organization's learning about how to view its customer segments and how to think about the probabilities for elements such as churn and win-backs.

BALANCING SHAREHOLDER VALUE WITH CUSTOMER VALUE

After developing the necessary customer relationship management structures, metrics, and calculations, the executive team begins the important work of strategic decision making to maximize customer profitability. This section examines how these decisions must balance shareholder and customer value, evaluate customer financial value in terms of loyalty behaviors, and weigh the tradeoffs between the creation or destruction of customer and shareholder value.

Evaluating Customers by Combining Their Financial Value with Loyalty Characteristics

Knowing customer loyalty is important because the degree of loyalty directly influences the amount of spending that may be required to retain the customer as an existing customer. Advanced-analytics companies use business intelligence (BI) software technologies to understand psycho-demographic characteristics of customers to predict their future behavior. The CIO is often the catalyst to recognize the need for BI tools for purposes like these. It is not unusual for the customer analytics departments in companies with progressive BI tools to claim the accuracy of their customer "survival" (i.e., defections) projections is reliably high. They can almost predict by name which customer is likely to defect—the question remains, is it worth the extra cost to attempt to retain them? Are they worth it for the shareholders to benefit?

The lower portion of Exhibit 6.5 equated the two-axis data points of the upper and middle portions into a single customer financial value score in order to combine the customer financial value information with nonfinancial information about degrees of a customer's loyalty. Exhibit 6.13 places the high-to-low rank-ordered customer financial value score from the lower portion of Exhibit 6.5 on the vertical axis and combines it with a customer loyalty score on the horizontal axis. With both pieces of information reported about a customer, then the location of that customer's intersection in the Exhibit 6.6 grid implies the level (and associated cost) of offering incentives, deals, discounts, and the like to retain the customer's ongoing revenue stream from their purchases. Less loyal customers will require, if deemed worth it to do so, relatively higher retention spending—and vice-versa. The controllable variable becomes how much to spend.

How does the integration of customer financial value and loyalty translate into decisions and actions? Stepping back, companies must realize that the spending budget for sales and marketing is critical, but that spending must be treated as a preciously scarce resource to be aimed at generating the highest long-term profits. This means answering questions like, *"Which type* of customer is attractive to newly acquire, retain, grow, or win back? And which types are not?"* Then,

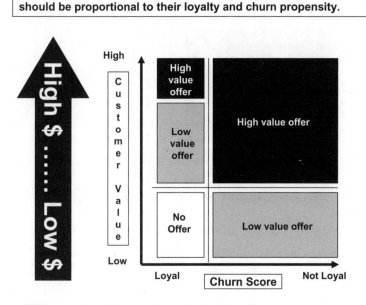

The spending on "actions" to acquire or retain customers should be proportional to their loyalty and churn propensity.

Exhibit 6.13: Combining Customer Value with Loyalty

after identifying the valid types of customers to target (and rejecting those types to not target), *"How much* should we spend attracting, retaining, growing, or recovering each targeted customer segment?" The last question is the needed calculus that leads us to our next point: maximizing shareholder wealth.

Tradeoff between Customer Value and Shareholder Value Creation or Destruction

That last question includes determining how much sales and marketing spending is too much or too little. This is the first derivative of calculus—similar to what acceleration is to velocity. It is about the next increment of change—up or down. What impact do I get by spending an extra dollar or Euro on each customer or by reducing that planned spending by an extra dollar or Euro?

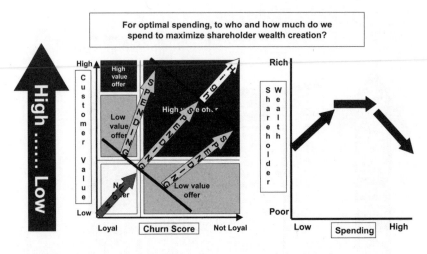

Exhibit 6.14: Value and Loyalty Trade-Off Analysis to Optimize Spending

Exhibit 6.14 expands on Exhibit 6.13 by indicating that not only can there be various levels of marketing spending for each segment, but also that too much or too little spending can destroy shareholder wealth. The added graph on the right side of the exhibit visually displays these tradeoffs as an optimization problem intended to maximize shareholder wealth. Combining customer financial value scores with customer loyalty measures can determine the optimal level of marketing and sales retention spending for each customer cluster. However, today most senior managers treat customer intelligence analytics as a harmless curiosity in a permanent phase of development and trials. As a result, these senior managers wonder if their situation is "should we know?" or "do we know?" It is incumbent on the CIO to educate senior management that these types of analytics are increasingly being adopted and to avoid falling so far behind the competition that they could get a head-start jump where they cannot be caught.

A company constantly interacts with its customers and their loyalty, both by actively pursuing them with new offers or deals and by passively assigning them to a customer segment which is entitled to a set of dormant offers—no actions or deals. How much is too much or too little? Excess spending can in some cases lead to shareholder wealth destruction. You can overspend on a customer to retain their loyalty, but potentially at a permanently lower (perhaps negative) long-term return on investment spending per customer. On the other hand, insufficient spending on a customer can also lead to shareholder wealth destruction. This is because the company risks losing that under-served customer to a competitor or risks its reduced spending frequency or amounts purchased, thus sacrificing the customer lifetime value for that customer.

Are there skeptics that suggest CLV math is too much ivory tower? Of course there are. Even the academics have yet to deeply explore these interdependent relationships. Here is a quote from an academic journal:

> Customer value management can be regarded as the key driver of Shareholder Value . . . (but) surprisingly, although being of obvious importance, literature taking a more comprehensive view of customer valuation has only recently been appearing. A composite picture of customers and investors is hardly found in business references.[5]

However, such skepticism may be unwarranted. For example, although survival analysis modeling, a component of CLV, appears challenging, increasing companies involved with subscription renewal customers are achieving competency with these projections. Further, the concept of integrating customer value and shareholder value is being addressed by the leading authorities in the field of customer relationship management, Don Peppers and Martha Rogers. Here is a quote from their 2005 book, *Return on Customer*:

> A higher promotion budget might improve customer acquisition. But each new acquisition will be more expensive. It's possible to wind up spending more than a new incremental(ly lower profit) customer will ever be worth.

> Creating value from customers is an optimization problem. Often, however, the tradeoffs occur in terms of generating increased future cash flows with adverse results of reduced current cash flows, or vice-versa . . . If CLV doesn't improve enough to offset increased costs, then value will be destroyed, even as loyalty improves.[6]

By integrating customer relationship management with shareholder wealth creation and destruction, both of these topics are placed into the context of PM.

CLV or Only Customer Profitability? When Is CLV Applicable?

CLV is understandably perceived as difficult to calculate with any degree of certainty. It is also perceived as hard to use. Hence, those managers who are cognizant that customers generate different profit levels relative to their sales typically only have confidence in a customer's *current* profitability—that is, if their accountants are measuring it—which most do not.

So is it feasible to measure CLV, and is it practical to try? For some companies, periodic customer profitability reporting with ABC can be a sufficiently good proxy or surrogate for the CLV measure. This could preclude any need to get more sophisticated. Others may see usefulness in calculating CLV, but wonder if the climb is worth the view—that is, will the benefits from using the data outweigh the administrative effort to collect and compute the data, plus train employees how to use it?

Companies with ABC systems have proven they can repeatedly and reliably report and score customer profitability information. The benefits with actual customer profitability reporting come from the insight managers and analysts gain by comparing profiles of customers with varying degrees of profitability. This information alone, particularly for business-to-business (B2B) companies whose customers do not experience lifecycles, may be sufficient to formulate new marketing strategies and to budget future marketing spending for higher payback.

CLV is *more* applicable when a company has a database with customer profiles and their transaction history data. That is, the company already knows a lot about them. CLV is *less* applicable if a company works through B2B sales channels that preclude a *direct* relationship, and hence intelligence, with end-consumers.

That is, it may be sufficient to simply begin with measuring current profitability for existing customers rather than advance to the more sophisticated CLV.

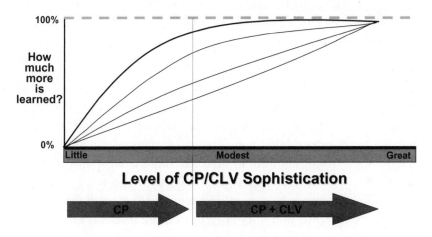

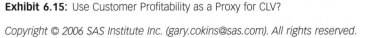

Exhibit 6.15: Use Customer Profitability as a Proxy for CLV?

Exhibit 6.15 illustrates the rate of learning about a customer's value relative to the level of analytical sophistication. It implies that much can be learned just with measuring customer profitability and applying rank-orders to formulating marketing strategies. Beyond that, adding CLV insights about future potential can add to the learning and enhance formulating even better marketing strategies.

There should be little argument, given the power of computers and data warehouses, that computing CLV with some degree of accuracy is feasible.

THE CFO AND CIO MUST SHIFT EMPHASIS

Customer value and profitability management require changes to the conventional working structures of traditional executive teams. The CMO becomes the customer advocate, and as the primary stewards of enterprise BI data and systems, the CIO and CFO provide the CMO's team with integrated information about the best customers and sales prospects. This section addresses the intersection between BI and PM with ways that the CIO can optimize the balance between customer and shareholder value creation.

The CFO and CIO Must Serve the CMO and Sales Director

This discussion began by stating that senior management has had unquestioned views that marketing and advertising is something the company must spend money on—but how much money? How much is too much? Where is the highest payback to focus and where to avoid? It is inevitable that the answers to these questions require a contribution from the business analysts using managerial accounting techniques. The day is coming that the CFO, supported by the CIO, must now turn his or her attention from operations and cost control to support the CMO and sales director to more intelligently focus on the right kinds of customers and sales prospects.

The CIO faces challenges because there is confusion today about what the difference is between mainstream BI[7] and PM. Are BI and PM synonymous? Is BI a part of PM? Or is PM a part of BI?

This ambiguity arises because the underlying inputs, processes, outputs, and outcomes of an organization—whether a public sector government agency or a commercial business—may arguably have some parts that belong to BI, while others belong to PM. The key word in that sentence was "arguably." This argument arises because IT-centric people often see an enterprise as a ravenous consumer of billions of bytes of data intended to manage the business (a BI view). In contrast, leaders, managers, and employee teams typically view the same enterprise as an organism with a purpose and mission (a PM view); they desire solutions and applications that achieve results. How can BI and PM be reconciled? It is important that CIOs assist their organizations in answering this question.

How Do Business Intelligence and Performance Management Relate to Each Other?

There are two things related to this topic that most people can agree upon: (1) BI involves raw data that must first be *integrated* from disparate source systems and then *transformed* into information; and (2) BI and PM *leverage* that information. In this context, information is much more valuable than data points, because integrating and transforming data using calculations and pattern discovery results in potentially meaningful information that can be used for decisions. The key point here is to apply analytics with BI and PM for better decision making. For example, an automobile manufacturer's warranty claims can be globally analyzed to detect a design problem. In another instance, the history of an individual's credit card purchase transaction data can be converted to information that, in turn, can be used for decisions by retailers to better serve the customer or provide customized offers to sell more to them.

A survey by the global technology consulting firm Accenture reported that senior U.S. executives are increasingly more disenchanted with their analytic and BI capabilities.[8] Although they acknowledged that their BI (regardless of how they personally define it) provides a display of data in terms of reporting, querying, searching, and visual dashboards, they felt their mainstream BI still fell short. An organization's interest is not just to *monitor* the dials; it is, more importantly, to *move* the dials. That is, just reporting information does not equate to managing for better results; what is needed are actions and decisions to *improve* the organization's performance. Having mainstream BI capability is definitely important; however, it often came about as the result of departments needing advances that the IT function could not provide. Extending BI across the organization so that mini-BI applications can talk is a mission-critical differentiator for organizational success and competitiveness. Some organizations refer to this extension as "big BI" to emphasize the importance of using analytic analysis with BI information, and the portfolio of methodologies that comprise PM.

Professor Tom Davenport of Babson College authored a January 2006 *Harvard Business Review* article proposing that the next differentiator for competitive advantage will be predictive analytics.[9] He has coined the phrase, "competing on analytics." His premise is that change at all levels has accelerated so much that reacting after-the-fact is too late and risky. He asserts that organizations must anticipate change to be proactive rather than reactive, and the primary way is through robust quantitative analysis that is forward-looking.

Predictive analytics becomes an obvious feature for BI and PM to help an organization understand where it has been and why, and then to determine strategy-aligned actions for decision-making with realistic target-setting.

Managing and improving are not the same things. Many people manage like coaching a sports team, and they get by. *Improving*, on the other hand, is how an organization wins. To differentiate BI from PM, PM can be viewed as *deploying* the power of BI, but the two are inseparable. Think of PM as an *application* of BI. PM adds context and direction for BI. BI is an enterprise information platform for querying, reporting, and much more, which when combined with the methodologies of PM makes them both the foundation to drive organizational improvement with analytics. PM drives the strategy and leverages all of the processes, methodologies, metrics, and systems that monitor, manage, and most importantly, *improve* enterprise performance. Together, BI and PM form the bridge, powered by analytics, that connects data to decisions.

With PM, the strategy spurs the application of technology, methodologies, and software. As methodologies—which are typically implemented or operated in isolation of each other—are integrated, the strength and power of PM grows. Technologies, such as software that the CIO is responsible for installing, support the methodologies. Software is an essential enabler, but the critical part is in the thinking. That is, one must understand the assumptions used in configuring commercial software and, more importantly, have a vision of the emerging possibilities to apply the new knowledge that BI and PM produce.

Ultimately it is advisable that organizations not waste valuable energy debating BI versus PM—they may get caught up in semantics—and agree that PM deploys the power in BI with its enterprise information platform, so that organizations can advance from managing to improving.

Optimizing the Balance between Customer Value and Shareholder Value

To maximize shareholder wealth, the company must dig much deeper than predicting income statements and balance sheets to compute "free cash flow" as the financial community does today. They must look at CLV and return-on-customer concepts as the core determinant (i.e., driver) of shareholder wealth creation, combined with these other factors—customers. CVM is a "bottom up" rather than a "top down" calculation. In summary, it is essential to have the analytical tools, such as for customer segmentation, loyalty analysis, forecasting, and ABC for calculating customer value, reducing internal debates, and making tradeoff decisions. It is inevitable that a company's executive team will navigate shareholder wealth creation based on facts, not hunches and intuition.

APPENDIX 6A: ACTIVITY-BASED COSTING IS A COST REASSIGNMENT NETWORK

In complex support-intensive organizations, there can be a substantial chain of indirect activities prior to the work activities that eventually trace into the *final cost objects*. These chains result in activity-to-activity assignments, and they rely on *intermediate* activity drivers in the same way that final cost objects rely on activity drivers to reassign costs into them based on their diversity and variation.

The *direct costing* of indirect costs is no longer, as it was in the past, an insurmountable problem given the existence of integrated ABC/M software, like the SAS Institute's SAS Activity-Based Management (ABM) software. ABC allows *intermediate* direct costing to a local process or to an internal customer or required component that is causing the demand for work. ABC cost flow networks no longer have to "hit the wall" from limited spreadsheet software that is restricted by columns-to-rows math. ABC/M software is arterial in design. Eventually via this expense assignment and tracing network, ABC reassigns 100% of the costs into the final products, service lines, channels, customers, and business sustaining costs. In short, ABC connects customers to the unique resources they consume—and in proportion to their consumption.

The ABC cost assignment network in Exhibit 6A.1 consists of the three modules connected by cost assignment paths. This network calculates the cost of cost objects (e.g., outputs, product lines, service lines, or customers). It is basically a "snapshot" view of the business conducted during a specific time period. (Lifecycle costing is described under the section, "Measuring Customer Lifetime Value.")

Resources, at the top of the cost assignment network, are the capacity to perform work because they represent all the available means upon which work activities can draw. Resources can be thought of as the organization's checkbook; this is where all the period's expenditure transactions are accumulated into buckets of spending. Examples of resources are salaries, operating supplies, or electrical power. These are the period's cash outlays and amortized cash outlays, such as for depreciation, from a prior period. It is during this step that the applicable resource drivers are developed as the mechanism to convey resource costs to the activity.

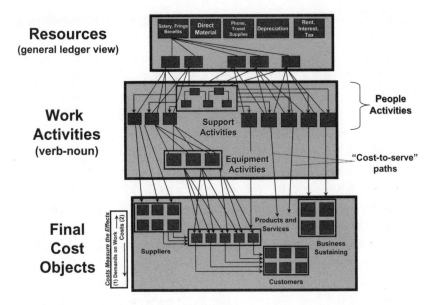

Exhibit 6A.1: ABC/M Cost Assignment Network

"Expenses" must be distinguished from "costs." They are not the same thing. All costs are *calculated* costs. It is important to recognize that assumptions are always involved in the conversion and translation of expenses into costs. The assumptions stipulate the basis for the calculation. Expenses occur at the point of acquisition with third parties, including employee wages. This is when money (or its obligation) exits the company. At that special moment, "value" does not fluctuate; it is permanently recorded as part of a legal exchange. From the expenses, all costs are *calculated* representations of how those expenses flow through work activities and into outputs of work.

In sum, resources are traced to work activities. It is during this step that the applicable resource drivers are developed as the mechanism to convey resource expenses into the activity costs.

A popular basis for tracing or assigning resource expenses is the time (e.g., number of minutes) that people or equipment use to perform activities. Note that the terms *tracing* or *assigning* are preferable to the term *allocation*. This is because many people associate the *allocation* with a redistribution of costs that have little to no correlation between source and destinations; hence to some organizations overhead cost allocations are felt to be arbitrary and are viewed cynically.

The activity module is where work is performed. It is where resources are converted into some type of output. The activity cost assignment step contains the structure to assign activity costs to cost objects (or to other activities), utilizing activity drivers as the mechanism to accomplish this assignment.

Cost objects, at the bottom of the cost assignment network, represent the broad variety of outputs and services where costs accumulate. The customers are *the final-final cost objects*; their existence ultimately creates the need for a cost structure in the first place. Cost objects are the persons or things that benefit from incurring work activities. Examples of cost objects are products, service lines, distribution channels, customers, and outputs of internal processes. Cost objects can be thought of as *the what* or *for whom* work is done.

Once established, the cost assignment network is useful in determining how the diversity and variation of things, such as different products or various types of customers, can be detected and translated into how they uniquely consume the activity costs that draw on resource expenses.

NOTES

1. Peter F. Mathias and Noel Capon, "Managing Strategic Customer Relationships as Assets," *Velocity* 5 no 2 (1st quarter, 2003): 46.
2. Michael E. Porter, *Competitive Advantage: Creating and Sustaining Superior Performance*, (New York: Free Press, 1985).
3. Don Peppers and Martha Rogers, Ph.D., *Return on Customer: Creating Maximum Value from Your Scarcest Resource*, (New York: Currency/DoubleDay, 2005) page 9. Return on Customer[SM] and ROC[SM] are registered service marks of Peppers & Rogers Group, a division of Carlson Marketing Group.
4. Junxiang Lu, "Modeling Customer Lifetime Value Using Survival Analysis," www2.sas.com/proceedings/sugi28/120-28.pdf.
5. T. Bayon, J. Gutsche, and H. Bauer, "Customer Equity Marketing" *European Management Journal* (June 2002) page 213.
6. See note 3, pages 12–13.
7. The information technology community distinguishes between "little" business intelligence for query and reporting and "big" business intelli-

gence for the platform where information is stored and managed. This chapter's emphasis is on the latter.

8. Accenture.com, 2005 News Release; "Companies Need to Improve Business Intelligence Capabilities to Drive Growth, Accenture Study Finds," www. accenture.com/xd/xd.asp?it=enweb&xd=_dyn%5Cdynamicpressrelease_ 809.xml.

9. Thomas H. Davenport, "Competing on Analytics," *Harvard Business Review*, January 2006.

CHAPTER **7**

Evolution of Networks into Networking

Karl Schubert

EVOLUTION OF NETWORKS INTO NETWORKING: COMPUTATIONAL, DATA, BUSINESS, AND PERSONAL

Over the past nearly 40 years, *networks*—that is, communications, computational, data, and business networks—have become an increasingly important part of our professional lives. Over just the past ten years they have become critical—as they have woven themselves into the fabric of our day-to-day lives. Advances in *network technology* have become the catalyst for the evolution of *networking* as an everyday aspect of the personal and professional life of the CIO.

Communications networks capacity has grown by orders of magnitude as have corporate and personal bandwidth access needs, but the cost of using this bandwidth has also diminished significantly. Between 1999 and 2008 the cost of bandwidth has decreased from $1,197 per 1,000 mbps to $130 mbps—nearly an order of magnitude reduction.[1]

At the same time, as the cost of bandwidth has gone down by one order of magnitude, the *availability* of high-speed bandwidth has

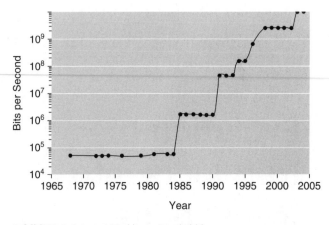

Exhibit 7.1: Internet Backbone Bandwidth

Source: *Raymond Kurzweil,* The Singularity is Near *(New York, NY: Penguin Group, 2005). Ray Kurzweil, http://singularity.com/charts/page81.html.*

increased *at least two orders of magnitude* over the same period, as shown in Exhibit 7.1. In other words, the overall change in this ten-year period was more than *three orders of magnitude.* In the early 2000s, it was oftentimes said that bandwidth would be free. Relatively speaking, this consideration must be understood in the cost and access context of that period of IT industry development.

Voice communications have changed significantly over this same period—from use of "land lines" to cell phones, where nearly anyone can own a telephone number of their choosing that permanently belongs to the them, regardless of where they live. The explosion of voice communications over the data networks (VoIP or Voice over IP) for business and personal communications is phenomenal. Users have the ability to call into and from these networks into the public telecommunications networks through applications such as Skype and Vonage. An added capability with these applications is that they make it feasible to teleconference with multiple parties and even with video. This is unimaginably different from the Picturephones Western Electric displayed in 1964.

Computational network capacity has also grown orders of magnitude over the past three decades and shows no signs of slowing down. Whenever a prediction has been made that the limits of computation have been reached, new breakthroughs and approaches reset the prediction. What thirty years ago needed an entire room to house a substation to power and a building chiller to cool, now fits in your hand and runs at ambient temperature. Data network capacity growth has been at a higher rate than nearly anyone could have foreseen, and the costs to store, access, and transfer data have done so, too.

The ability to store, retrieve, move, and *share* incredible amounts of data at lightning speed has opened up the online marketplace for businesses far beyond the original vision for Electronic Data Interchange (EDI).[2] This has enabled businesses to affordably keep their data online, and to be able to mine that data for additional business opportunities. This IT trend has also *enabled* customers to keep their records and mementos (tax records, music, photographs) online and share with their families and friends.

Business networks capacity has grown in the past thirty years from being Basically point-to-point to universal connectivity and availability. Customers can now connect from and to nearly anywhere and have that connection be as fast as needed. At the same time, it is very difficult in today's world to do business without being on the network, and there are significant untapped network capacities and technological breakthroughs on the horizon that will greatly increase such access. Thirty years ago, it would not have been possible to videoconference a half-dozen people and/or sites around the world, and what little videoconferencing that enterprise employees actually utilized required very sophisticated rooms with very expensive equipment (more than $1 million) to yield very poor results. Today, a six-person or six-site videoconference can be initiated by an individual on a personal workstation connected to the network right from a home office using the camera, microphone, and speakers that come standard with laptop computers—all for under $1,000.

Personal networks have emerged over the past thirty years with remarkably accelerated capacities over the past 20 years. These networks started with online access to the privileged few through services such as CompuServe,[3] Prodigy,[4] and AOL,[5] growing to have millions of subscribers by the 1990s and evolving to more basic online communities from the early twenty-first century. Providing the fuel for the use of these personal networks has been the general public's access to personal computers, capacity growth and cost reductions, training on the use of computers in K-12 schools, the proliferation of cell phones, digital photography, and last but not least, online sharing sites such as Facebook, MySpace, LinkedIn, Plaxo, Flickr, Shutterfly, SnapFish, and many others. All age groups—young, middle-aged, elderly—use personal networks. Naturally, enterprises also leverage personal networks.

In a recent study of long-term trends, researchers summarized their findings.

> The exponentially advancing price/performance capability of computing, storage, and bandwidth is driving an adoption rate for our new "digital infrastructure" that is two to five times faster than previous infrastructures, such as electricity and telephone networks.

> More than just bits and bytes, this digital infrastructure consists of institutions, practices, and protocols that together organize and deliver the increasing power of digital technology to business and society.[6]

It is this delivery of technology and capability to business and society that lies at the heart of the dilemma for CIOs and CTOs today: Businesses want and need access to *networks* (electronic communities) to reach—that is network with—their current and potential customers. Businesses are concerned that access to these same networks by their employees could pose a security or competitive risk through direct or indirect disclosure or productivity losses by employees being distracted by non-business activities. This chapter explores best practice answers for CIOs who allow employees to have what they want while strategically enabling enterprise IT values and policies, and reflects the most comprehensive range of considerations as expressed by the CIO Council's Information Security and Identity Management Committee and Network and Infrastructure Security Subcommittee: "The decision to embrace social media technology is a risk-based decision, not a technology-based decision. It must be made based on a strong business case, supported at the appropriate level . . . considering its . . . space, threats, technical capabilities, and potential threats."[7]

ADVANCES IN COMPUTATIONAL AND DATA NETWORKS

Thirty years ago, most commercial data was stored on computer tapes, and this data was accessible only by sequentially moving through the tape. For the most part, a computer operator mounted these tapes by hand. This typically took several minutes, unless the operator knew the request was coming and had the tape ready. Then, once mounted, the computer program's search for the right data on the tape could take several more minutes. The operator would repeat this procedure with as many tapes as necessary until the data were finally located. Today, enterprises of all sizes store most of their commercial data on disk drives in storage systems with *orders of magnitude* more data capacity that is accessible *randomly* (i.e., *immediately* for all practical purposes) and *without human intervention*.

Also, thirty years ago, most commercial data could only be stored, retrieved, and used by someone who had direct access to the hardware and the data—physical presence. Today, most enterprises store commercial data in facilities that are network-connected, and access is controlled by a combination of prior authorization and ability to connect to where the data is stored. This access ranges from the cornucopia of data accessible by anyone on the Internet to secure applications that access data on private networks—all with personal computers and some of the more sophisticated cellular phones.

Computational networks have evolved through a combination of scientific and engineering advances in both the computing network themselves (processors and servers), and storage networks (disk drives, subsystems, and switches). No single approach to building these components has had a greater effect than the use of commercial-off-the-shelf (COTS) technology. COTS technology approaches have proven to provide significant cost advantages in the manufacture, service, and evolution of information technology in recent years, most highly visible in the area of personal computers and smartphones, and more recently, with computer servers and computer disks. A combination of technological innovation, manufacturing, and production advances along in the context of widespread commercialization in business- and mission-critical applications have enabled this shift from highly

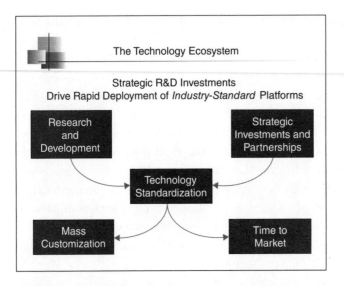

Exhibit 7.2: The Technology Ecosystem: Leveraging COTS

Source: *Karl Schubert, "Delivering on Strategic Value Propositions in Product-Based Corporations." The Institute of Management Accountants 2001 CFO/Controller Conference, Orlando, Florida.*

proprietary and costly technology to cost-effective COTS technology, as shown in Exhibit 7.2.

This technology standardization has come about through a combination of focused research, development, strategic partnerships, and investments by the commercial technology industries. The beneficiaries have been the users of these technology-based products in terms of improved costs, performance evolution, and effectiveness regarding price and performance, reduced ongoing service, and support costs. These technologies have been successful in commercial and non-commercial environments. The basis for projecting the advances in these "technology ecosystems" has its roots in a phenomenon now known as Moore's Law.

In 1965, Dr. Gordon E. Moore, co-founder of Intel, hypothesized that approximately every two years, the number of transistors that will be able to be placed onto an integrated circuit would double with a roughly linear correlation between the number of transistors and the speed of the processor chip, as shown in Exhibit 7.3. Now referred

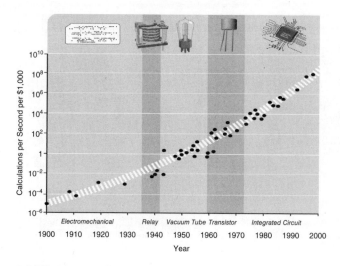

Exhibit 7.3: Moore's Law

Source: Raymond Kurzweil, The Singularity is Near *(New York, NY: Penguin Group, 2005). Ray Kurzweil, http://singularity.com/charts/page81.html.*

to as Moore's Law, this performance phenomenon continues to hold true as today's faster, more compact, and more cost-effective servers rapidly become obsolete. The combined impact of Moore's Law on *performance and capability,* broad commercialization on *quantity,* and the application to business-critical applications on reliability, availability, and serviceability (RAS) has resulted in a cascading effectiveness far beyond what would be suggested by Moore's Law alone. Pundits have forecast the demise of Moore's Law every decade since its advent. However, those same challenges have provided added motivation for more and faster scientific and engineering breakthroughs. There appears to be no end in sight.[8]

ADVANCES IN STORAGE AND DATA NETWORKS

Data storage has evolved in many ways since IBM introduced the first commercial disk drive system in 1956. The IBM RAMAC (Random Access Memory Accounting and Control) 305, as shown in Exhibit 7.4, was equipped with an IBM 350 disk storage unit that had a list purchase price of approximately $39,000 for 5 MB or, in the present

Exhibit 7.4: IBM 350 Disk Storage Unit

Reprint Courtesy of International Business Machines Corporation, © 2009 International Business Machines Corporation.

case, equivalent to $7.8 million per GB. To achieve 5 MB of capacity required 50 magnetic disk platters that rotated at 1,200 RPM and could deliver data at 8.8 KiloBytes (KB) per second.[9]

In contrast, today's high-capacity server-class hard disk drive (HDD) installed in a storage subsystem sells for a list purchase price of approximately $700 for 600GB (600,000 MB) or approximately $1.17 per GB. To achieve 600GB of capacity requires 4 magnetic disk platters that can rotate at up to 15,000 RPM and deliver data at 6 GB per second or 6,000,000 KB per second.[10] In the past 40 years, HDD capabilities have grown exponentially: total HDD capacity has increased by more than 500,000 percent, and HDD prices have decreased by more than 1,000,000 percent per GB. Originally applied to integrated circuits, Moore's Law has also been an effective predictor of data storage capacity, as shown in Exhibit 7.5.

Data access speeds have also increased significantly due to the increases in capacity per platter, number of platters, rotating speed of the platters, magnetic read/write head positioning speed, and hardware interface speed increases. The primary cost drivers for storage are (1) capacity, (2) speed, and (3) availability. Several waves of change in the storage industry have supported these cost drivers, as

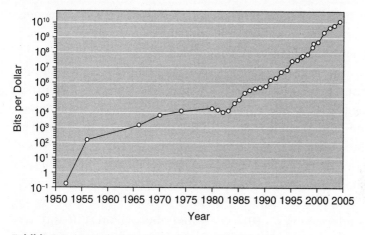

Exhibit 7.5: Magnetic Data Storage Bits per FY 2000 Dollars

Source: *Raymond Kurzweil,* The Singularity is Near *(New York, NY: Penguin Group, 2005). Ray Kurzweil, http://singularity.com/charts/page81.html.*

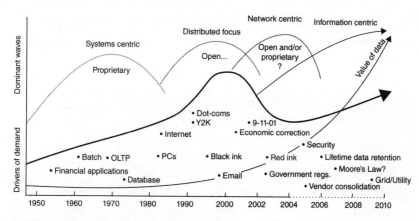

Exhibit 7.6: Storage Industry Waves of Change

Source: *Fred Moore, "Notable Events in the IT/Storage Industry, A Historical Summary," presented at Diskcon Conference, September 2006, Santa Clara, CA, USA.*

shown in Exhibit 7.6, representing a movement from proprietary technologies to open technologies. The significant increase in the amount of generated data that must be stored from email, Internet applications, businesses, and many other applications as mandated by government regulations and business policies, has led to an exponential increase in the volume of commercial, government, and military data that shows no signs of slowing down.

One of the primary drivers of cost and capacity is *areal density*. Areal density is the number of bits that can be stored in the surface area of the hard disk drive, typically stated in gigabits per square inch (Gb/sq. in.) From the introduction of the HDD in the mid-1950s (with the IBM 305) through to the current generation of HDDs, areal density has increased by almost 8 orders of magnitude. While industry pundits have regularly and chronically predicted that the end of areal density improvements is near, history shows that new and innovative means of storing information on HDDs will continue, and areal density will continue to increase, as shown in Exhibit 7.7.[11]

The compound annual growth rate (CAGR) for areal density has generally outpaced what would have been predicted by application of Moore's Law. The bottom line, therefore, is that storage is getting faster, less expensive, and has higher capacity per HDD (see Exhibit 7.8). It is a good thing, too. There is no shortage of commercial and social networking application material to be stored and managed.

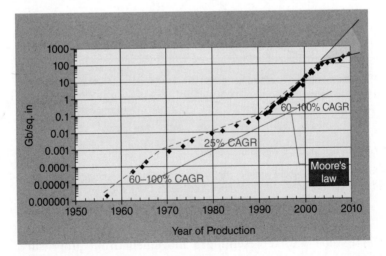

Exhibit 7.7: Full History Disk Areal Density

Reprint Courtesy of International Business Machines Corporation, © 2003 International Business Machines Corporation.

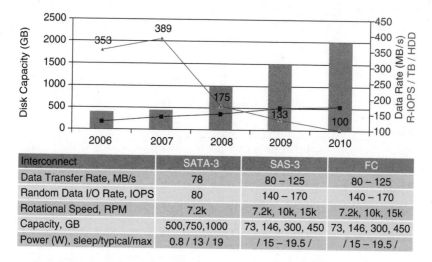

Interconnect	SATA-3	SAS-3	FC
Data Transfer Rate, MB/s	78	80 – 125	80 – 125
Random Data I/O Rate, IOPS	80	140 – 170	140 – 170
Rotational Speed, RPM	7.2k	7.2k, 10k, 15k	7.2k, 10k, 15k
Capacity, GB	500,750,1000	73, 146, 300, 450	73, 146, 300, 450
Power (W), sleep/typical/max	0.8 / 13 / 19	/ 15 – 19.5 /	/ 15 – 19.5 /

Exhibit 7.8: 3.5″ Form Factor Hard Disk Drive Performance and Capacity Trends

BUSINESS IMPACTS OF BUSINESS NETWORKING

In their guidelines report for social networking in the United States government, Crane and colleagues define social media as social software that connects people spontaneously and interactively, and they reference four usage models for social media (see Exhibit 7.9):

1. Inward Sharing—defined as sharing information within an organization through the use of tools such as SharePoint and Wikis.

2. Outward Sharing—defined as sharing information with groups external to the organization through the use of tools such as Groove and Huddle.

3. Inbound Sharing—defined as a means of soliciting information from groups external to the organization through the use of tools such as polls and "crowdsourcing."

4. Outbound Sharing—defined as a means of providing and sharing information to groups external to the organization through the use of such tools as LinkedIn, Plaxo, Facebook, and Twitter.

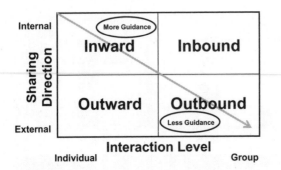

Exhibit 7.9: Relationship between Social Networking Interaction and Guidance

Source: Earl Crane and members of the Web 2.0 Security Working Group, "Guidelines for Secure Use of Social Media by Federal Departments and Agencies, Version 1.0," CIO Council Committee Report, Information Security and Identity Management Committee, Network and Infrastructure Security Subcommittee, Web 2.0 Security Working Group, September 2009, page 8, management.energy.gov/documents/SecureSocialMedia.pdf.

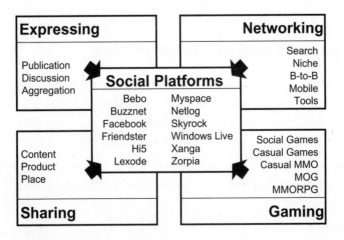

Exhibit 7.10: Social Media Landscape

Adapted from Fred Cavazza, "Social Media Landscape," June 9, 2008, www.fredcavazza.net/2008/06/09/social-media-landscape/.

Each of these usage models has a role in business networks and can positively or adversely affect a business. Most of these usage models are represented in the myriad of social media programs shown in Exhibit 7.10. Given the types and quantity of non–business related social media and social networking outlets, it is no surprise that CIOs are concerned.

Is the intersection of social networking and business new? Not by any means. In the early 1980s, IBM created what we called a "computer conferencing facility," or "conference disk," for short. The first two facilities, called *IBMPC* and *IBMVM*, brought together the IBM Personal Computer development community and the IBM Virtual Machine operating system development communities, respectively.[12] These were preceded and paralleled by IBM customer-based "conference disks" called VMSHARE and PCSHARE; VMSHARE was created in August 1976.[13] IBM was greatly concerned about simultaneously giving product development, research, and the field access to the same information with IBMVM and IBMPC: confidential information would find its way to customers and clients. Interestingly enough, although the same concern existed relative to providing email to IBM employees ten years earlier, by the early 1980s nearly everyone who needed (and wanted) email had it and many who did *not* want it had it too. IBM was run by email, and IBM's internal research and development communities were run with email and "conference disks." In fact, the first PCs allowed to have connections to outside networks had a hardwired switch that physically switched-off the internal network and switched-on the external network. Although this approach only lasted about a year (once it was realized that that was not enforceable at home), it demonstrated the level of corporate concern.

Fast forward thirty years, and companies have concerns about access to social media at work for the same reasons as IBM had in the 1980s, and now these employees have full access outside the work environment. While corporations are understandably concerned, their anxiety is exacerbated by the computer software security industry with white papers inciting fear, uncertainty, and doubt.[14]

A study by Robert Half surveyed more than 1,400 CIOs from U.S. companies with more than 100 employees to examine their company policies for employees visiting social networking sites (e.g., Facebook, MySpace and Twitter) while at work. As shown in Exhibit 7.11, more than half of the companies *completely* prohibit such access. The Fourth Estate has reported similar concerns.

- "FACEBOOK FIRED: 8% of U.S. Companies Have Sacked Social Media Miscreants"[15]

Prohibit completely	54%
Permitted for business purposes only	19%
Permitted for limited personal use	16%
Permitted for any type of personal use	10%
Don't know/no answer	1%
Total	**100%**

Exhibit 7.11: CIOs on Social Network Sites Access at Work

*Source: Robert Half Technology, "Whistle—But Don't Tweet—While You Work,"
October, 2009, www.roberthalftechnology.com/PressRoom?pressrelease_5
.request_type=RenderPress release&pressrrelease_5.releaseId=2531.*

- "45% of Employers Now Screen Social Media Profiles"[16]
- "STUDY: 20% Increase in Companies Blocking Social Media Sites"[17]
- "Marines Ban Facebook and MySpace, Pentagon Considers It"[18]
- "Domino's YouTube Video: YouTube Can Get You Fired, Too"[19]

These headlines give vivid support to those CIOs and CTOs who have concerns about social media in the workplace and reinforce those who refuse to deal with it at all. However, the number of available places for employees to get to social media sites is ever increasing, even when they are banned at work. According to *The Economist*, the number of wireless Internet (WiFi) hotspots worldwide has grown from 53,700 in 2004 to over 286,000 in late 2009, and the number is still rising at this same incredible rate.[20] By the end of 2009, there were more than 200 hotspots per million people in the United States, more than 450 in Great Britain, more than 400 in France, more than 250 in South Korea, more than 230 in Taiwan, and more than 25 in China. (Considering the size of population of China, 25 per million people is still a *significant number* of WiFi hotspots.)

The concerns most often cited by CIOs and CTOs about this kind of access include:

- Lost productivity from time spent on social networking sites
- Leaking of intellectual property or confidential business information
- Ensuring privacy and avoiding misuse of personal information made available through social networking sites

Unstated in these concerns are the ever-present cultural barriers, but there are signs of change on the horizon. On February 25, 2010, the Department of Defense released an official policy on social networking.[21,22] The memorandum makes it policy that the U.S. Defense Department non-classified networks enable the use of Internet-based social networking capabilities (e.g., Facebook, Twitter, LinkedIn) across all agencies in the DoD. It cautions due diligence regarding malicious activity and "prohibited content sites" (such as gambling and pornography), and the policy delegates some temporary operational flexibility where required to ensure missions are safeguarded and circumstances of severe bandwidth constraints. Another key mandate in this mandate states, "This policy recognizes that Internet-based capabilities are integral to operations across the Department of Defense."[23] Examples of allowable access by these unclassified networks and their users include YouTube, Facebook, MySpace, Twitter, and Google Apps—just to name a few.

BUSINESS IMPACTS OF SOCIAL NETWORKING

If there was ever any question about the inevitability of emerging links between businesses, employees, customers or clients, and social networking, Microsoft dispelled that question once and for all by announcing that it was adding social links to its Outlook email application.[24] Called Outlook Social Connector (OSC), the capability allows users to work with and view their LinkedIn contacts in a manner fully integrated with Outlook. Microsoft also announced that it would be adding integration features for Facebook and MySpace. Twitter and other social networking applications are sure to follow.

Social networking and applications are relatively new as a capability, and the related technology and commercial uses are still evolving. By virtue of its very purpose, social networking technology brings people and organizations of like interests and needs together, creating opportunities to provide information and/or share information limited only by human imagination. CIOs and their C-Suite peers are still learning whether or not the enterprise and its customers can profit from that connectivity. What about the return on investment? Invest in what? How quickly? As a strategic IT enabler, social networking technology is still a work-in-progress. Many companies are investing in multiple means of social networking to cover their bets. Since CIOs and CTOs typically have to invest their limited resources prudently, how do you decide where to invest? You have to look at the trends and have the infrastructure ready by the time your enterprise and IT organization needs it, because you will not have time to make it available if you wait until you are asked or directed. Robert Stephens, founder of the Geek Squad and a VP at Best Buy, agrees:

> The CIO's job is to serve the organization's goal. If not the CEO, the CMO is where that starts. It's about talking and listening to the customers, and that's the marketing team. The CIO, in absence of input from the leadership, can deduce what would be required by looking at technology trends and what's technically possible and extrapolating from there. We know people use mobiles so we should probably have a mobile platform capability. Don't wait for the marketing department to ask. That's how the CIO can lead with the thought leadership and yet remain neutral to how it's being used. Put it in a technology roadmap and tell the marketing department that it's there for their use. If the CIO waits for the CMO to ask for something that requires technology, by the time the CIO can build it out, it will be way behind. The CIO needs to predict the future by watching the trends and implementing the infrastructure so that it's ready when the CMO needs the capability. CIOs probably got caught unaware with social networking because the change moved so quickly—it isn't like things used to be.[25]

How important is social networking? Do you see it as another means to communicate with your team, employees, or customers? You should. The enterprise internal communications and external marketing movements are shifting rapidly in that direction, and to be effective, the CIO and CTO need to make certain that this communication path is open and ready to go when the enterprise becomes ready to harness the opportunities.

There will be resistance, but like all radically disruptive technologies, resistance is futile. CIOs and IS/IT organizations have been focused on protecting the enterprise network, and this has made us all paranoid and change-averse for valid reasons (in the past). The strategic challenge for the new users of social networking is to figure out how to discriminate among all the information sources relentlessly bombarding customers and employees at all levels of the enterprise. Robert Stephens likens Twitter to citizens band (CB) radio except that it's electronic: With CB radio, people lost all record of any information and recommendations that they made to each other (e.g., where to eat, what to watch out for), but with Twitter—a similarly principled, more reliable, more accessible technology—every conversation is preserved for as long as the users want it to store them. As with all that information, discrimination becomes increasingly important. Social networking has turned the world into an open microphone where just about anyone can listen to anything if they try hard enough.

Information discrimination is difficult (if not impossible) to automate because as a group, social network participants have a mind of their own. The CIO must work with the IT organization to develop discrimination as an inherent part of the job description, and this means working with the IT organization staff to develop positive, broadminded, inclusive forms of professional discrimination. Robert Stephens observes, "There is a real downside to discrimination: if you set up your customized version of the Apple iPad to only give you articles on topics that you want to read (like a specialized tailored version of the *New York Times*), you will miss the opportunity where journalists take you in serendipitous directions. It's important to have the unexpected experience as human beings."

Imagine the possibilities. In-store customers with questions or problems can use a social network established by the enterprise that allows customer-facing employees to immediately find and serve the customer's specific need. A properly configured social networking service would allow a customer walking through the store to make use of "augmented reality" by pointing a mobile phone camera at an item so that it can be scanned to retrieve information about that item, including competitive pricing. Best practice CIOs and CTOs anticipate these trends, and have already become familiar with a new social meme: "There's an app for that."

Infrastructure makes these social networking opportunities possible, and a new technology based on virtual reality research from the 1980s called "Virtual Worlds" enables development of this kind of IT infrastructure.

VIRTUAL WORLDS: SECOND LIFE

Virtual worlds—the natural bases for virtual reality—are not new. They have their base in ideas by researchers from the late 1950s, who believed that computers could be used for digital display in addition to being used as number crunchers.[26] As with many "futuristic" technologies, going from vision to reality in this area was led by the U.S. military and the Advanced Research Projects Agency. The first step was the development of flight simulators, military tank driving simulators, and military ship steering simulators for training purposes. Computer graphics improvements and early experimentation with head-mounted helmet displays in the 1970s provided better visual feedback, but it was not until the 1980s that computing power, digital displays, and software became advanced enough to create realistic detailed virtual worlds.

On a nearly parallel course, commercial interest in virtual reality (and virtual worlds) was driven by the equally powerful entertainment industry, and the newly created computer games industry, with its yet unenvisioned influence. Network television shows and Hollywood movies such as Paramount's *Star Trek: The Next Generation* and Disney's *Tron* showed the general public depictions of virtual worlds and virtual realities sometimes referred to as *cyberspace*—a term coined by author William Gibson.[27] We subsequently witnessed the creation of *SimCity*, a 1980s city-building simulation game. By the early 1990s, another developer produced a similar prototype 3D world called *CyberTown*, which, while simplistic to us now, demonstrated the potential for online human interactions and transactions through an interactive town square, public services, a bank with a working model of an ATM, a travel agency complete with 3D globe, and much more. CyberTown first introduced the concept of "avatars," 3D graphic representations of personal, customizable human surrogate images that represent computer users in the virtual world.

By the mid-1990s, the CyberTown virtual world was commercially launched, as was another 3D virtual reality platform called *Activeworlds*. While CyberTown did not ultimately succeed in the commercial environment, it made significant technological inroads. Activeworlds allows users to create their own personal online environments and develop a virtual office or building environment in 3D by allowing employee users to create avatars for themselves and their clients. Typical applications were for remote and distributed forms of education and training priorities (i.e., virtual distance learning). In 2006, Activeworlds was released to the general public, and remains active today.[28] In 2000, the strategic life-simulation computer game, *The Sims*, was first released for personal computers. By the end of 2002, *The Sims Online* was launched to wide commercial acclaim.

In late 2001, *LindenWorld* was launched, and by mid-2003 it had already evolved and was re-launched as *Second Life* (SL). Over the next several years, SL grew through grassroots, word-of-mouth efforts, and by early 2007 it came to the attention of mainstream news and media. Since then, the number of *residents* (as they call their users) has grown exponentially in terms of both personal and commercial use.[29] Many enterprises now consider this population to be their mainstream, preferred customers and even leverage it in terms of customer relationship management (CRM) and new commercial opportunities with its over 100 million users, more than 270 terabytes of content, one billion user hours per year, and more than $300 million in revenue. In July 2008, Linden Lab and IBM announced a major partnership in the development of virtual worlds and interoperability between Linden Lab's *Second Life* and the *OpenSim* virtual world on which IBM was developing commercial applications.[30] In December 2008, IBM reported that it had saved $320,000 by holding two of its major events for their IBM Academy of Technology for over 200 of its members—and 75 percent of the second event's participants declared it successful.[31,32]

Many major corporations have—or have had—a presence in SL, such as IBM, SUN Microsystems, Sony, Cigna, BMW, Coca-Cola, and the San Francisco Exploratorium Museum, not to mention thousands of other companies and tens of millions registered individual users worldwide. Many of these enterprises and individual concerns use their global and local presence to establish educational forums and to conduct internal and external "distributed meetings" in place of teleconferences, videoconferences, and in-person travel to achieve their objectives as key enterprise stakeholders (see Chapter 5 for other examples).

Enterprising educational applications have been created *in-world*, too.[33] For example, a theatre class at Ohio State University created an automated production of Edgar Allan Poe's *Masque of the Red Death*. The Centers for Disease Control and Prevention, NASA, the Information Resources Management College at the National Defense University, the National Oceanic and Atmospheric Administration (NOAA), and the U.S. Navy have all built presences on SL.[34] Cigna Healthcare has created an SL virtual world called, "The Cigna Virtual Healthcare Community,"[35] as has IBM, called, "Virtual Healthcare Island."[36] In mid-2008, the American Cancer Society raised approximately $200,000 with 1,000 runners on 89 running teams through a Relay for Life on SL.[37] These applications come and go as the SL environment, methods for use, and commercial approaches by companies evolve. Also, with a major international application in October 2008, IBM announced a partnership with the Palace Museum in Beijing, China, called, "The Forbidden City: Beyond Space and Time," creating an online virtual world that represents a three-dimensional replica of the palace grounds. This replica allows visitors to take guided tours, interact with each other, and interrogate museum volunteers, staff, and automated characters.

In an article in the *Times*, the management consulting firm McKinsey and Company was quoted as saying, "virtual worlds were on the cusp of a major expansion—particularly as a way to reach younger customers," and that companies were "ignoring them at their peril."[38] One of the major issues with SL in a business environment is that of user control and confidentiality of sensitive (business confidential) conversations and interactions. To address this, Linden Labs has announced a hardware device that allows enterprises to create their own SL world on their own networks and behind their own firewalls. Is this the future of conference calls and online conference applications? That remains to be seen. Faster processors and faster bandwidth provide a richer, more realistic, and more real-time, immersive user experience. However, these improvements are counterbalanced by richer and more compute- and bandwidth-intensive interactions and graphics in these environments. Many pundits believe that the experience is not yet intuitive enough, so while there are millions of worldwide users, SL remains a venue for the more technically literate, and more experimental for business applications. The future, though, could be significantly different.

The Army Research Laboratory is funding research at Rensselaer Polytechnic Institute to study social and cognitive networks: the Center for Social and Cognitive Networks as part of the Collaborative Technology Alliance (CTA) of the Army Research Laboratory.[39] Co-participants in the program include IBM, Northeastern University, City University of New York, Harvard University, MIT, New York University, Northwestern University, University of Notre Dame, University of Maryland, and Indiana University. They bring together top social scientists, neuroscientists, and cognitive scientists with leading physicists, computer scientists, mathematicians, and engineers to uncover, model, understand, and foresee the complex social interactions that take place in today's society. "All aspects of social networks, from the origin of adversarial networks to gauging the level of trust with vast social networks will be investigated within the center."[40] In particular, the collaborative study will provide valuable insights into levels of social trust by the Internet community, and understanding about how individual interactions affect and are shaped by their thoughts and behaviors. Just how people in social networks build trust and how that trust affects the sharing and use of information are important areas to be covered by this research, too.

Will virtual worlds reach "critical mass?" Data showing SL membership and usage statistics consistently show a range of 40,000 to 80,000 concurrent logins with a median just slightly less than 60,000, approximately 10,000 new sign-ups per day, and a total number of "residents" at 1.4 million and growing.[41] With the improvements in computing power and network bandwidth, the barriers to a good virtual experience are being eliminated. With the introduction and acceptance of mainstream tablet computers such as the Apple iPad and the HP Slate for under $1,000, virtual worlds are easily accessible and portable for business and training uses.

Virtual, anonymous IT worlds indirectly further the notion of democratization and a flattening—or reinvention—of the knowledge hierarchy on individual and cultural levels: a socialization of information. What does this mean for CIOs and CTOs?

DEMOCRATIZATION AND SOCIALIZATION OF INFORMATION

After an experience he documented in his 2004 book, *The Cult of the Amateur: How Today's Internet is Killing Our Culture*, Andrew Keen gained insight into what he calls, "The Great Seduction," democratized media, democratized "Big Experts," and the transformation through Web 2.0 to "noble amateurs . . . where Wikipedia met MySpace met YouTube. Everyone was simultaneously broadcasting themselves, but nobody was listening."[42] In fact, Wikipedia is a prime example of the risks of dependence on democratized information. As Keen points out:

> Look at Wikipedia, the Internet's largest cathedral of knowledge. Unlike editors at a professional encyclopedia like the *Britannica*, the identity of the volunteer editors on Wikipedia is unknown. These citizen editors out-edit other citizen editors in defining, redefining, then reredefining truth, sometimes hundreds of times a day.[43] . . . Amateur hour has arrived and the audience is now running the show.[44] . . . these noble amateurs' (will) democratize . . . the dictatorship of expertise. So instead of a dictatorship of experts, we'll have a dictatorship of idiots.[45]

What distinguishes an *expert* from an *amateur*? And, why is it important to CIOs and CTOs? An amateur is a citizen in the general public who contributes, writes, blogs, wikis, or podcasts about news, opinions, analysis, and other topics. But amateurs are not held accountable for what they say, how they say it, or the accuracy of their writings. In fact, many amateurs produce their materials anonymously under pseudonyms. Their "user-generated content" may also appear in online encyclopedias or other online forums with the appearance of credibility and refereed authority.

An *expert* is a professional—an academic, an recognized industry consultant or employee, a journalist, or an editor—who may contribute Web content through the same forums as an amateur but is held accountable for what they say, how they say it, and the factual accuracy of their writings. In fact, regardless of their stature, experts can be criticized and even fired for false reporting or serious errors of professional standards, analysis, fact, or judgment. They write and contribute under their real names, and their contributions appear in credible, refereed publications and online sites.

For the IT professionals and companies staking their reputations and businesses (and even the safety of others) on factual information, sorting fact from fiction and amateurs from experts is serious business. Universities and professional societies have been moving to strongly advise against or actually ban the use of non-refereed online citation sources (such as wikis—like Wikipedia, blogs, etc.). For example, Purdue University's "Reference List: Electronic Sources (Web Publications)" cites the American Psychological Association (APA) as the reference method for citing electronic sources and for wikis: "Please note that the *APA Style Guide to Electronic References* warns writers that wikis (like Wikipedia, for example) are collaborative projects which cannot guarantee the verifiability or expertise of their entries."[46]

Universities became alarmed and responded vigorously to an incident in 2007 when a contributor to Wikipedia edited the online article profiling the comedian Sinbad, reporting that the actor had died. Sinbad himself was called on to clear up the confusion.[47] While a seemingly trivial case of misinformation (Internet vandalism is a more appropriate term for this particular incident), the event was one of the first times that information credibility made the mass market news in terms of how easy it is to publish misleading and incorrect information as factual on some Web sites. Consider how difficult it can be in technical and medical subjects to know the basis for an article or blog, for example, where there is no qualified peer review.

In an online Harvard Business School article, the process and problems of online information posting and credibility became even more public.[48] Harvard Business School Professor Andy McAfee proposed the concept of "Enterprise 2.0" as a means by which businesses could use Web 2.0 technologies. An enterprising Wikipedia "contributor" started an article on the subject, and it was promoted into the online encyclopedia. Some time later it was identified by another Wikipedia contributor (or "Wikipedian," as they refer to themselves) as an article that did not meet Wikipedia's standards and therefore labeled it as an "Article for Deletion" or "AfD." After a series of back-and-forth changes in status from "not deleted" to being a re-nominated AfD, Professor McAfee realized that the AfD label was not about the validity of the article and topic but more about the opposing authors' personal views: "It seemed to me that some of the people arguing against it were entrenched, and they were using Wikipedia's policies as doors, as barriers, without being willing to engage in a real debate about them. So the policies had become for them a way to keep out articles they just personally didn't like."[49] This experience sparked Professor McAfee to co-author a Harvard Business School Case Study on how Wikipedia governs itself (or doesn't).[50]

Corporations are also examining the use of non-refereed online sources. Larry Sanger, co-founder of Wikipedia, addressed the issue of the knowledge of experts versus the "wisdom" of amateurs, and founded and launched *Citizendium* in September 2006 to address the issue head-on.[51] *Citizendium* is "staffed" by enlisting real experts to author, review, approve, and settle disputes concerning articles within their area of expertise, and there are "constables" who deal with those who break the rules. *Citizendium* reflects the *Encyclopedia Britannica* approach, recognizing that some people simply know more than others about specific topics—that a degreed engineer knows more about how to design a bridge than a high-schooler. In other words, it *is* important to understand the source of information and the qualifications of the person or persons providing opinions in areas where business decisions are being made.

In 2007, *Wired.com* reported that a substantial number of companies and organizations were editing their own and others' entries through the use of a program called "Wikipedia Scanner," which matches anonymous edits with the IP addresses from which they were made.[52] Common edits were to add positive materials that read like press releases or to delete critical material. Because these edits can be anonymous, they are not restricted to qualified contributors or to the companies themselves. *CNN.com International* cited that Microsoft had solicited an online blogger to correct (for pay) inaccuracies in an article about an open-source document standard proposal early in 2009.[53]

THE WISDOM OF CROWDS?

Is it possible that the "galactic masses"—if they applied themselves to a difficult problem—could come up with solutions to problems that an expert or group of experts could not? That is the premise made by *New Yorker* magazine business columnist James Surowiecki in his book, *The Wisdom of Crowds*, ". . . under the right circumstances, groups are remarkably intelligent, and are often smarter than the smartest people in them."[54] According to Surowiecki, there are four key elements that govern the success of a "wise crowd":

1. Diversity of those in the crowd, which provides different backgrounds and viewpoints from those in the crowd
2. Independence of those in the crowd from each other, which keeps them from being biased by the opinion of strong personalities or single leaders
3. Decentralization
4. A method for bringing together the views of the crowd

The idea that crowds can be wise is counterintuitive to many, and the jury is still out. Surowiecki provides many examples of how tapping into the crowd solves the seemingly unsolvable. One of his favorite examples is based on an account documented in the book *Blind Man's Bluff*, an account describing the location of the lost submarine, *U.S.S. Scorpion*.[55] The *Scorpion* disappeared on its way back to port in May 1968, and there was a significant amount of uncertainty in where to even start looking. Rather than go to the top experts in the field, the naval officer in charge created potential scenarios for what might have happened and where the submarine might have gone down. He then assembled a team with a wide range of skills (e.g., salvagers, submarine specialists, mathematicians) and asked them to work together and come up with their best probability estimate for each scenario. They were asked to guess on why the submarine disappeared, the distance and direction it traveled from the point of last contact, and circumstances relevant to locating the ship and crew. When the team returned and reported their estimates and guesses, the naval officer used their various scenarios collectively to build a composite scenario. The submarine was found, approximately 220 yards from where the composite predicted.

Importantly, this "wise crowd" was *not* a random sampling of the "galactic masses." It was a collection of educated and knowledgeable people who had a basis of expertise from which to work. They were not "world-renowned experts," but neither were they chosen randomly off the street. Thomas W. Malone, the director of the Center for Collective Intelligence at the Massachusetts Institute of Technology, has observed, "There is a misconception that you can sprinkle crowd wisdom on something and things will turn out for the best. That's not true. It's not magic."[56]

The advantages of the "wise crowd," also known as "crowdsourcing," were demonstrated in a contest sponsored by Netflix, the rental movie company. The Netflix Prize was established in 2006 with the goal to improve the Web site's movie recommendations to subscribers by 10 percent; the incentive was a $1 million prize. Web site-generated recommendations are based on the customer's viewing habit data, and an improvement in the recommendations was expected to improve customer satisfaction.[57] The prize was awarded to team "BellKor's Pragmatic Chaos." While the guidelines for who could compete was completely open-ended, the winner was a seven-person team composed of statisticians, machine learning experts, and computer engineers from the United States, Austria, Canada, and Israel, who were led by the statisticians from AT&T Research. This team was by no means a random collection of the "galactic masses." This was a very wise and carefully chosen "crowd."

In a recent study, researchers looked at three Web sites that aggregate voter input: IMDB (the Internet Movie Database), Amazon, and BookCrossings.[58] Their study evaluated the mechanisms that each site used for voting and analyzed the aggregate voting behavior. Their results suggested that:

- Web sites with higher barriers to vote introduce a relatively high number of one-off voters

- Web sites with higher barriers to vote appear to attract mostly experts
- One-off voters tend to vote on popular items
- Experts mostly vote for obscure, low-rated items

The bottom line of their analysis: The voting is dominated by the few—not by the many, and that a community of voting experts is much less biased despite the absence of quality control mechanisms. Google search and online "hotlists" such as Digg.com return results that are *popular*—not that are necessarily true, reliable, or pertinent to the wishes of the searcher. There are widespread reports that the ordered rankings of these results can be influenced (and even manipulated) by a very small number of people.[59]

Should a CIO or CTO be concerned about the quality, veracity, truthfulness, and accuracy of information available online? Absolutely. Scientific equations, engineering rules of thumb, cost estimates, best practices, and legal regulations are only accepted and used when the source is known. Ease of online availability and access does not relax this requirement. For your own organization, it can be as simple as creating guidelines for acceptable sources of information and requirements for verifying the origin of the information. As Andrew Keen puts it, "... technology doesn't create human genius."[60]

Then there are the other classes of online information: the professional networking site such as LinkedIn and Plaxo, the in-between online networking site such as Twitter, and the social networking site such as Facebook and MySpace (even corporations and professional groups are creating a strategic, competitive presence on the social networking sites as discussed in Chapter 1). Once again, is it the role of the CIO or CTO to force the same on the rest of the enterprise or IT organization?

THE NEW REALITY

With the evolutionary information technology changes over the past twenty years, and the pace at which IT continues to evolve, CIOs and CTOs must remain current and experience increasing pressures to control, moderate, manage, and enable network and network applications access. Unfortunately, many CEOs and CFOs (and even some

CIOs and CTOs) interpret this to mean "control," and for many, this means risk management: no social networking Web sites and applications available within their companies. As described earlier, this was the approach taken in the early days of email applications (even by technology companies), and of course, from today's perspective, it was an unrealistic and untenable position.

Some unlikely sectors have taken forward-thinking stands that might help risk-averse corporate C-Suite executives open their minds to the competitive advantages of social media. The U.S. government and military have chosen to take a decidedly business-oriented approach to dealing with this "new reality." A recent White Paper, "Guidelines for Secure Use of Social Media by Federal Departments and Agencies," clearly defines such guidelines:

> The goal of the IT organization should not be to say "No" to social media Web sites and block them completely, but to say "Yes, following security guidance," with effective and appropriate information assurance security and privacy controls. The decision to authorize access to social media Web sites is a business decision and comes from a risk management process made by the management team with inputs from all players.[61]

This is a prudent approach. It should *not* solely be the IS/IT organization's responsibility to determine whether or not a capability should be available to an organization or its employees. That responsibility belongs to the senior executive team. It *is* the responsibility of the IS/IT organization to provide proper security, privacy, and auditing to protect management, employees, and information assets. The U.S. Department of Defense believes that it can manage this—and if they can do it, so can most free enterprise CIOs and CTOs.

Whether or not a particular enterprise executive team agrees with the usefulness and appropriate business applications of these tools, new private and corporate cultural realities increasingly embrace their potential, and entrepreneurs have captured the hearts and minds of the general public by producing new applications daily. Access to many, if not all, of these personal and business applications, is available not only for computers but through Internet-connected mobile phones, smartphones, PDAs, and network-connected personal music players such as Apple iPods and Microsoft Zunes. Whether or not these devices are company-purchased or managed, employees carry them into the workplace. So, blocking access to social networking Web sites and applications over an enterprise network does not actually prevent the employees from accessing them. Such practices only serve to drive employee social network access to their personal mobile devices. On the surface, this may appear to be an acceptable solution: out of sight, out of mind. However, all the risks are still there for security, privacy, and intellectual property loss.

The more realistic approach is to create policies, practices, guidelines, and education around personal and professional access to and use of social networking Web sites and applications. The CIO Council believes that these realistic approaches should be general enough to apply to current and future technologies, and should be focused on providing a context and guidelines for behavior:

> Policies should not be based on specific technology, as technology changes rapidly. Rather, policies should be created to focus on user behavior, both personal and professional, and to address information confidentiality, integrity, and availability when accessing data or distributing government information. Procedures should be created and updated frequently to address the rapid changes in specific technologies.[62]

Can your employees be trusted to follow the rules and guidelines? Excellent question. Do you trust them to follow your existing rules and guidelines for personal computers, office supplies, travel expenses, and so on? Most likely, "yes"—with appropriate monitoring and selective auditing. The same approach applies in the new social networking reality.

Is the CIO's and IT organization's primary motivation for embracing the new reality a form of compulsory resignation, or is there some hidden opportunity—some silver lining—something more? There is more. Many Fortune 500 companies are using social media to learn from their customers, to support their marketing strategy, and to build their business as in the Best Buy examples from Chapter 1. Many take a metered approach, starting small to learn, and iteratively improving as they find what works for them with their customers. For example, at Newell Rubbermaid: "The more we engage with our consumers, the more we learn and the more we can expand our social media efforts. I cannot emphasize enough how important it is to start small, be flexible and be willing to pull back and change if something does not work."[63]

One aspect of the new IT reality is that social networking Web sites have become more than just message boards; they have come to be viewed as *places*: permanent destinations that allow people and organizations of like interests to *gather together*, just as if they were doing so in person. What makes this sense of community particularly attractive is multimedia capability: pictures, text, sound, video, music, and more. What makes these sites useful is that their integrated multimedia capabilities have been made so accessible and easy to use by people of all ages who require very little, if any, technical skills.

Many of these capabilities were available in the 1980s, when businesses used computer conferencing disks such as IBMVM. They weren't pretty or easy to use, and they were not widely available. Today's applications such as Facebook and MySpace are available to anyone with an Internet connection, and are in use by school children and octogenarians alike, right beside organizations, professional societies, companies, and the media. Through the use of fan pages and interest groups, many people (especially today's young adults) get their professional and personal news intermixed through and "at" these virtual *places*: "Older adults go online to find information, the younger crowd go online to live. The boundaries between private and public and between offline and online are blurring. . . ."[64]

Another key element of social networking Web sites and applications is that the sense of community and commonality bringing people to these *places* can be strategically leveraged:

- ▪ **Twitter:** Through the use of applications such as *TweetDeck*, an individual can collect messages, or "tweets," from similar topic areas together for the equivalent of a running ticker tape of opinion around a topic. Many of these tweets are sent from and received by mobile phones and PDAs. For example, you can follow IT profession-related tweets from *CIO Magazine*.[65]

- **Facebook:** A prominent "news feed" option at the top of every users home page includes updates provided by organizations for which users and their friends have "Become a Fan." For example, you can join "CIO Forum" and be informed on discussions and topics of interest from *CIO Magazine*.[66]
- **LinkedIn:** There are a number of special interest and discussion groups for CIOs and CTOs here. For example, a search for "CIO" returns hundreds of groups that welcome participation, and *CIO Magazine*'s "CIO Forum" was at the top of the list. Likewise, a search for "CTO" also returns hundreds of groups that welcome CTOs, and *The Enterprise Architecture Network*, with more than 40,000 members, was at the top of this list.

The new reality is that these *places* are valuable, and their personal and business uses are exploding. CIOs and CTOs can now get timely, relevant information tailored to their *professional needs*. There are usually many people in the IT organization who would also profit from access to these professional social networks.

ADAPTING TO THE NEW REALITY

The statistics on the rise and acceptance of social media are unequivocal: *Facebook* grew from 100 million to 200 million users in less than 8 months, currently has over 300 million users, and growth continues. *Twitter* grew from 1 million users to 7 million users in the same period, currently has over 75 million users, and growth continues. *LinkedIn* currently has over 60 million registered users, and growth continues.[67] Social networking technologies are here to stay, so best practice CIOs are prudently adapting to the new reality, and they approach any other new technology or application from the perspective of executive leadership responsibilities with a commitment to enable stakeholder enterprise value: with deliberate education, planning, processes, procedures, and guidelines. Keen confirms this notion: "Indeed, what defines 'the very best minds' available, whether they are cultural critics or scientific experts is their ability to go beyond the 'wisdom' of the crowd and mainstream public opinion and bestow on us the benefits of their hard-earned knowledge."[68]

Because we cannot know the validity or integrity of the information we read on much of the Internet, we are forced to read everything with a skeptical and critical eye—and how critical that is depends on the knowledge of the reader rather than the other way around. This is a key dilemma for business use of democratized and socialized information.

With these ever-changing personal and business communications styles and concepts of *places*, a whole new generation of technology and non-technology workers are comfortable with—and even assume—a 24/7 always on/always available connected lifestyle, and this generation is *not* age specific. They are more "experience specific." Some of this comes through the anonymity of the Internet, and some of it comes through the use of popular Internet applications such as reviewers on BarnesandNoble.com or Amazon.com, virtual worlds such as SL, blogs, or other online communities. Gartner calls this group "Generation V"—"V" for "Virtual."[69] Generation V has a more independent (and perhaps "newer") view of their personal and employee personas. They see themselves as having their own *personal* intellectual property, and that they own their contacts and relationships with others. For example, what used to be kept on a Rolodex and was taken from job to job (if you were allowed to take it with you) is now kept on your cell phone, your email address books, and your LinkedIn or Facebook network friend lists.

Generation V will not honor a forced requirement to use social networking solutions solely behind a firewall because they see that policy as an intrusion into their personal life because of the significant blurring between their personal and professional lives with "always available" Internet access. It is physically impossible to prevent Generation V from using social networking Web sites and applications in the workplace, even if they are not available through the corporate network. Over time, some of these applications actually become extremely useful for competitive enterprise strategies, and in hindsight, some enterprises wonder how they ever lived without them. One example is VoIP for phone calls and teleconferences, using computers and the Internet to connect people all over the world for no additional cost other than the cost of the computer and the Internet connection. Another example is the use of instant messaging (IMing) for immediate, short communications among employees within a company or cross-company; procurement departments and vendors commonly use IMing to identify materials availability and cost on immediate need items. Yet less than five years ago, many enterprises blocked the use of Skype and IMing, fearing loss of control (among other reasons). These are technologies that have matured and can be managed, monitored, and logged for audit purposes—all unobtrusively. The newer technologies, such as social networking Web sites and applications, are not yet mature and are still evolving, as is the pattern of use and even the usefulness to employees and enterprises.

One possible evolution is a shift from email distribution lists to blogging, where the blog updates occur either through email distributions or through Really Simple Syndication (RSS) feeds read through "newsreader" applications. Newsreaders come as standalone applications or in standard business email applications such as Microsoft's Outlook and Entourage. A similar shift happened from email to conference disks in the 1980s and 1990s. It was common then to have both email for one-way or "broadcast" communications and the conference disks for communal, similar-interest group communications. As with many things in life, technology trends repeat themselves.

Because the new social networking reality is only gaining momentum in our private and workplace lives, it is important for CIOs and CTOs to focus on managing risks of sensitive data leaving the enterprise, regardless of the path that it may leave. CIOs and CTOs must ensure that all employees understand their personal workplace responsibilities in maintaining confidentiality and privacy through policies and guidelines that assist this understanding.

ROLE OF IS/IT IN ADAPTING TO THE NEW REALITY

It is not the CIO's responsibility to *decide* whether or not social networking should be available to an enterprise. Yet, the CIO and the IS/IT organization can be of significant help in identifying, planning, implementing, managing, monitoring, and auditing social networking Web sites and applications used by enterprise employees and for use with and by external partners or customers. Many enterprises are not aware of such IS/IT capabilities, and the CIO must consequently sell executive leadership on social networking possibilities. The first step in gaining trust, comfort, and interest is to take an enlightened approach to social networking: move to *social controls* rather than increasing use of *rules and technology controls* to meet your business, privacy, and intellectual property needs. In other words, peer pressure and self-policing can be very effective.

Many enterprises already have guidelines for internal and external email and written communications. Those guidelines should be directly applied to social networking Web site and application access and use. This approach forces the employees to actually *think* about what information they are sharing and how they are sharing it. The responsibility is in the employees' hands, as it should be. Employees find ways around the "control" when the control is merely technical, such as one example from the early 1980s: Our IS/IT group's conference disk required that any code updates be included with an explanation about the addition or change. While most participants complied conscientiously, two group members "fulfilled" the requirement of the software by entering a single period (".") rather than entering a cogent explanation. After the conference disk manager changed the requirement to a 20-character minimum, the two employees would simply enter 20 random characters. Eventually, the requirement was removed but the two were socially pressured to comply by the *entire* rest of the team. I was a member of that team and have seen the same behavior repeatedly in different contexts over the past 30 years. Clear policy explanations and peer pressure compliance cultures are very effective. Where they fail, conditions of employment must be invoked.

It is easy to understand the difficulties in accepting a hands-off approach to controls. Over the past 20 years, increasingly restrictive and widely-deployed control applications and practices have generated an industry-wide, market-based climate that pressures IS/IT organizations to fear new less restrictive alternatives. Once headed down this control-heavy path, CIOs inevitably conclude that "more is better" to ensure that the IS/IT organization is covered. After all, who's the first person brought under the bright lights after an apparent information asset security breach? Yet increased technology security controls rarely prevent such a breach because the majority of these breaches are by insiders who have legitimate system access.[70] When asked about information and data security, retailers said that their greatest concern is unauthorized access to their systems by *insiders*:

- 70%: insider gets unauthorized access
- 60%: outsider gets unauthorized access
- 48%: use of stolen credit card
- 42%: breach at a third party
- 30%: phishing attack
- 26%: lost or stolen employee laptop or mobile device
- 24%: malware on employee's PCs

So, what is the CIO to do? Create effective controls, guidelines, checks, and balances that allow you to add value and to enable your business to meet its goals. These effective social controls ("rules" and "guidelines") have several key attributes:

- No more rules and guidelines than absolutely required. This ensures that the rules and guidelines are easy to remember.
- All rules and guidelines follow common sense and are intuitive. This ensures that all employees can understand and internalize the rules and guidelines. Rules and guidelines should be defined in a way that encourages active and positive participation, collaboration, and allows for constructive criticism. This approach *enables* productivity rather than stifling participation.
- Employees have a means to report offensive participation or improper use. This ensures that the "self-policing" has a reporting mechanism.

Once the rules and guidelines are established, it is important to monitor and manage participation and use to ensure compliance. The best way to do this is through monitoring for good behavior and audits for compliance. Find opportunities to publicize contributions in a positive manner; they go a long ways towards reinforcing proper behavior and participation. Improper employee behavior usually stimulates the reflexive urge to increase controls and/or restrictions. This response will not ensure elimination of the behavior, and it creates penalties for and reduces the productivity of the majority—compliant employees.

Resist the temptation. Instead, deal with the improper behavior through counseling, training, and individual sanctions. Social controls are effective because the participants are *not* anonymous. These controls focus on informing participants about specific expectations in these environments that encourage use and participation. Rules should address major enterprise risk factors such as harassment, foul language, representations of corporate commitments, and sexually explicit text and images. The same expectations apply for corporate policies and ethical behavior. All policies and guidelines can be published as part of the general IS/IT access agreements that employees generally sign and that can be updated and redistributed on a regular basis to remind participants of their importance. Gartner recommendations are clear on this practice: "When formulating governance strategies for social sites, it's easy to focus on controls and restrictions and lose sight of the fundamental goal of building a thriving and self-sustaining community. Assess all governance policies, rules and mechanisms for their impact on the growth of community participation. . . . Managing an appropriate balance between freedom and control is crucial. . . ."[71]

Following the general rules and guidelines, particular enterprise "communities" will more than likely require additional specialized policies. For example, policies for the IS/IT organization are usually different than those of the financial or human resources departments. There may be additional specialized guidelines for corporate officers and for the marketing team. Similarly, the rules and guidelines directed at intra-organization social networking and external-to-the-organization social networking must be clarified. Social media have become permanent fixtures of the workplace, and prudent adaptation to this new reality, with its emerging opportunities and hidden risks, the best practice CIO approaches this increasingly concrete virtual business reality like any other new technology or application: through education, planning, processes, procedures, and guidelines.

NOTES

1. John Hagel, III, John Seely Brown, and Lang Davison, *Measuring the Forces of Long-Term Change: The 2009 Shift Index*, Deloitte Center for the Edge, 2009, page 29.

2. www.edissweb.com/.

3. CompuServe Interactive Services, Incorporated,1999, www.fundinguniverse .com/company-histories/CompuServe-Interactive-Services-Inc-Company-History.html.

4. Prodigy Communications Corporation, 2000, www.fundinguniverse.com/ company-histories/Prodigy-Communications-Corporation-Company-History.html.

5. Funding Universe, "Company Histories," 2004, www.fundinguniverse.com/ company-histories/AOL-Time-Warner-Inc-Company-History.html.

6. John Hagell, III, John Seely Brown, and Lang Davison, "Measuring the Forces of Long-Term Change: The 2009 Shift Index," September 23, 2009, www.deloitte.com/assets/Dcom-UnitedStates/Local%20Assets/ Documents/us_tmt_ce_ShiftIndex_072109ecm.pdf.

7. Earl Crane and members of the Web 2.0 Security Working Group, "Guidelines for Secure Use of Social Media by Federal Departments and Agencies, Version 1.0," CIO Council Committee Report, Information Security and Identity Management Committee, Network and Infrastructure Security Subcommittee, Web 2.0 Security Working Group, September 2009, page 19, management.energy.gov/documents/SecureSocialMedia. pdf.

8. National Physics Laboratory, "Research Shows There Could Be No End in Sight for Moore's Law." December 9, 2008, www.physorg.com/ news148054154.html.

9. IBM Corporation, "IBM 350 disk storage unit." IBM Archives/Exhibits/ IBM Storage/Storage Reference Room/Storage product profiles, 2009, www-03.ibm.com/ibm/history/exhibits/storage/storage_350.html.

10. Seagate Technology, "Cheetah 15K.7 Data Sheet, Publication DS1677.2-0907US," July 2009, www.seagate.com/docs/pdf/datasheet/disc/ds_cheetah _15k_7.pdf.

11. E. Grochowski and R. D. Halem, "Technological Impact of Magnetic Hard Disk Drives on Storage Systems," *IBM Systems Journal*, Volume 442, Issue 2, 2003.

12. Davis Foulger, "Medium as Process: The Structure, Use, and Practice of Computer Conferencing on IBM's IBMPC Computer Conferencing Facility: An Overview," 1991, http://davis.foulger.info/papers/dissummary .htm.

13. Rob van der Heij, "Welcome to the VMSHARE Archives," August, 1998, http://vm.marist.edu/~vmshare/.

14. MessageLabs division of Symantec, "Employee Web Use and Misuse: Companies, their employees and the Internet," White Paper, Symantec Corporation, 2008, 4.

15. Adam Ostrow, "FACEBOOK FIRED: 8% of US Companies Have Sacked Social Media Miscreants," August 10, 2009, http://mashable.com/2009/08/10/social-media-misuse.

16. Jennifer Van Grove, "45% of Employers Now Screen Social Media Profiles," August 19, 2009, http://mashable.com/2009/08/19/social-media-screening/.

17. Jennifer Van Grove, "STUDY: 20% Increase in Companies Blocking Social Media Sites," August 21, 2009, http://mashable.com/2009/0821/social-networks-blocked/.

18. "Marines Ban Facebook and MySpace, Pentagon Considers It," *Wall Street Journal*, August 5, 2009, http://blogs.wsj.com/digits/2009/08/05/marines-ban-facebook-and-myspace-pentagon-considers-it/.

19. Stan Schroeder, "Domino's YouTube Video: YouTube Can Get You Fired, Too." April 15, 2009, http://mashable.com/2009/04/15/youtube-fired/.

20. Economist.com. "Well Connected," November 17, 2009, www.economist.com/research/articlesBySubject/PrinterFriendly.cfm?story_id=14896700.

21. Office of the Assistant Secretary of Defense (Public Affairs), "DOD Releases Policy for Responsible Use of Internet-based Capabilities." February 26, 2010, www.defense.gov/releases/release.aspx?releaseid=13338.

22. William J. Lynn, III, "Directive-Type Memorandum (DTM) 09-026-Responsible and Effective Use of Internet-Based Capabilities." *Deputy Secretary of Defense.* February 25, 2010, www.defense.gov/NEWS/DTM%2009-026.pdf.

23. *Ibid*, page 1.

24. Jeffrey Schwartz, "Microsoft Adds Social Links to Outlook." *Redmond Channel Partner* online, February 17, 2010, http://rcpmag.com/articles/2010/02/17/microsoft-adds-social-links-to-outlook.aspx?sc_lang=en.

25. Robert Stephens, this and subsequent quotations from a personal interview by Karl Schubert, January 13, 2010.

26. The Board of Trustees of the University of Illinois, *Virtual Reality: History*, October 24, 1995, http://archive.ncsa.illinois.edu/Cyberia/VETopLevels/VR.History.html.

27. William Gibson, *Burning Chrome* (New York: Arbor House, 1986).

28. www.activeworlds.com/.

29. Underlying, Incorporated, "Second_Life Timeline," www.dipity.com/rhiannonsl/Second_Life.

30. Linden Lab, "Linden Lab and IBM Achieve Major Virtual World Interoperability Milestone." July 8, http://lindenlab.com/pressroom/releases/07_08_08.

31. Virtual Worlds News, "IBM Saves $320,000 with Second Life Meeting," February 27, 2009, www.virtualworldsnews.com/2009/02/ibm-saves-320000-with-second-life-meeting.html.

32. Irving Wladawsky-Berger, "'Serious'" Virtual Worlds Applications," December 1, 2008, http://blog.irvingwb.com/blog/2008/12/serious-virtual-worlds-applications.html.

33. SL-ed blog crew, "SLED Blog," December 23, 2008, www.sl-education blog.org/.

34. Gautham Nagesh, "Virtual Connections," July 1, 2008, www.govexec .com/features/0708-01/0708-01s2.htm.

35. Dean Takahashi, "Cigna Deploys a Second Life Island for Health Education," July 1, 2008, http://social.venturebeat.com/2008/07/01/cigna -deploys-a-second-life-island-for-health-education/.

36. Virtual Worlds News, "IBM Opens Healthcare Island in Second Life," February 25, 2008, www.virtualworldsnews.com/2008/02/ibm-opens-healt.html.

37. Wagner James Au, "Second Life Residents Raise Record-Making $200,000 In Linden Dollars For American Cancer Society," July 21, 2008, http:// nwn.blogs.com/nwn/2008/07/second-life-res.html.

38. Jonathan Richards, "McKinsey: Ignore Second Life at Your Peril," April 23, 2008, http://technology.timesonline.co.uk/tol/news/tech_and_web/ article3803056.ece.

39. Gabrielle DeMarco, "Rensselaer to Lead Multimillion Dollar Research Center for Social and Cognitive Networks," Rensseleaer Polytechnic Institute, October 29, 2009, www.eurekalert.org/pub_releases/2009-10/ rpi-rtl102309.php.

40. *Ibid.*

41. http://dwellonit.taterunino.net/sl-statistical-charts/.

42. Andrew Keen, *The Cult of the Amateur: How Today's Internet is Killing Our Culture,* (New York: Doubleday, 2007) pages 14–15.

43. *Ibid.,* page 20.

44. *Ibid.,* page 34.

45. *Ibid.,* page 35.

46. Purdue University, Reference List: Electronic Sources (Web Publications), March 3, 2010, http://owl.english.purdue.edu/owl/resource/560/10/.

47. Matt Reilly, "Source of the Problem: College Departments Begin to Ban Wikipedia as Cited Reference in Academic Work, SU Leaves it up to Professors." *The Daily Orange,* March 7, 2010, www.dailyorange.com/ 2.8657/source-of-the-problem-college-departments-begin-to-ban -wikipedia-as-cited-reference-in-academic-work-su-leaves-it-up-to-professors-1.1233904.

48. Sean Silverthorne, "HBS Cases: How Wikipedia Works (or Doesn't)." *Harvard Business School Working Knowledge—Research & Ideas*, July 23, 2007, http://hbswk.hbs.edu/item/5605.html.

49. *Ibid.*

50. Karim R. Lakhani and Andrew P. McAfee "Wikipedia (A)," *Harvard Business School Public Case Studies*, 2007, http://courseware.hbs.edu/public/cases/wikipedia/.

51. www.citizendium.org.

52. John Borland, "See Who's Editing Wikipedia—Diebold, the CIA, a Campaign," August 14, 2007, www.wired.com/politics/onlinerights/news/2007/08/wiki_tracker.

53. CNN.com International, "Use with Caution: The Perils of Wikipedia," CNN.com International / technology, January 6, 2009, http://edition.cnn.com/2007/TECH/11/02/perils.wikipedia/.

54. James Surowiecki, *The Wisdom of Crowds* (New York, Anchor Books, 2005), page xiii.

55. Sherry Sontag, Christopher Drew, and Annette Lawrence Drew, *Blind Man's Bluff: The Untold Story of American Submarine Espionage* (New York: Harper Collins, 1999).

56. Steve Lohr, "The Crowd is Wise (When It's Focused)," *New York Times*, July 18, 2009, www.nytimes.com/2009/07/19/technology/internet/19unboxed.html.

57. Netflix, "Netflix Prize," September 21, 2009, www.netflixprize.com//index.

58. Vassilis Kostakos, "Is the crowd's wisdom biased?" *2009 International Conference on Computational Science and Engineering.* IEEE, September 1, 2009, 251–255, http://arxiv.org/abs/0909.0237v5.

59. Michiko Kakutani, "Books of the Times: The Cult of the Amateur," *The New York Times Review of Books*, June 29, 2007, www.nytimes.com/2007/06/29/books/29book.html?_r=1.

60. See note 42, page 204.

61. See note 7, page 6.

62. See note 7, page 6.

63. Jennifer Leggio, "10 Fortune 500 Companies Doing Social Media Right," ZDNet, September 28, 2009, http://blogs.zdnet.com/feeds/?p=1761.

64. Amanda Gefter, "The Difference Between 'Real' and Online Is No Longer Clear-Cut," *New Scientist*, September 16, 2006, pages 179–183.

65. http://twitter.com/CIOonline.

66. www.facebook.com/group.php?sid=0fbfca0634ddd6f0a3ff0578269c8344&gid=16140755250&ref=search.

67. Stan Schroeder, "The Web in Numbers: The Rise of Social Media," April 17, 2009, http://mashable.com/2009/04/17/web-in-nunbers-social-media/.

68. See note 42, page 44.

69. Adam Sarner, "How 'Generation V' Will Change Your Business," January 3, 2008, www.gartner.com/DisplayDocument?doc_cd=153798.

70. Avivah Litan, "PCI Compliance Remains Challenging and Expensive," Research Report, Gartner, Inc., 2008.

71. Anthony Bradley and Nikos Drakos, "Establishing Policies for Social Application Participation," Research Report, Gartner, Inc., 2008, page 8.

About the Editor

Joe Stenzel has worked as editor-in-chief of the *Journal of Strategic Performance Management* and *Cost Management*, two Thomson Reuters professional business periodicals, since 1997. A board-certified pediatrician, he also works as a mediator and child advocate in the Minnesota Family and Juvenile Court systems. Using his experience with individual human development, Joe has worked with a number of organizational and IT specialists on models of enterprise and cyber systems maturity staging, with the broader goal of integrating recurrent developmental and maturity principles into a sustainable management philosophy for global economic, government, and ecology systems. Joe has also authored four books for John Wiley & Sons: *Essentials of Cost Management, From Cost to Performance Management, CFO Survival Guide*, and *Lean Accounting: Best Practices for Sustainable Integration*. He lives in northern Minnesota with his wife and inspiration, Catherine.

Index